S0-AWL-596

Level 1 • Part 1

Integrated Chinese

中文听说读写

TEXTBOOK Simplified Characters

Third Edition

THIRD EDITION BY

Yuehua Liu and Tao-chung Yao
Nyan-Ping Bi, Liangyan Ge, Yaohua Shi

ORIGINAL EDITION BY

Tao-chung Yao and Yuehua Liu
Liangyan Ge, Yea-fen Chen, Nyan-Ping Bi,
Xiaojun Wang, Yaohua Shi

CHENG & TSUI COMPANY
BOSTON

Third Edition / fourth printing March 2011

16 15 14 13 12 11 4 5 6 7 8 9 10

Published by
Cheng & Tsui Company, Inc.
25 West Street
Boston, MA 02111-1213 USA
Fax (617) 426-3669
www.cheng-tsui.com
"Bringing Asia to the World"™
ISBN 978-0-88727-644-6 — ISBN 978-0-88727-638-5 (pbk.)

Cover Design: studioradia.com

Cover Photographs: Man with map © Getty Images; Shanghai skyline © David Pedre/iStockphoto; Building with masks © Wu Jie; Night market © Andrew Buko. Used by permission.

Interior Design: Wanda España, Wee Design

Illustrations: 洋洋兔动漫

Transportation photograph (p. 271, top): Courtesy of Kristen Wanner
Subway photograph (p. 271, bottom): Courtesy of Andrew Buko

Library of Congress Cataloging-in-Publication Data

Integrated Chinese = [Zhong wen ting shuo du xie]. Traditional character edition. Level 1, part 1 / Yuehua Liu ... [et. al]. — 3rd. ed.
p. cm.
Chinese and English.
Includes indexes.
Parallel title in Chinese characters.
ISBN 978-0-88727-645-3 — ISBN 978-0-88727-639-2 (pbk.) — ISBN 978-0-88727-644-6 — ISBN 978-0-88727-638-5 (pbk.) 1. Chinese language—Textbooks for foreign speakers—English. I. Liu, Yuehua. II. Title: Zhong wen ting shuo du xie.

PL1129.E5I683 2008
495.1—dc22

2008062308

The *Integrated Chinese* series includes books, workbooks, character workbooks, audio products, multimedia products, teacher's resources, and more. Visit **www.cheng-tsui.com** for more information on the other components of *Integrated Chinese*.

Printed in Canada.

The Integrated Chinese Series

Textbooks Learn Chinese language and culture through ten engaging lessons per volume. Includes dialogues and narratives, culture notes, grammar explanations, and exercises.

Workbooks Improve all four language skills through a wide range of integrated activities that accompany the lessons in the textbook.

Character Workbooks Practice writing Chinese characters and learn the correct stroke order.

Teacher's Handbooks Create a successful language program with sample syllabi, lesson plans, classroom activities, sample tests and quizzes, and teaching tips.

Audio CDs Build listening comprehension with audio recordings of the textbook narratives, dialogues, and vocabulary, plus the pronunciation and listening exercises from the workbooks.

The Integrated Chinese Companion Site

www.integratedchinese.com

Find everything you need to support your course in one convenient place.

- FREE teacher resources
- Password-protected answer keys
- Image gallery
- Links to previews and demos
- Supplementary readings
- Sentence drills

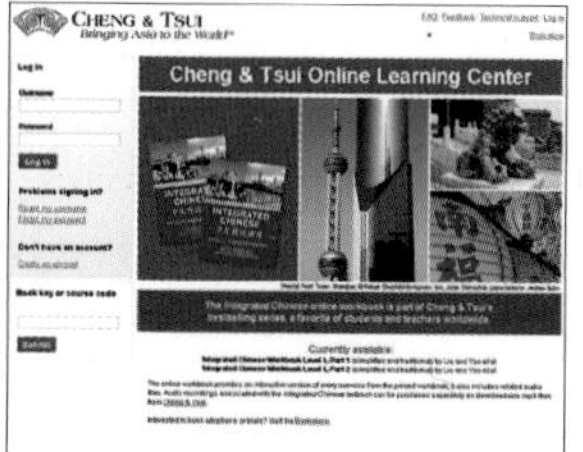

Online Workbooks

Complete the exercises from the printed workbooks using a dynamic, interactive platform. Includes instant grading and intuitive course management.

eTextbooks

Display these downloadable versions of the printed textbooks on interactive whiteboards or your personal computer. Search, bookmark, highlight, and insert notes.

Textbook DVDs

Watch the *Integrated Chinese* story unfold with live-action videos of the textbook dialogues and cultural segments for each lesson.

BuilderCards

Reinforce and build vocabulary using flashcards. Features all essential vocabulary from Level 1.

Find other publications to supplement your *Integrated Chinese* course. See page xi for more information about graded readers, listening comprehension workbooks, character guides, and reference materials.

To order call 1-800-554-1963 or visit www.cheng-tsui.com.

Contents

More Companions for Integrated Chinese

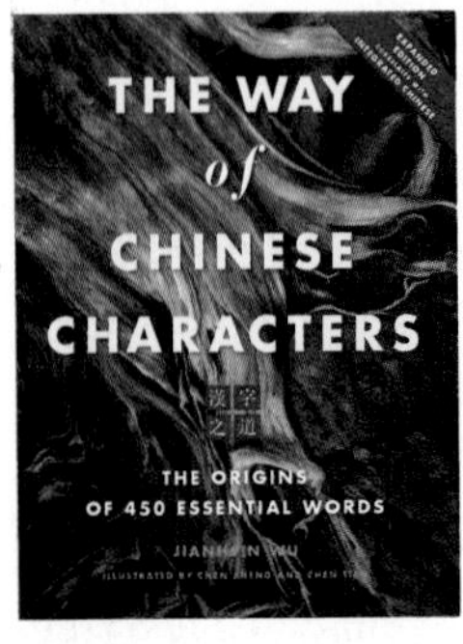

The Way of Chinese Characters
The Origins of 450 Essential Words

By Jianhsin Wu, Illustrated by Chen Zheng, Chen Tian

Learn characters through a holistic approach.

Making Connections
Enhance Your Listening Comprehension in Chinese

By Madeline K. Spring

Improve listening skills using everyday conversations.

Tales and Traditions
Readings in Chinese Literature Series

Compiled by Yun Xiao, et al.

Read level-appropriate excerpts from the Chinese folk and literary canon.

Readings in Chinese Culture Series

By Qun Ao, Weijia Huang

Increase reading and cultural proficiency with level-appropriate essays about Chinese culture.

Integrated Chinese BuilderCards
Much More than Vocabulary Flashcards

By Song Jiang, Haidan Wang

Reinforce and build vocabulary with flashcards.

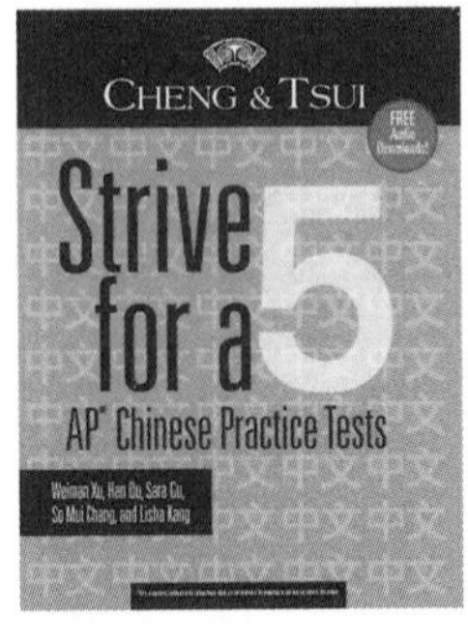

Strive for a 5
AP Chinese Practice Tests*

By Weiman Xu, Han Qu, Sara Gu, So Mui Chang, Lisha Kang

Prepare for the AP exam with eight practice tests, tips, and more.

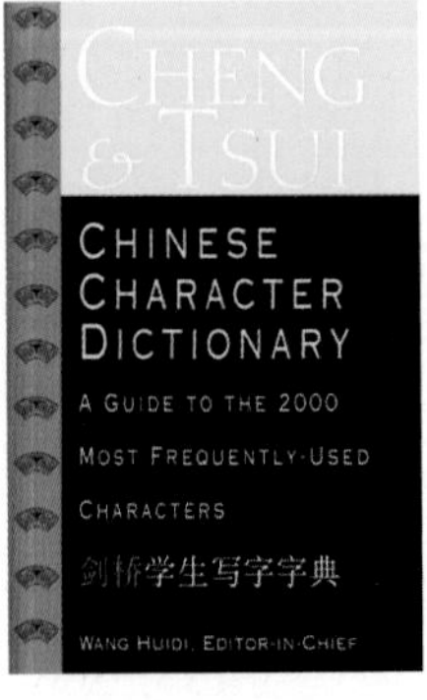

Cheng & Tsui Chinese Character Dictionary
A Guide to the 2000 Most Frequently Used Characters

Edited by Wang Huidi

Master the 2,000 most-used characters.

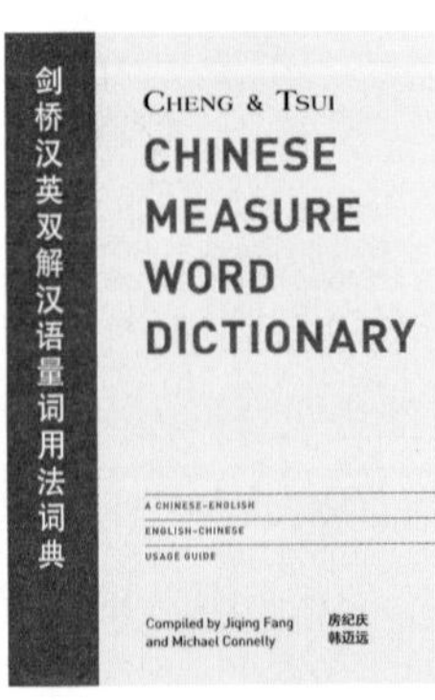

Cheng & Tsui Chinese Measure Word Dictionary
A Chinese-English English-Chinese Usage Guide

Compiled by Jiqing Fang, Michael Connelly

Speak and write polished Chinese using this must-have reference.

Visit www.cheng-tsui.com to view samples, place orders, and browse other language-learning materials.

*Advanced Placement and AP are registered trademarks of the College Board, which was not involved in the production of, and does not endorse, this product.

Publisher's Note

When *Integrated Chinese* was first published in 1997, it set a new standard with its focus on the development and integration of the four language skills (listening, speaking, reading, and writing). Today, to further enrich the learning experience of the many users of *Integrated Chinese* worldwide, Cheng & Tsui is pleased to offer this revised and updated third edition of *Integrated Chinese.* We would like to thank the many teachers and students who, by offering their valuable insights and suggestions, have helped *Integrated Chinese* evolve and keep pace with the many positive changes in the field of Chinese language instruction. *Integrated Chinese* continues to offer comprehensive language instruction, with many new features and useful shared resources available on our website at **www.cheng-tsui.com**.

The Cheng & Tsui Chinese Language Series is designed to publish and widely distribute quality language learning materials created by leading instructors from around the world. We welcome readers' comments and suggestions concerning the publications in this series. Please contact the following members of our Editorial Board, in care of our Editorial Department (e-mail: editor@cheng-tsui.com).

Preface to the Third Edition

It has been over ten years since *Integrated Chinese* (*IC*) came into existence in 1997. During these years, amid all the historical changes that took place in China and the rest of the world, the demand for Chinese language teaching-learning materials has been growing dramatically. We are greatly encouraged by the fact that *IC* not only has been a widely used textbook at the college level all over the United States and beyond, but also has become increasingly popular with advanced language students at high schools. Over the years, regular feedback from the users of *IC*, both students and teachers, has greatly facilitated our repeated revisions of the series. Following its second edition published in 2005 that featured relatively minor changes and adjustments, the third edition is the result of a much more extensive revision.

Changes in the Third Edition

Manageable Number of Lessons

Level 1 now contains 10 lessons in Part 1 and 10 lessons in Part 2 for maximum flexibility. Based on the reports from many teachers that they could not finish all the lessons in the Level 1 volumes within one academic year, we have, for the third edition, eliminated the chapters "At the Library" and "At the Post Office," as the language contents in these chapters have become somewhat obsolete. The chapter "Hometown" has also been removed, but part of its content has been incorporated into other chapters.

Revised Storyline

In the present edition, a new, connected storyline about a diverse group of students strings together all the dialogues and narratives in the lessons throughout Level 1. The relationships among the main characters are more carefully scripted. We want the students to get to know the characters well and to find out how things develop among them. We hope that, by getting to know more about each cast member, the students will be more involved in the process of learning the language.

Current Vocabulary

As in the earlier editions, the third edition makes a special effort to reflect students' life. Additionally, we have updated some of the vocabulary items and expressions in the hope of keeping pace with the evolution of contemporary Chinese and enhancing students' ability to communicate. In the meantime, we have deleted some words and expressions that are of relatively lower frequencies of usage. As a result, the total number of vocabulary items for the series is moderately reduced. The grammar sequence, however, remains fundamentally unchanged.

Clear Learning Objectives and Engaging Learner-Centered Approach

Ever since its inception in 1997, *IC* has been a communication-oriented language textbook which also aims at laying a solid foundation in language form and accuracy for students. The third edition holds fast to that pedagogic philosophy. On top of that, it has adopted a task-based teaching approach, which is intended to intensify students' motivation and heighten their awareness of the learning objectives in each chapter. Each lesson includes Learning Objectives and Relate and Get Ready questions at the beginning to focus students' study. At the end of each lesson, there is a Progress Checklist to be used by students in self-testing their fulfillment of the learning objectives.

It is our hope that these changes will enable students to learn Chinese in a more efficient and pragmatic way and develop their language proficiency and problem-solving abilities in real-life situations. In their feedback to us, many users of previous editions of *IC* noted that, more than many other Chinese language textbooks, *IC* was effective in developing students' abilities to use the language. While making every effort to retain that merit in the new edition, we have endeavored to place language acquisition in a real-world context and make *IC* all the more conducive to active use of the language in the classroom and, more importantly, beyond it.

Contextualized Grammar and Interactive Language Practice

The somewhat mechanical drills on sentence patterns in the earlier editions are now replaced by Language Practice exercises based on simulated real-life situations. In particular, we have increased the number of interactive exercises and exercises that serve the purpose of training students' abilities in oral communication and discourse formation. Similar changes are also to be seen in the *Integrated Chinese* Workbook, which offers new exercises that are more distinctly communication-oriented and more closely aligned with the learning objectives of each chapter. The exercises in the workbook cover the three modes of communication as explained in the "Standards for Foreign Language Learning in the 21st Century": interpretive, interpersonal and presentational. To help the user locate different types of exercises, we have labeled the workbook exercises in terms of the three communication modes.

Linguistically and Thematically Appropriate Cultural Information and Authentic Materials

In comparison with the earlier editions, there is more cultural information in the third edition. The revised texts provide a broader perspective on Chinese culture, and important cultural features and topics are discussed in the "Culture Highlights." In the meantime, more up-to-date language ingredients, such as authentic linguistic materials, new realia, and new illustrations, are introduced with a view towards reflecting cultural life in the dynamic and rapidly changing contemporary China. We believe that language is a carrier of culture and a second/foreign language is acquired most efficiently in its native cultural setting. Based on that conviction, we have attempted to offer both linguistic and cultural information in a coherent, consistent manner and simulate a Chinese cultural environment in our texts, especially those that are set in China.

All-New, Colorful, and User-Friendly Design

Where design and layout are concerned, the third edition represents a significant improvement, intended to better facilitate its use by both teachers and students. We have taken full advantage of colors to highlight different components of each chapter, and have brought in brand-new illustrations and photos to complement the content of the text. The book has also been thoroughly redesigned for optimal ease of use.

Updated Audio Recordings

Throughout this book, you will see an audio CD icon next to the main texts, vocabulary, and pronunciation exercises. This symbol indicates the presence of audio recordings, which are available on the companion audio CD set.

Acknowledgments

During the course of preparing for the third edition, we accumulated more academic and intellectual debts than any acknowledgment can possibly repay. We wish to express our deep gratitude to all those who helped us in so many different ways. In particular, our heartfelt thanks go to the two editors, Ying Yang of the University of California Berkeley and Zoe Wu of Pasadena City College, as well as Craig Butler of Hong Kong International School, Chengzhi Chu of the University of California Davis, colleagues and friends at Beijing Language and Culture University, and Laurel Damashek at Cheng & Tsui.

As authors, we take great pleasure in the contributions that *IC* has made to Chinese teaching and learning over the past ten years, and we also feel the weight of responsibility. In retrospect, *IC* has traversed a long way since its earliest incarnation, yet we know its improvement will not end with the present edition. We promise to renew our efforts in the future, and we expect to continue to benefit from the invaluable comments and suggestions we receive from the users.

An Overview of the New Features of the Third Edition

Chapter Opener

Each lesson opens with an illustration that highlights the theme for the lesson.

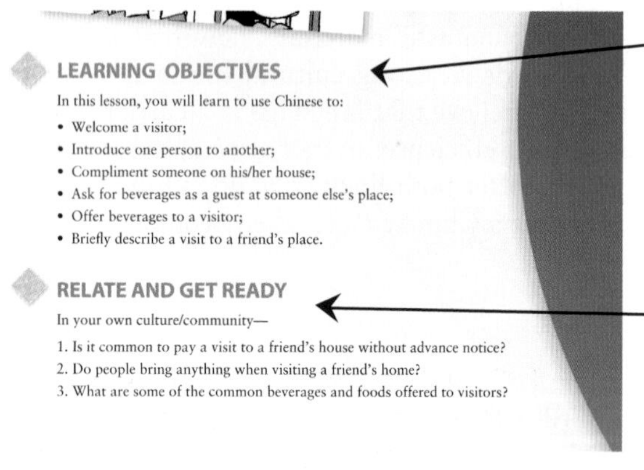

LEARNING OBJECTIVES

In this lesson, you will learn to use Chinese to:

- Welcome a visitor;
- Introduce one person to another;
- Compliment someone on his/her house;
- Ask for beverages as a guest at someone else's place;
- Offer beverages to a visitor;
- Briefly describe a visit to a friend's place.

RELATE AND GET READY

In your own culture/community—

1. Is it common to pay a visit to a friend's house without advance notice?
2. Do people bring anything when visiting a friend's home?
3. What are some of the common beverages and foods offered to visitors?

Learning Objectives for every lesson help students focus their study and envision what they will have accomplished at the end of the lesson.

The self-reflective questions in **Relate and Get Ready** help students to reflect on similarities and differences between their native language and culture and Chinese language and culture.

Dialogue Design

Each dialogue or narrative begins with an illustration depicting the scene.

For the main characters, instead of the characters' names, their avatar icons appear in the dialogue. This helps the students get acquainted with the characters more quickly.

Language Notes and Grammar Callouts

Bái Yīng'ài, nǐ jiā yǒu jǐ kǒu rén?

Wǒ jiā yǒu liù kǒu rén. Wǒ bàba, wǒ māma, yí ge gēge, liǎng ge mèimei hé wǒ. Lǐ Yǒu, nǐ jiā yǒu jǐ kǒu rén?

Wǒ jiā yǒu wǔ kǒu rén: bàba, māma, dàjiě, èrjiě hé wǒ. Nǐ bàba māma zuò shénme gōngzuò?

Wǒ bàba shì lǜshī, māma shì Yīngwén lǎoshī, gēge, mèimei dōu shì dàxuéshēng.

Wǒ māma yě shì lǎoshī, wǒ bàba shì yīshēng.

syllable, it is pronounced in the fourth tone, e.g., 一张 (yì zhāng, a sheet), 一盘 (yì pán, one plate), 一本 (yì běn, one volume).

④ Unlike *and*, 和 (hé) cannot link two clauses or two sentences: 我爸爸是老师，*和我妈妈是医生 (Wǒ bàba shì lǎoshī, *hé wǒ māma shì yīsheng).

⑤ The pause mark, or series comma, 、 is often used to link two, three or even more parallel words or phrases, e.g., 爸爸、妈妈、两个妹妹和我 (bàba, māma, liǎng ge mèimei hé wǒ; dad, mom, two younger sisters and I). For further

The **Language Notes** are clearly marked and numbered in green circles, and placed next to the dialogue for ease of reference.

The **grammar points** are highlighted and numbered in red to draw the students' attention to the language forms covered in the Grammar section of each lesson.

Vocabulary Section

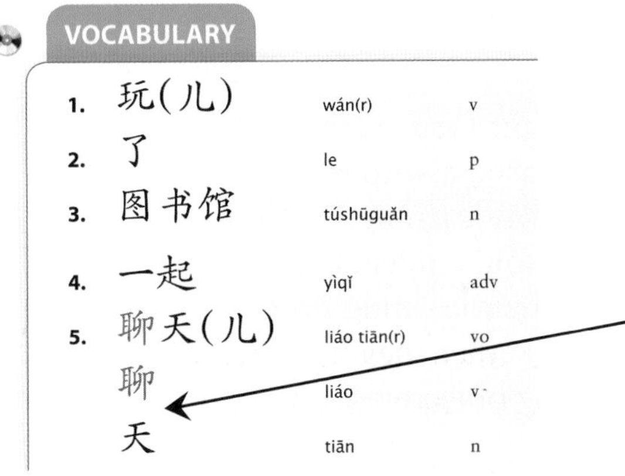

VOCABULARY

1.	玩(儿)	wán(r)	v
2.	了	le	p
3.	图书馆	túshūguǎn	n
4.	一起	yìqǐ	adv
5.	聊天(儿)	liáo tiān(r)	vo
	聊	liáo	v
	天	tiān	n

A low-frequency character that the teacher may decide not to have the students practice writing is shown in a shaded gray color.

Language Practice

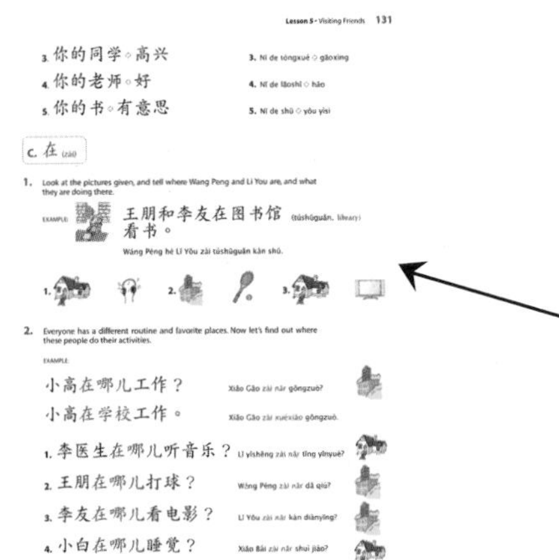

Lesson 5 • Visiting Friends 131

3. 你的同学◇高兴 3. Nǐ de tóngxué ◇ gāoxìng

4. 你的老师◇好 4. Nǐ de lǎoshī ◇ hǎo

5. 你的书◇有意思 5. Nǐ de shū ◇ yǒu yìsi

C. 在 (zài)

1. Look at the pictures given, and tell where Wang Peng and Li You are, and what they are doing there.

EXAMPLE: 王朋和李友在图书馆 (túshūguǎn, library) 看书。
Wáng Péng hé Lǐ Yǒu zài túshūguǎn kàn shū.

1. 2. 3.

2. Everyone has a different routine and favorite places. Now let's find out where these people do their activities.

EXAMPLE:
小高在哪儿工作？ Xiǎo Gāo zài nǎr gōngzuò?
小高在学校工作。 Xiǎo Gāo zài xuéxiào gōngzuò.

1. 李医生在哪儿听音乐？ Lǐ yīshēng zài nǎr tīng yīnyuè?
2. 王朋在哪儿打球？ Wáng Péng zài nǎr dǎ qiú?
3. 李友在哪儿看电影？ Lǐ Yǒu zài nǎr kàn diànyǐng?
4. 小白在哪儿睡觉？ Xiǎo Bái zài nǎr shuì jiào?

In addition to role plays and partner activities, this section also includes contextualized drill practice with the help of visual cues.

New sentence patterns are highlighted in blue.

Culture Highlights

writes horizontally from left to right. But the traditional way of writing is still kept alive in calligraphy.

This is a store sign which was commissioned more than one hundred years ago. It is read from right to left, and it's the name of the person who established the store. Can you recognize his family name?

Should this sign be read from the left to the right or from the right to the left?

Photos or other authentic materials accompany the culture notes.

Customized Learning: How About You?

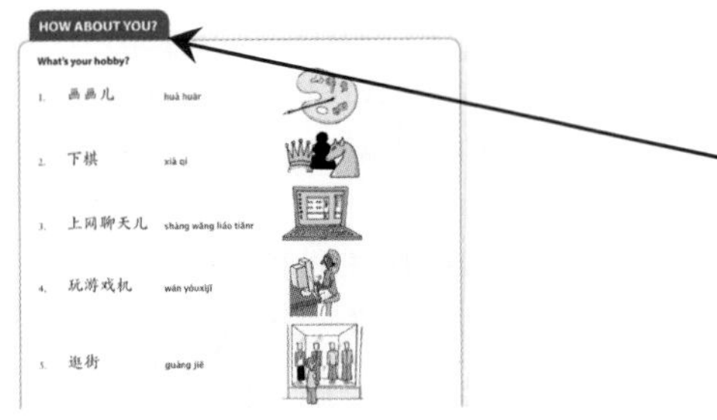
HOW ABOUT YOU?

What's your hobby?

1. 画画儿 huà huàr
2. 下棋 xià qí
3. 上网聊天儿 shàng wǎng liáo tiānr
4. 玩游戏机 wán yóuxìjī
5. 逛街 guàng jiē

Beginning students need not be overwhelmed by additional vocabulary items that do not seem to be very useful or relevant to them. However, they should be given opportunities to select and learn words and phrases that relate to their own interests and experiences. **How About You?** provides this personalized vocabulary space.

Self-Reflection: Progress Checklist

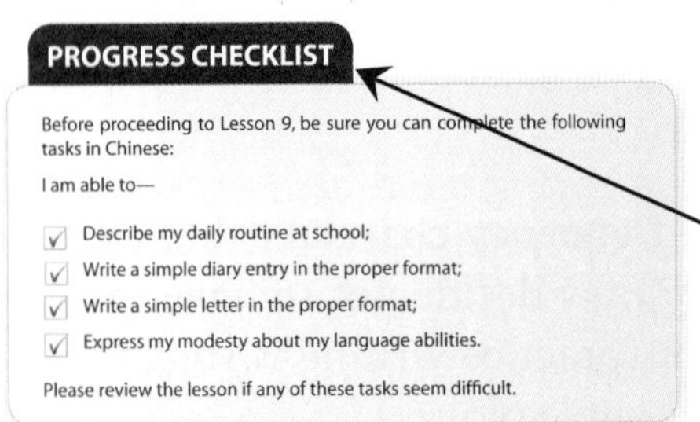
PROGRESS CHECKLIST

Before proceeding to Lesson 9, be sure you can complete the following tasks in Chinese:

I am able to—

- ✓ Describe my daily routine at school;
- ✓ Write a simple diary entry in the proper format;
- ✓ Write a simple letter in the proper format;
- ✓ Express my modesty about my language abilities.

Please review the lesson if any of these tasks seem difficult.

It's important for students to be engaged learners who feel responsible for their own learning. At the end of each lesson, students are asked to check on their learning progress and evaluate whether they have achieved the learning objectives.

Functional Expressions: That's How the Chinese Say It!

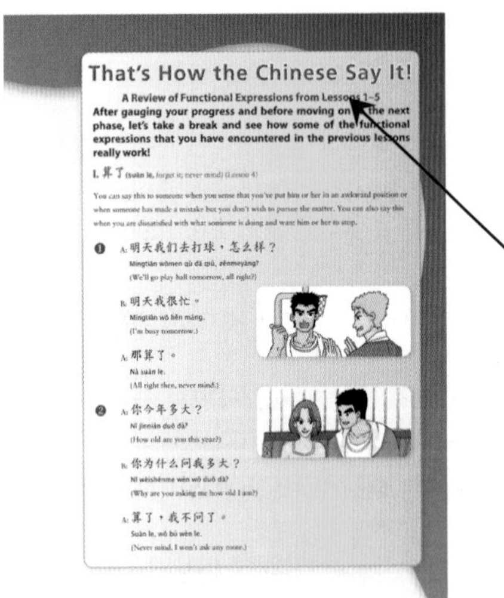
That's How the Chinese Say It!

A Review of Functional Expressions from Lessons 1–5

After gauging your progress and before moving on to the next phase, let's take a break and see how some of the functional expressions that you have encountered in the previous lessons really work!

I. 算了 (suàn le, *forget it; never mind*) (Lesson 4)

You can say this to someone when you sense that you've put him or her in an awkward position or when someone has made a mistake but you don't wish to pursue the matter. You can also say this when you are dissatisfied with what someone is doing and want him or her to stop.

❶ A: 明天我们去打球，怎么样？
Míngtiān wǒmen qù dǎ qiú, zěnmeyàng?
(We'll go play ball tomorrow, all right?)

B: 明天我很忙。
Míngtiān wǒ hěn máng.
(I'm busy tomorrow.)

A: 那算了。
Nà suàn le.
(All right then, never mind.)

❷ A: 你今年多大？
Nǐ jīnnián duō dà?
(How old are you this year?)

B: 你为什么问我多大？
Nǐ wèishénme wèn wǒ duō dà?
(Why are you asking me how old I am?)

A: 算了，我不问了。
Suàn le, wǒ bú wèn le.
(Never mind. I won't ask any more.)

After every five lessons, **That's How the Chinese Say It** provides a review of the functional expressions that have appeared in the texts. It includes additional linguistic and cultural contexts to demonstrate the use of these expressions.

Preface to the Second Edition

The *Integrated Chinese* series is an acclaimed, best-selling introductory course in Mandarin Chinese. With its holistic, integrated focus on the four language skills of listening, speaking, reading, and writing, it teaches all the basics beginning and intermediate students need to function in Chinese. *Integrated Chinese* helps students understand how the Chinese language works grammatically, and how to use Chinese in real life.

The Chinese title of *Integrated Chinese*, which is simply 中文听说读写(*Zhōngwén Tīng Shuō Dú Xiě*), reflects our belief that a healthy language program should be a well-balanced one. To ensure that students will be strong in all skills, and because we believe that each of the four skills needs special training, the exercises in the *Integrated Chinese* Workbooks are divided into four sections of listening, speaking, reading, and writing. Within each section, there are two types of exercises, namely, traditional exercises (such as fill-in-the-blank, sentence completion, translation, etc.) to help students build a solid foundation, and communication-oriented exercises to prepare students to face the real world.

How *Integrated Chinese* Has Evolved

Integrated Chinese (IC) began, in 1993, as a set of course materials for beginning and intermediate Chinese courses taught at the East Asian Summer Language Institute's Chinese School, at Indiana University. Since that time, it has become a widely used series of Chinese language textbooks in the United States and beyond. Teachers and students appreciate the fact that IC, with its focus on practical, everyday topics and its numerous and varied exercises, helps learners build a solid foundation in the Chinese language.

What's New in the Second Edition

Thanks to all those who have used *Integrated Chinese* and given us the benefit of their suggestions and comments, we have been able to produce a second edition that includes the following improvements:

- ▲ Typographical errors present in the first edition have been corrected, and the content has been carefully edited to ensure accuracy and minimize errors.
- ▲ The design has been revised and improved for easier use, and the Textbooks feature two colors.
- ▲ **Revised illustrations** and **new photos** provide the reader with visual images and relevant cultural information.
- ▲ Many **new culture notes** and examples of **functional expressions** have been added.
- ▲ **Grammar and phonetics explanations** have been rewritten in more student-friendly language.
- ▲ **Workbook listening and reading sections** have been revised.
- ▲ **A new flexibility for the teaching of characters** is offered. While we believe that students should learn to read all of the characters introduced in the lessons, we are aware that different Chinese programs have different needs. Some teachers may wish to limit the number of characters for which students have responsibility, especially in regards to writing requirements. To help such teachers, we have identified a number of lower-frequency Chinese characters and marked them with a pound sign (#) in the vocabulary lists. Teachers might choose to accept *pinyin* in place of these characters in homework and tests. The new edition adds flexibility in this regard.

- ▲ **The Level 1 Workbooks** have been reorganized. The Workbook exercises have been divided into two parts, with each part corresponding to one of the dialogues in each lesson. This arrangement will allow teachers to more easily teach the dialogues separately. They may wish to use the first two or three days of each lesson to focus on the first dialogue, and have students complete the exercises for the first dialogue. Then, they can proceed with the second dialogue, and have students complete the exercises for the second dialogue. Teachers may also wish to give separate quizzes on the vocabulary associated with each dialogue, thus reducing the number of new words students need to memorize at any one time.
- ▲ **Level 2 offers full text in simplified and traditional characters.** The original Level 2 Textbook and Workbook, which were intended to be used by both traditional- and simplified-character learners, contained sections in which only the traditional characters were given. This was of course problematic for students who were principally interested in learning simplified characters. This difficulty has been resolved in the new edition, as we now provide both traditional and simplified characters for every Chinese sentence in both the Textbook and the Workbook.

Basic Organizational Principles

In recent years, a very important fact has been recognized by the field of language teaching: the ultimate goal of learning a language is to communicate in that language.

Integrated Chinese is a set of materials that gives students grammatical tools and also prepares them to function in a Chinese language environment. The materials cover two years of instruction, with smooth transitions from one level to the next. They first cover everyday life topics and gradually move to more abstract subject matter. The materials are not limited to one method or one approach, but instead they blend several teaching approaches that can produce good results. Here are some of the features of *Integrated Chinese* which make it different from other Chinese language textbooks:

Integrating Pedagogical and Authentic Materials

All of the materials are graded in *Integrated Chinese*. We believe that students can grasp the materials better if they learn simple and easy to control language items before the more difficult or complicated ones. We also believe that students should be taught some authentic materials even in the first year of language instruction. Therefore, most of the pedagogical materials are actually simulated authentic materials. Real authentic materials (written by native Chinese speakers for native Chinese speakers) are incorporated in the lessons when appropriate.

Integrating Written Style and Spoken Style

One way to measure a person's Chinese proficiency is to see if s/he can handle the "written style" (书面语, shūmiànyǔ) with ease. The "written style" language is more formal and literal than the "spoken style" (口语, kǒuyǔ); however, it is also widely used in news broadcasts and formal speeches. In addition to "spoken style" Chinese, basic "written style" expressions are gradually introduced in *Integrated Chinese*.

Integrating Traditional and Simplified Characters

We believe that students should learn to handle Chinese language materials in both the traditional and the simplified forms. However, we also realize that it could be rather confusing and overwhelming to teach students both the traditional and the simplified forms from day one. A reasonable solution to this problem is for the student to concentrate on one form, either traditional or simplified, at the first level, and to acquire the other form during the second level. Therefore, for Level 1, *Integrated Chinese* offers two editions of the Textbooks and the Workbooks, one using traditional characters and one using simplified characters, to meet different needs.

We believe that by the second year of studying Chinese, all students should be taught to read both traditional and simplified characters. Therefore, the text of each lesson in Level 2 is shown in both forms, and the vocabulary list in each lesson also contains both forms. Considering that students in a second-year Chinese language class might come from different backgrounds and that some of them may have learned the traditional form and others the simplified form, students should be allowed to write in either traditional or simplified form. It is important that the learner write in one form only, and not a hybrid of both forms.

Integrating Teaching Approaches

Realizing that there is no one single teaching method which is adequate in training a student to be proficient in all four language skills, we employ a variety of teaching methods and approaches in *Integrated Chinese* to maximize the teaching results. In addition to the communicative approach, we also use traditional methods such as grammar-translation and direct method.

Online Supplements to Integrated Chinese

Integrated Chinese is not a set of course materials that employs printed volumes only. It is, rather, a network of teaching materials that exist in many forms. Teacher keys, software, and more are available from www.cheng-tsui.com, Cheng & Tsui Company's online site for downloadable and web-based resources. Please visit this site often for new offerings.

Other materials are available at the IC website, http://eall.hawaii.edu/yao/icusers/, which was set up by Ted Yao, one of the principal *Integrated Chinese* authors, when the original edition of *Integrated Chinese* was published. Thanks to the generosity of teachers and students who are willing to share their materials with other *Integrated Chinese* users, this website is constantly growing, and has many useful links and resources. The following are some of the materials created by the community of *Integrated Chinese* users that are available at the *Integrated Chinese* website.

- ▲ Links to resources that show how to write Chinese characters, provide vocabulary practice, and more.
- ▲ *Pinyin* supplements for all *Integrated Chinese* books. Especially useful for Chinese programs that do not teach Chinese characters.
- ▲ Preliminary activities for an activity book for *Integrated Chinese* Level 1 (in progress), by Yea-fen Chen, Ted Yao and Jeffrey Hayden. (http://eall.hawaii.edu/yao/AB/default.htm)
- ▲ Teacher's resources.

About the Format

Considering that many teachers might want to teach their students how to speak the language before teaching them how to read Chinese characters, we decided to place the *pinyin* text before the Chinese-character text in each of the eleven lessons of the Level 1 Part 1 Textbook.

Since *pinyin* is only a vehicle to help students learn the pronunciation of the Chinese language and is not a replacement for the Chinese writing system, it is important that students can read out loud in Chinese by looking at the Chinese text and not just the *pinyin* text. To train students to deal with the Chinese text directly without relying on *pinyin*, we moved the *pinyin* text to the end of each lesson in the Level 1 Part 2 Textbook. Students can refer to the *pinyin* text to verify a sound when necessary.

We are fully aware of the fact that no two Chinese language programs are identical and that each program has its own requirements. Some schools will cover a lot of material in one year while some others will cover considerably less. Trying to meet the needs of as many schools as possible, we decided to cover a wide range of material, both in terms of vocabulary and grammar, in *Integrated Chinese*. To facilitate oral practice and to allow students to communicate in real-life situations, many supplementary vocabulary items are added to each lesson. However, the characters in the supplementary vocabulary sections are not included in the Character Workbooks. In the Character Workbooks, each of the characters is given a frequency indicator based on the *Hànyǔ Pínlǜ Dà Cídiǎn* (汉语频率大辞典). Teachers can decide for themselves which characters must be learned.

Acknowledgments

Since publication of the first edition of *Integrated Chinese,* in 1997, many teachers and students have given us helpful comments and suggestions. We cannot list all of these individuals here, but we would like to reiterate our genuine appreciation for their help. We do wish to recognize the following individuals who have made recent contributions to the *Integrated Chinese* revision. We are indebted to Tim Richardson, Jeffrey Hayden, Ying Wang and Xianmin Liu for field-testing the new edition and sending us their comments and corrections. We would also like to thank Chengzhi Chu for letting us try out his "Chinese TA," a computer program designed for Chinese teachers to create and edit teaching materials. This software saved us many hours of work during the revision. Last, but not least, we want to thank Jim Dew for his superb professional editorial job, which enhanced both the content and the style of the new edition.

As much as we would like to eradicate all errors in the new edition, some will undoubtedly remain, so please continue to send your comments and corrections to editor@cheng-tsui.com, and accept our sincere thanks for your help.

Scope and Sequence

Lessons	Topics & Themes	Sections & Contexts	Learning Objectives & Functions
Introduction		1. Chinese Language and Dialects 2. Syllabic Structure and Pronunciation of Modern Standard Chinese 3. The Chinese Writing System 4. Useful Expressions	1. Learn about the Chinese language 2. Become familiar with basic Chinese pronunciation 3. Know basic information about the Chinese writing system 4. Use common expressions in the classroom and daily life
1	Greetings	1. Exchanging Greetings 2. Asking about Someone's Nationality	1. Exchange basic greetings 2. Request a person's last name and full name, and provide your own 3. Determine whether someone is a teacher or a student 4. Ascertain someone's nationality
2	Family	1. Looking at a Family Photo 2. Asking about Someone's Family	1. Employ basic kinship terms 2. Describe a family photo 3. Ask about someone's profession 4. Say some common professions
3	Dates & Time	1. Taking Someone out to Eat on His/Her Birthday 2. Inviting Someone to Dinner	1. Tell and speak about time and dates 2. Talk about someone's age and birthday 3. Invite someone to dinner 4. Arrange a dinner date
4	Hobbies	1. Talking about Hobbies 2. Would You Like to Play Ball?	1. Say and write the terms for basic personal hobbies 2. Ask about someone's hobbies 3. Ask friends out to see a movie 4. Set up plans for the weekend
5	Visiting Friends	1. Visiting a Friend's Home 2. At a Friend's House	1. Welcome a visitor 2. Introduce one person to another 3. Compliment someone on his/her house 4. Ask for beverages as a guest at someone else's place 5. Offer beverages to a visitor 6. Briefly describe a visit to a friend's place

	Forms & Accuracy	Culture Highlights
	1. The Verb 姓 (xìng) 2. Questions Ending with 呢 (ne) 3. The Verb 叫 (jiào) 4. The Verb 是 (shì) 5. Questions Ending with 吗 (ma) 6. The Negative Adverb 不 (bù) 7. The Adverb 也 (yě)	Chinese names
	1. The Particle 的 (de) (I) 2. Measure Words (I) 3. Question Pronouns 4. 有 (yǒu) in the sense of "to Have" or "to Possess" 5. 有 (yǒu) in the sense of "to Exist" 6. The Usage of 二 (èr) and 两 (liǎng) 7. The Adverb 都 (dōu)	Chinese kinship terms Chinese education system
	1. Numbers (0, 1–100) 2. Dates and Time 3. Pronouns as Modifiers and the Usage of the Particle 的 (de) (II) 4. The Sentence Structure of 我请你吃饭 (Wǒ qǐng nǐ chī fàn) 5. Alternative Questions 6. Affirmative + Negative (A-not-A) Questions (I) 7. The Adverb 还 (hái)	Chinese calendar Chinese manner of counting age Chinese food symbolizing longevity
	1. Word Order in Chinese 2. Affirmative + Negative (A-not-A) Questions (II) 3. The Conjuction 那(么)(nà{me}) 4. 去 (qù) + Action 5. Questions with 好吗 (hǎo ma) 6. The Modal Verb 想 (xiǎng) 7. Verb+Object as a Detachable Compound	Chinese way of "splitting" the check Chinese pastimes
	1. 一下 (yí xià) and (一)点儿({yì} diǎnr) Moderating the Tone of Voice 2. Adjectives as Predicates 3. The Preposition 在 (zài) 4. The Particle 吧 (ba) 5. The Particle 了 (le) (I) 6. The Adverb 才 (cái)	Chinese civilities upon meeting for the first time Chinese tea

Lessons	Topics & Themes	Sections & Contexts	Learning Objectives & Functions
That's How the Chinese Say It!			1. Review functional expressions from lessons 1–5
6	**Making Appointments**	1. Calling One's Teacher 2. Calling a Friend for Help	1. Answer a phone call and initiate a phone conversation 2. Set up an appointment with a teacher on the phone 3. Ask for a favor 4. Ask someone to return your call
7	**Studying Chinese**	1. How Did You Do on the Exam? 2. Preparing for a Chinese Class	1. Comment on one's performance on an exam 2. Comment on one's character writing 3. Talk about one's experience in learning Chinese vocabulary and grammar 4. Talk about one's study habits 5. Remark on typical scenes from one's language class
8	**School Life**	1. A Diary: A Typical School Day 2. A Letter: Talking about Studying Chinese	1. Describe the routine of a student's life on campus 2. Write a simple diary entry 3. Write a brief letter in the proper format 4. Express your modesty in terms of your foreign language ability 5. Invite friends to go on an outing
9	**Shopping**	1. Shopping for Clothes 2. Exchanging Shoes	1. Speak about the color, size, and price of a purchase 2. Recognize Chinese currency 3. Pay bills in cash or with a credit card 4. Determine the proper change you should receive 5. Ask for a different size and/or color of merchandise 6. Exchange merchandise
10	**Transportation**	1. Going Home for the Winter Vacation 2. An Email: Thanking Someone for a Ride	1. Comment about several means of transportation 2. Explain how to travel from one station to another 3. Describe a traffic route 4. Express your gratitude after receiving a personal favor 5. Offer New Year's wishes

Forms & Accuracy	Culture Highlights
1. 算了 (suàn le) **2.** 谁呀 (shéi ya) **3.** 是吗 (shì ma)	
1. The Preposition 给 (gěi) **2.** The Modal Verb 要 (yào) (I) **3.** The Adverb 别 (bié) **4.** Time Expressions **5.** The Modal Verb 得 (děi) **6.** Directional Complements (I)	Chinese phone etiquette Chinese phone numbers Chinese names for the Chinese language
1. Descriptive Complements (I) **2.** The Adverbs 太 (tài) and 真 (zhēn) **3.** The Adverb 就 (jiù) (I) **4.** Double Objects **5.** Ordinal Numbers **6.** 有(一)点儿 (yǒu{yì}diǎnr) **7.** 怎么 (zěnme) in Questions **8.** The 的 (de) Structure (I) **9.** The Use of Nouns and Pronouns in Continuous Discourse	Chinese characters Chinese character writing Chinese writing brushes and other stationery
1. The Position of Time-When Expressions **2.** The Adverb 就 (jiù) (II) **3.** 一边…一边… (yìbiān...yìbiān...) **4.** Series of Verbs/Verb Phrases **5.** The Particle 了 (le) (II) **6.** The Particle 的 (de) (III) **7.** The Adverb 正在 (zhèngzài) **8.** 除了…以外，还…(chúle...yǐwài, hái...) **9.** 能 (néng) and 会 (huì) (I) Compared **10.** The Adverb 就 (jiù) (III)	Chinese letter format Chinese school year
1. The Modal Verb 要 (yào) (II) **2.** Measure Words (II) **3.** The 的 (de) structure (II) **4.** 多 (duō) Used Interrogatively **5.** Amounts of Money **6.** 跟/和…(不)一样 (gēn/hé... {bù} yíyàng) **7.** 虽然…，可是/但是…(suīrán..., kěshì/dànshì...)	Chinese salesclerks and waiters Chinese formal attire
1. Topic-Comment Sentences **2.** 或者 (huòzhě) and 还是 (háishi) **3.** 先 (xiān)…再 (zài)… **4.** 还是 (háishi)…(吧) (ba) **5.** 每 (měi)…都 (dōu) **6.** 要 (yào)…了 (le)	Chinese taxi drivers Chinese public transportation Chinese New Year

Lessons	Topics & Themes	Sections & Contexts	Learning Objectives & Functions
That's How the Chinese Say It!			1. Review functional expressions from Lessons 6–10
Indexes and Appendix		1. Vocabulary Index (Chinese-English) 2. Vocabulary Index (English-Chinese) 3. Vocabulary Index (By Grammar Category and by Lesson) 4. Appendix: Alternate Characters (Texts in Traditional Form)	

	Forms & Accuracy	Culture Highlights
	1. 喂 (wéi) 2. 没问题 (méi wèntí) 3. Expressing and Acknowledging Gratitude 4. 哪里，哪里 (nǎli, nǎli) or 是吗？(shì ma) 5. 就是它吧/就是他/她了(Jiù shì tā ba/ Jiù shì tā le) 6. 祝 (zhù)	

Abbreviations of Grammatical Terms

adj	adjective
adv	adverb
conj	conjunction
interj	interjection
m	measure word
mv	modal verb
n	noun
nu	numeral
p	particle
pn	proper noun
pr	pronoun
prefix	prefix
prep	preposition
qp	question particle
qpr	question pronoun
t	time word
v	verb
vc	verb plus complement
vo	verb plus object

Cast of Characters

Wang Peng:

王朋

A Chinese freshman from Beijing. He has quickly adapted to American college life and likes to play and watch sports.

Li You:

李友

Amy Lee, an American student from New York State. She and Wang Peng meet each other on the first day of classes and soon become good friends.

Gao Wenzhong:

高文中

Winston Gore, an English student. His parents work in the United States. He says he enjoys singing and dancing. He is also a big fan of Chinese cooking. He has a secret crush on Bai Ying'ai.

Gao Xiaoyin:

高小音

Jenny Gore, Winston's older sister. She has already graduated from college, and is now a school librarian.

Bai Ying'ai:

白英爱

Baek Yeung Ae, a friendly outgoing Korean student from Seoul. She finds Wang Peng very "cool" and very "cute".

Chang laoshi:

常老师

(Chang Xiaoliang) Originally from China, in her forties. Chang laoshi has been teaching Chinese in the United States for ten years.

Introduction

I. Chinese Language and Dialects

China is roughly the same size as the United States. There are numerous regional dialects of Chinese. These dialects, which are often mutually unintelligible, are usually divided into eight groups: Northern, Wu, Kejia (Hakka), Southern Min (Xiamen), Northern Min (Fuzhou), Yue (Cantonese), Xiang or Hunan, and Gan or Jiangxi.

Modern Standard Chinese is known as *Putonghua* ("common language") in mainland China; *Guoyu* ("national language"), but also *Huayu* ("language spoken by ethnic Chinese people"), in Taiwan and other Chinese-speaking communities such as Singapore and Malaysia. It is the *lingua franca* for intra-ethnic (among different Chinese dialect speakers) as well as inter-ethnic (among ethnic Chinese and other minority groups) communication in China. Its grammar is codified from the modern Chinese literary canon, while its pronunciation is based on the speech of Beijing.

China officially recognizes 56 ethnic groups. The largest group is the Han, which makes up over 90% of China's population. Many of the other 55 ethnic minorities speak their own distinct languages.

II. Syllabic Structure and Pronunciation of Modern Standard Chinese

A syllable of Modern Standard Chinese is usually composed of three parts: an initial consonant, a final consisting of vowels or vowels and ending consonants -[n] or -[ng], and a tone. The tone is superimposed on the entire syllable. A syllable may also have no initial consonant.

Chinese syllabic structure:

<table><tr><td rowspan="2">syllable =</td><td colspan="2">tone</td></tr><tr><td>(initial)</td><td>final</td></tr></table>

In this book, Chinese sounds are represented by *Hanyu Pinyin*—shortened to *Pinyin*. The *Pinyin* system uses twenty-five of the twenty-six letters of the Roman alphabet. Although *Pinyin* symbols are thus the same as English letters, the actual sounds they represent can be very different from their English counterparts. Over time, you will acquire a better appreciation of the finer details of Chinese pronunciation. This chapter is designed to help you become aware of these distinctions, though attaining more native-sounding pronunciation will take time and effort through extensive listening and practice.

A. Simple Finals:

There are six simple finals in Modern Standard Chinese:
a, o, e, i, u, ü

When it is pronounced by itself, a is a central vowel. The tongue remains in a natural, relaxed position. It sounds similar to a as in "fa la la" in English.

o is a rounded semi-high back vowel. The lips are rounded when pronouncing o. o seldom appears as a syllable by itself. Usually it compounds with the initials b, p, m, and f, and should be practiced with them. Because of the bilabial or labio-dental nature of b p m f, o sounds almost like a diphthong or double vowel uo. It glides from a brief u to o.

e is an unrounded semi-high back vowel. It may be helpful to first position the tongue as if to pronounce o, and then change the shape of the mouth from rounded to unrounded. At the same time spread the lips apart, as if you were smiling. This vowel is different from "e" in English, which is pronounced with the tongue raised slightly forward.

i is an unrounded high front vowel. Try to squeeze a smile and pull the corners of your mouth straight back. It is similar to the long vowel in the English word "sheep." However, the tongue is raised higher than it would be to pronounce its counterpart in English.

u is a rounded high back vowel. Pucker up your lips when pronouncing this sound. It is similar to the long vowel in the English word "coop," but the tongue is raised higher and retracted more.

ü is a rounded high front vowel. To produce this vowel, first position the tongue as if to pronounce i, then round the lips.

In the *Pinyin* system, besides the high front vowel, i also represents two additional special vowels. One is a front apical vowel, the other a back apical vowel—that is to say, they are articulated with the front and back part of the tongue respectively. Both of these vowels are homorganic with the very limited sets of initials with which they can co-occur (see below z, c, s and zh, ch, sh, and r). In other words, they are pronounced in the same area of the vocal tract as those consonants. You'll learn how to pronounce it simply by prolonging the sounds of the two groups of consonants.

B. Initials

There are twenty-one initial consonants in Modern Standard Chinese:

1.	**b**	**p**	**m**	**f**	4.	**j**	**q**	**x**	
2.	**d**	**t**	**n**	**l**	5.	**z**	**c**	**s**	
3.	**g**	**k**	**h**		6.	**zh**	**ch**	**sh**	**r**

B.1: b, p, m, f

b is different from its English counterpart. It is not voiced, as the vocal cords do not vibrate, and sounds more like the "p" in the English word "speak."

p is aspirated. In other words, there is a strong puff of breath when the consonant is pronounced. It is also voiceless.

m is produced in the same manner as the English m. It is voiced.

Pronounce f as you would in English.

Only the simple finals a, o, i, and u and the compound finals that start with a, o, i, or u can be combined with b, p, and m; only the simple finals a, o, and u and the compound finals which start with a, o, or u can be combined with f. When these initials are combined with o, there is actually a short u sound in between. For instance, the syllable bo (buo) actually includes a very short u sound between b and o.

Practice:

☐ **B.1.A**

ba	**bi**	**bu**	**bo**
pa	**pi**	**pu**	**po**
ma	**mi**	**mu**	**mo**
fa	**fu**	**fo**	

☐ **B.1.B b vs. p**

ba	**pa**	**bu**	**pu**
po	**bo**	**pi**	**bi**

☐ **B.1.C m vs. f**

ma	**fa**	**mu**	**fu**

☐ **B.1.D b, p, m, f**

bo	**po**	**mo**	**fo**
fu	**mu**	**pu**	**bu**

B.2: d, t, n, l

When pronouncing **d, t, n**, the tip of the tongue touches the gum of the upper teeth. The tongue is raised more to the back than it would be to pronounce their English counterparts. When pronouncing **l**, the tip of the tongue should touch the palate. **d** and **t** are voiceless, and **n** is nasal.

Only the simple finals **a**, **i**, **e**, and **u** and the compound finals which start with **a**, **i**, **e**, or **u** can be combined with **d**, **t**, **n**, and **l**; **n** and **l** can also be combined with **ü** and the compound finals which start with **ü**.

Practice:

☐ **B.2.A**

da	**di**	**du**	**de**	
ta	**ti**	**tu**	**te**	
na	**ni**	**nu**	**ne**	**nü**
la	**li**	**lu**	**le**	**lü**

☐ **B.2.B d vs. t**

da	**ta**	**di**	**ti**
du	**tu**	**de**	**te**

☐ **B.2.C l vs. n**

lu	**lü**	**nu**	**nü**
lu	**nu**	**lü**	**nü**

☐ **B.2.D d, t, n, l**

le	**ne**	**te**	**de**
du	**tu**	**lu**	**nu**

B.3: g, k, h

g is unaspirated and voiceless, and k is aspirated and voiceless. When pronouncing g and k, the back of the tongue is raised against the soft palate. The *Pinyin* g sounds like the "k" in the English word "sky."

h is voiceless. When pronouncing h, the back of the tongue is raised towards the soft palate. The friction is noticeable. With its English counterpart, however, the friction is not noticeable.

Only the simple finals a, e, and u and the compound finals that start with a, e, or u can be combined with g, k, and h.

Practice:

☐ **B.3.A**

gu	**ge**	**ga**
ku	**ke**	**ka**
hu	**he**	**ha**

☐ **B.3.B g vs. k**

gu	**ku**	**ge**	**ke**

☐ **B.3.C g vs. h**

gu	**hu**	**ge**	**he**

☐ **B.3.D k vs. h**

ke	**he**	**ku**	**hu**

☐ **B.3.E g, k, h**

gu	**ku**	**hu**
he	**ke**	**ge**

B.4: j, q, x

To make the j sound, first raise the flat center of the tongue to the roof of the mouth and position the tip of the tongue against the back of the bottom teeth, and then loosen the tongue and let the air squeeze out through the channel thus made. It is unaspirated and the vocal cords do not vibrate. Chinese j is similar to the English j as in "jeep," but it is unvoiced and articulated with the tip of the tongue resting behind the lower incisors. You also need to pull the corners of your mouth straight back to pronounce j.

q is pronounced in the same manner as j, but it is aspirated. Chinese q is similar to the English ch as in "cheese," except that it is articulated with the tip of the tongue resting behind the lower incisors. Don't forget to pull the corners of your mouth straight back.

To make the x sound, first raise the flat center of the tongue toward (but not touching) the hard palate and then let the air squeeze out. The vocal cords do not vibrate. x, like j and q, is articulated with the tip of the tongue resting behind the lower incisors. To pronounce x correctly, you also need to pull the corners of your mouth straight back, like squeezing a smile.

The finals that can be combined with j, q and x are limited to i and ü and the compound finals which start with i or ü. When j, q and x are combined with ü or a compound final starting with ü, the umlaut is omitted and the ü appears as u.

Practice:

☐ **B.4.A**

ji	**ju**
qi	**qu**
xi	**xu**

☐ **B.4.B j vs. q**

ji	**qi**	**ju**	**qu**

☐ **B.4.C q vs. x**

qi	**xi**	**qu**	**xu**

☐ **B.4.D j vs. x**

ji	**xi**	**ju**	**xu**

☐ **B.4.E j, q, x**

ji	**qi**	**xi**
ju	**qu**	**xu**

B.5: z, c, s

z is similar to the English ds sound as in "lids."

c is similar to the English ts sound as in "students." It is aspirated.

s is similar to the English s sound.

The above group of sounds is pronounced with the tongue touching the back of the upper teeth.

The simple finals that can be combined with z, c, s are a, e, u and the front apical vowel i. (*Not* the regular palatal high front vowel i.)

In pronouncing the syllables zi, ci and si the tongue is held in the same position throughout the syllable except that it is slightly relaxed as the articulation moves from the voiceless initial consonant to the voiced vowel.

Practice:

☐ **B.5.A**

za	**zu**	**ze**	**zi**
ca	**cu**	**ce**	**ci**
sa	**su**	**se**	**si**

☐ **B.5.B s vs. z**

sa	**za**	**su**	**zu**
se	**ze**	**si**	**zi**

☐ **B.5.C z vs. c**

za	**ca**	**zi**	**ci**
ze	**ce**	**zu**	**cu**

☐ **B.5.D s vs. c**

sa	**ca**	**si**	**ci**
su	**cu**	**se**	**ce**

☐ **B.5.E z, c, s**

sa	**za**	**ca**
su	**zu**	**cu**
se	**ze**	**ce**
si	**zi**	**ci**
za	**cu**	**se**
ci	**sa**	**zu**
su	**zi**	**ce**

B.6 zh, ch, sh. r

To make the zh sound, first curl up the tip of the tongue against the hard palate, then loosen it and let the air squeeze out the channel thus made. It is unaspirated and the vocal cords do not vibrate. zh sounds rather like the first sound in "jerk," but it is unvoiced and produced with the tip of the tongue raised against the hard palate.

ch is pronounced in the same manner as zh, but ch is aspirated. ch sounds rather like the "ch" in "chirp" except that it is produced with the tip of the tongue raised against the hard palate.

To make the sh sound, turn up the tip of the tongue toward (but not touching) the hard palate and then let the air squeeze out. The vocal cords do not vibrate. sh sounds rather like the "sh" in "shirt" and "Shirley" except that it is produced with the tip of the tongue raised against the hard palate.

r is pronounced in the same manner as sh, but it is voiced, therefore the vocal cords vibrate. You can pronounce it simply by prolonging sh, but make sure your lips are not rounded.

The finals that can be combined with zh, ch, sh, r are a, e, u and the back apical vowel i, as well as the compound finals which start with a, e, or u. In pronouncing the syllables zhi, chi, shi and ri the tongue is held in the same position throughout the syllable except that it is slightly relaxed as the articulation moves from the initial consonant to the vowel.

Practice:

☐ **B.6.A**

zha zhu zhe zhi
cha chu che chi
sha shu she shi
ru re ri

☐ **B.6.B zh vs. sh**

sha zha shu zhu

☐ **B.6.C zh vs. ch**

zha cha zhu chu

☐ **B.6.D ch vs. sh**

chu shu sha cha

☐ **B.6.E zh, ch, sh**

shi zhi chi shi
she zhe che she

☐ **B.6.F sh vs. r**

shu ru shi ri

☐ **B.6.G r vs. l**

lu ru li ri

☐ **B.6.H sh, r, l**

she re le re

☐ **B.6.I zh, ch, r**

zhe re che re

☐ **B.6.J zh, ch, sh, r**

sha cha zha
shu zhu chu ru
zhi chi shi ri
che zhe she re

A Reference Chart for Initials

	UNASPIRATED STOPS	ASPIRATED STOPS	NASALS	FRICATIVES	VOICED CONTINUANTS
Labials	b	p	m	f	w*
Alveolars	d	t	n	l	
Dental sibilants	z	c		s	
Retroflexes	zh	ch		sh	r
Palatals	j	q		x	y*
Velars	g	k		h	

* See explanations of w and y in the "Spelling Rules" section on the next page.

C. Compound Finals:

1.	**ai**	**ei**	**ao**	**ou**					
2.	**an**	**en**	**ang**	**eng**	**ong**				
3.	**ia**	**iao**	**ie**	**iu***	**ian**	**in**	**iang**	**ing**	**iong**
4.	**ua**	**uo**	**uai**	**ui****	**uan**	**un*****	**uang**	**ueng**	
5.	**üe**	**üan**	**ün**						
6.	**er**								

* The main vowel **o** is omitted in the spelling of the final **iu (iu = iou)**. Therefore, **iu** represents the sound **iou**. The **o** is especially conspicuous in third and fourth tone syllables.
** The main vowel **e** is omitted in the final **ui (ui = uei)**. Like **iu** above, it is quite conspicuous in third and fourth tone syllables.
*** The main vowel **e** is omitted in **un (un = uen)**.

In Chinese, compound finals are composed of a main vowel and one or two secondary vowels, or a main vowel and one secondary vowel followed by one of the nasal endings -n or -ng. When the initial vowels are a, e, and o, they are stressed. The vowels following are soft and brief. When the initial vowels are i, u, and ü, the main vowels come after them. i, u and ü are transitional sounds. If there are vowels or nasal consonants after the main vowels, they should be unstressed as well. In a compound final, the main vowel can be affected by the phonemes before and after it. For instance, the a in ian is pronounced with a lower degree of aperture and a higher position of the tongue than the a in ma; and to pronounce the a in ang the tongue has to be positioned more to the back of the mouth than the a elsewhere.

When pronouncing the e in ei, the tongue has to be positioned a bit toward the front and a bit higher than pronouncing the simple vowel e alone. The e in ie is pronounced with a lower position of the tongue than the e in ei. When pronouncing the e in en and the e in a neutral tone like the second syllable of gēge, the tongue position should be in the center, like the e in "the."

As noted above, in *Pinyin* orthography some vowels are omitted for the sake of economy, e.g., i(o)u, u(e)i. However, when pronouncing those sounds, the vowels must not be omitted.

SPELLING RULES

1. If there is no initial consonant before i, i is written as a semi-vowel, y. Thus ia, ie, iao, iu, ian, iang become ya, ye, yao, you (note that the o cannot be omitted here), yan, yang. Before in and ing, add y, e.g., yin and ying.
2. If there is no initial consonant before ü, add a y and drop the umlaut: yu, yuan, yue, yun.
3. u becomes w if it is not preceded by an initial, e.g., wa, wai, wan, wang, wei, wen, weng, wo. u by itself becomes wu.
4. ueng is written as ong if preceded by an initial, e.g., tong, dong, nong, long. Without an initial, it is weng.
5. In order to avoid confusion, an apostrophe is used to separate two syllables with connecting vowels, e.g., nǚ'ér (daughter) and the city Xī'ān (nǚ and ér, Xī and ān are separate syllables). Sometimes an apostrophe is also needed when there are confusions even if the two syllables are not connected by vowels, e.g., fáng'ài (to hinder) and fāng'àn (plan; scheme).

Practice

C.1: ai **ei** **ao** **ou**

pai	**lei**	**dao**	**gou**
cai	**mei**	**sao**	**shou**

C.2: an en ang eng ong

☐ **C.2.A an vs. ang**

tan	**tang**	**chan**	**chang**
zan	**zhang**	**gan**	**gang**

☐ **C.2.B en vs. eng**

sen	**seng**	**shen**	**sheng**
zhen	**zheng**	**fen**	**feng**

☐ **C.2.C eng vs. ong**

cheng chong deng dong

zheng zhong keng kong

C.3: ia iao ie iu ian in iang ing iong

☐ **C.3.A ia vs. ie**

jia jie qia qie

xia xie ya ye

☐ **C.3.B ian vs. iang**

xian xiang qian qiang

jian jiang yan yang

☐ **C.3.C in vs. ing**

bin bing pin ping

jin jing yin ying

☐ **C.3.D iu vs. iong**

xiu xiong you yong

☐ **C.3.E ao vs. iao**

zhao jiao shao xiao

chao qiao ao yao

☐ **C.3.F an vs. ian**

chan qian shan xian

zhan jian an yan

☐ **C.3.g ang vs. iang**

zhang jiang shang xiang

chang qiang ang yang

C.4: ua uo uai ui uan un uang

☐ **C.4.A ua vs. uai**

shua shuai wa wai

☐ **C.4.B uan vs. uang**

shuan shuang chuan chuang

zhuan zhuang wan wang

☐ **C.4.C un vs. uan**

dun duan kun kuan

zhun zhuan wen wan

☐ **C.4.D uo vs. ou**

duo dou zhuo zhou

suo sou wo ou

☐ **C.4.E ui vs. un**

tui tun zhui zhun

dui dun wei wen

C.5: üe üan ün

☐ **C.5.A ün vs. un**

jun zhun yun wen

☐ **C.5.B üan vs. uan**

xuan shuan juan zhuan

quan chuan yuan wan

☐ **C.5.C üe**

yue que jue

C.6: er

ger*

* Due to the lack of words with first tone in them, the word "ger" (ge with r ending) is here to give the reader a feel for it. See **D.1 Practice III** below for more examples.

D. Tones

Every Chinese syllable has a tone.

D.1: Four Tones and Neutral Tone:

There are four tones in Modern Standard Chinese: the first tone, the second tone, the third tone, and the fourth tone.

The first tone is a high level tone with a pitch value of 55 (see chart below); its tone mark is "¯".

The second tone is a rising tone with a pitch value of 35; its tone mark is "ˊ".

The citation form of the third tone has a pitch value of 214. However, in normal speech it almost always occurs as a "half third tone" with a pitch value of 21. Its tone mark is "ˇ". Please see **D.2: Tone Sandhi** for discussions on how to pronounce third tone syllables in succession.

The fourth tone is a falling tone with a pitch value of 51; its tone mark is "ˋ".

In addition to the four tones, there is also a neutral tone (qīngshēng) in Modern Standard Chinese. Neutral tone words include those that do not have fundamental tones (e.g., the question particle ma), and those which do have tones when pronounced individually, but are not stressed in certain compounds (e.g., the second ba in bàba or "father"). There are no tone marks for neutral tone syllables. A neutral tone syllable is pronounced briefly and softly, and its pitch value is determined by the stressed syllable immediately before it. A neutral tone following a first tone syllable, as in māma (mother), carries a pitch tone of 2. When it follows a second tone syllable, a third tone syllable, or a fourth tone syllable, its pitch value will be 3, 4, and 1 respectively.

Tones are very important in Chinese. The same syllable with different tones can have different meanings. For instance, mā is mother, má is hemp, mǎ is horse, mà is to scold, ma is an interrogative particle. The four tones can be diagrammed as follows:

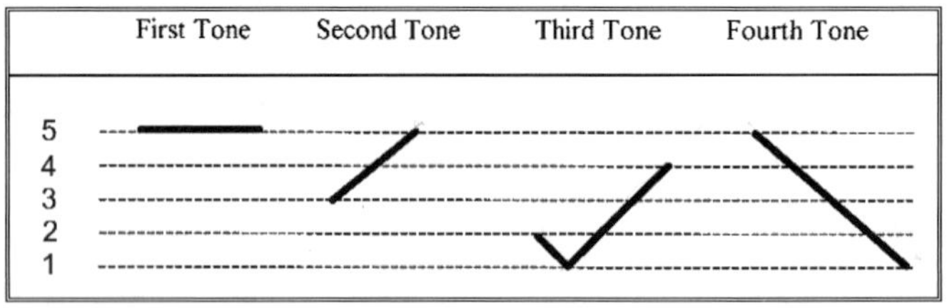

First Tone Second Tone Third Tone Fourth Tone

5
4
3
2
1

Tone marks are written above the main vowel of a syllable. The main vowel can be identified according to the following sequence: a-o-e-i-u-ü. For instance, in ao the main vowel is a. In ei the main vowel is e. There is one exception: when i and u are combined into a syllable, the tone mark is written on the second vowel: iù, uì.

D.1 Practice I: Monosyllabic Words

☐ **1.A Four Tones**

bī	**bí**	**bǐ**	**bì**
pū	**pú**	**pǔ**	**pù**
dà	**dǎ**	**dá**	**dā**
shè	**shě**	**shé**	**shē**
tí	**tī**	**tǐ**	**tì**
kè	**kě**	**kē**	**ké**
jǐ	**jí**	**jì**	**jī**
gú	**gù**	**gū**	**gǔ**

☐ **1.B 1st vs. 2nd**

zā	**zá**
chū	**chú**
hē	**hé**
shī	**shí**

☐ **1.C 1st vs. 3rd**

tū	**tǔ**
mō	**mǒ**

☐ **1.D 1st vs. 4th**

fā	**fà**
dī	**dì**

	xī	xǐ
	shā	shǎ
☐	1.E	2nd vs. 1st
	hú	hū
	xí	xī
	zhé	zhē
	pó	pō
☐	1.G	2nd vs. 4th
	lú	lù
	mó	mò
	cí	cì
	zhé	zhè
☐	1.I	3rd vs. 2nd
	chǔ	chú
	kě	ké
	xǐ	xí
	qǔ	qú
☐	1.K	4th vs. 1st
	jì	jī
	là	lā
	sù	sū
	hè	hē
☐	1.M	4th vs. 3rd
	sà	sǎ
	zì	zǐ
	kù	kǔ
	zhè	zhě

	qū	qù
	kē	kè
☐	1.F	2nd vs. 3rd
	gé	gě
	tí	tǐ
	jú	jǔ
	rú	rǔ
☐	1.H	3rd vs. 1st
	tǎ	tā
	mǐ	mī
	gǔ	gū
	chě	chē
☐	1.J	3rd vs. 4th
	bǒ	bò
	nǐ	nì
	chǔ	chù
	rě	rè
☐	1.l	4th vs. 2nd
	nà	ná
	zè	zé
	jù	jú
	lǜ	lǘ

D.1 Practice II: Bisyllabic Words

2.a	1st+1st:	chūzū	tūchū	chūfā
2.b	1st+2nd:	chātú	xīqí	chūxí
2.c	1st+3rd:	shēchǐ	gēqǔ	chūbǎn
2.d	1st+4th:	chūsè	hūshì	jīlǜ
2.e	2nd+1st:	shíshī	qíjī	shíchā
2.f	2nd+2nd:	jíhé	shépí	pígé
2.g	2nd+3rd:	jítǐ	bóqǔ	zhélǐ
2.h	2nd+4th:	qítè	fúlì	chíxù
2.i	3rd+1st:	zǔzhī	zhǔjī	lǐkē
2.j	3rd+2nd:	pǔjí	zhǔxí	chǔfá
2.k	3rd+4th:	lǚkè	gǔlì	tǐzhì

2.l	4th+1st:	zìsī	qìchē	lùshī
2.m	4th+2nd:	fùzá	dìtú	shìshí
2.n	4th+3rd:	zìjǐ	bìhǔ	dìzhǐ
2.o	4th+4th:	mùdì	xùmù	dàdì

D.1 Practice III: Words with "er" sound

3.a	érzi	érqiě
3.b	ěrduo	mù'ěr
3.c	shí'èr	èrshí

D.2: Tone Sandhi

If two third tone syllables are spoken in succession, the first third tone becomes second tone. This tone change is known as *tone sandhi* in linguistics. For instance,

xǐlǐ	→	xílǐ	(baptism)
chǐrǔ	→	chírǔ	(shame)
qǔshě	→	qúshě	(accept or reject)

Note: Following standard *Pinyin* practice, we do not change the tone marks from third to second tone. Initially the student might have to consciously remember that the first syllable actually is pronounced in the second tone, but through practice and by imitating the teacher, it will soon become an automatic habit.

D.2 Practice

chǔlǐ	→	chúlǐ	gǔpǔ	→	gúpǔ
bǐnǐ	→	bínǐ	jǔzhǐ	→	júzhǐ
zǐnǚ	→	zínǚ	zhǐshǐ	→	zhíshǐ

D.3: Neutral Tone

The neutral tone occurs in unstressed syllables. It is unmarked. For instance,

chēzi (car)	māma (mom)	chúzi (cook)
shūshu (uncle)	lǐzi (plum)	shìzi (persimmon)

D.3 Practice

1. māma	gēge	shīfu	chūqu
2. dízi	bóbo	bízi	chúle
3. lǐzi	qǐzi	dǐzi	fǔshang
4. bàba	dìdi	kèqi	kùzi

E. Combination Exercises

I.

shān	xiān	sān
cháng	qiáng	cáng
zhǐ	jǐ	zǐ
lüè	nüè	yuè
kè	lè	rè

II.

Zhōngguó	xīngqī	lǜshī	zhàopiàn
zàijiàn	tóngxué	xǐhuan	diànshì
yīnyuè	kělè	yǎnlèi	shàngwǔ
cèsuǒ	chūntiān	xiàwǔ	bànyè
gōngkè	kāishǐ	rìjì	cāntīng
zuìjìn	xīwàng	yīsheng	chūzū
zhōumò	guānxi	dòufu	jiéhūn
liúxué	nǚ'ér	shénme	suīrán
wǎngqiú	xǐzǎo	niánjí	yóuyǒng

III. The Chinese Writing System

A. The Formation of Chinese Characters

Unlike English, which is an alphabetic language, Chinese writing is represented by "characters," each of which represents a syllable. Characters are traditionally divided into the following six categories:

1. 象形 xiàngxíng pictographs, pictographic characters

EXAMPLES:

人		rén	person
山		shān	mountain
日		rì	sun
月		yuè	moon
木		mù	tree

2. 指事 **zhǐshì** **self-explanatory characters**

EXAMPLES:

上	二	shàng	above
下	二	xià	below

3. 会意 **huìyì** **associative compounds**

EXAMPLES:

明		míng	bright
休		xiū	rest

4. 形声 **xíngshēng** **pictophonetic characters (with one element indicating meaning and the other sound)**

EXAMPLES: 江，河，饭，姑

5. 转注 **zhǎnzhù** **mutually explanatory characters**

EXAMPLES: 老，考

6. 假借 **jiǎjiè** **phonetic loan characters**

EXAMPLES: 来，我

A popular myth is that Chinese writing is pictographic, and that each Chinese character represents a picture. It is true that some Chinese characters evolved from pictures, but these comprise only a small proportion of the characters. The vast majority of Chinese characters are pictophonetic characters consisting of a radical and a phonetic element. The radical often suggests the meaning of a character, and the phonetic element indicates its original pronunciation, which may or may not represent its modern pronunciation.

B. Basic Chinese Radicals

Although there are more than fifty thousand Chinese characters in existence, one only needs to know two or three thousand to be considered literate. Mastering two or three thousand characters is, of course, still a rather formidable task. However, the learning process will be more effective and easier if one knows well the basic components of Chinese characters. Traditionally, Chinese characters are grouped together according to their common components known as "radicals" (部首，bùshǒu). The 214 "Kangxi radicals" have been the standard set of radicals since the publication of the great *Kangxi Dictionary* (康熙字典, Kāngxī Zìdiǎn) in 1716, although some contemporary dictionaries, which treat simplified characters as primary forms, have reduced that number to 189. By knowing the radicals and other basic components well, you will find recognizing, remembering and reproducing characters much easier. Knowing the radicals is also a must when using dictionaries that arrange characters according to their radicals. The following is a selection of forty radicals that everybody should know well when starting to learn characters.

Chinese radical	Pinyin	English	Examples
1. 人（亻）	rén	person	今，他
2. 刀（刂）	dāo	knife	分，到
3. 力	lì	power	加，助
4. 又	yòu	right hand; again	友，取
5. 口	kǒu	mouth	叫，可
6. 囗**	wéi	enclose	回，因
7. 土	tǔ	earth	在，坐
8. 夕	xī	sunset	外，多
9. 大	dà	big	天，太
10. 女	nǚ	woman	婆，好
11. 子	zǐ	son	字，孩
12. 寸	cùn	inch	寺，封
13. 小	xiǎo	small	少，尖
14. 工	gōng	labor; work	左，差
15. 幺	yāo	tiny; small	幻，幼
16. 弓	gōng	bow	引，弟
17. 心（忄）	xīn	heart	想，忙
18. 戈	gē	dagger-axe	我，或
19. 手（扌）	shǒu	hand	拿，打
20. 日	rì	sun	早，明
21. 月	yuè	moon	期，朗
22. 木	mù	wood	李，杯
23. 水（氵）	shuǐ	water	汞，洗
24. 火（灬）	huǒ	fire	烧，热

	Radical	Pinyin	Meaning	Examples
25.	田	tián	field	男，留
26.	目	mù	eye	看，睡
27.	示 (礻)	shì	show	票，社
28.	糸 (纟)	mì	fine silk	素，红
29.	耳	ěr	ear	聋，聊
30.	衣 (衤)	yī	clothing	袋，衫
31.	言 (讠)	yán	speech	誓，说
32.	贝	bèi	cowrie shell	贵，财
33.	走	zǒu	walk	趣，起
34.	足	zú	foot	跳，跑
35.	金 (钅)	jīn	gold	鉴，钱
36.	门	mén	door	间，闷
37.	隹	zhuī	short-tailed bird	难，集
38.	雨	yǔ	rain	零，雲
39.	食 (饣)	shí	eat	餐，饭
40.	马	mǎ	horse	骑，骂

(** = used as radical only, not as a character by itself)

弓	弓字旁
子	子字旁
女	女字旁
纟	绞丝旁

马	马字旁
扌	提手旁
艹	草字头
大	大字头

Two Chinese radical charts.

C. Basic Strokes

The following is a list of basic strokes:

Basic stroke	Chinese	Pinyin	English	Examples
1. "丶"	点	diǎn	dot	小，六
2. "一"	横	héng	horizontal	一，六
3. "丨"	竖	shù	vertical	十，中
4. "丿"	撇	piě	downward left	人，大
5. "㇏"	捺	nà	downward right	八，人
6. "㇀"	提	tí	upward	我，江
7. "乛"	横钩	hénggōu	horizontal hook	你，字
8. "亅"	竖钩	shùgōu	vertical hook	小，你
9. "㇂"	斜钩	xiégōu	slanted hook	戈，我
10. "㇕"	横折	héngzhé	horizontal bend	五，口
11. "𠃊"	竖折	shùzhé	vertical bend	七，亡

Note: With the exception of the "**tí**" stroke (which moves upward to the right) and the "**piě**" stroke (which moves downward to the left), all Chinese strokes move from top to bottom, and from left to right.

D. Stroke Order

Following is a list of rules of stroke order. When writing a Chinese character, it is important that you follow the rules. Following the rules will make it easier for you to accurately count the number of strokes in a character. Knowing the exact number of strokes in a character will help you find the character in a radical-based dictionary. Also, your Chinese characters will look better if you write them in the correct stroke order!

1. From left to right (川，人)
2. From top to bottom (三)
3. Horizontal before vertical (十)
4. From outside to inside (月)
5. Middle before two sides (小)
6. Inside before closing (日，回)

Note: Learn the correct stroke order of the characters introduced in this book by using the *Integrated Chinese Level 1 Part 1 Character Workbook*.

IV. Useful Expressions

A. Classroom Expressions

The following is a list of classroom expressions that you will hear every day in your Chinese class.

1.	Nǐ hǎo!	How are you? How do you do?
2.	Lǎoshī hǎo!	How are you, teacher?
3.	Shàng kè.	Let's begin the class.
4.	Xià kè.	The class is over.
5.	Dǎ kāi shū.	Open the book.
6.	Wǒ shuō, nǐmen tīng.	I'll speak, you listen.
7.	Kàn hēibǎn.	Look at the blackboard.
8.	Duì bu duì?	Is it right?
9.	Duì!	Right! Correct!
10.	Hěn hǎo!	Very good!
11.	Qǐng gēn wǒ shuō.	Please repeat after me.
12.	Zài shuō yí biàn.	Say it again.
13.	Dǒng bu dǒng?	Do you understand?
14.	Dǒng le.	Yes, I/we understand; I/we do.
15.	Zàijiàn!	Good-bye!

B. Survival Expressions

The following is a list of important expressions that will help you survive in a Chinese language environment. A good language student is constantly learning new words by asking questions. Learn the following expressions well and start to acquire Chinese on your own!

1.	Duìbuqǐ!	Sorry!
2.	Qǐng wèn...	Excuse me...; May I ask...
3.	Xièxie!	Thanks!
4.	Zhè shì shénme?	What is this?
5.	Wǒ bù dǒng.	I don't understand.
6.	Qǐng zài shuō yí biàn.	Please say it one more time.
7.	"..." Zhōngwén zěnme shuō?	How do you say "..." in Chinese?
8.	"..." shì shénme yìsi?	What does "..." mean?
9.	Qǐng nǐ gěi wǒ...	Please give me...
10.	Qǐng nǐ gàosu wǒ...	Please tell me...

C. Numerals

Having good control of the Chinese numerals will facilitate your dealing with real life situations such as shopping, asking for time and dates, etc. You can get a head start by memorizing 1 to 10 well now.

1.	yī	one	一
2.	èr	two	二
3.	sān	three	三
4.	sì	four	四
5.	wǔ	five	五
6.	liù	six	六
7.	qī	seven	七
8.	bā	eight	八
9.	jiǔ	nine	九
10.	shí	ten	十

Do you know the names of the strokes below? Can you write them properly?

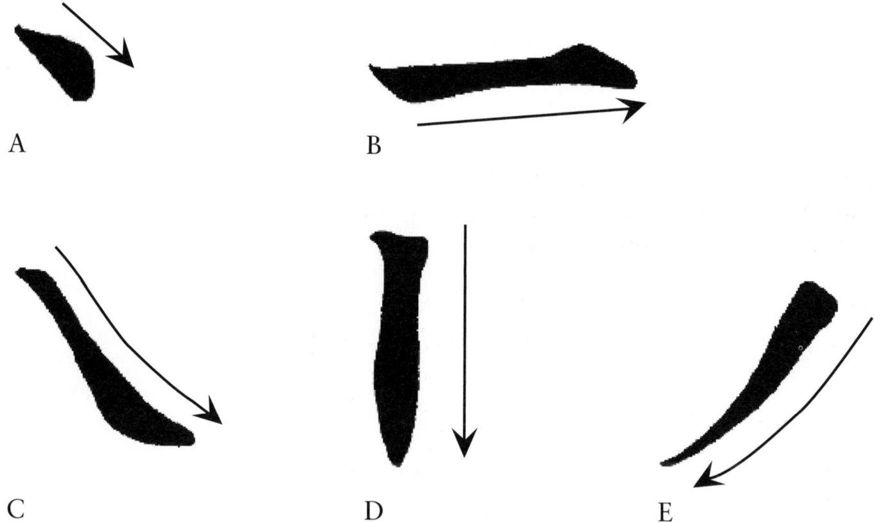

LESSON 1 Greetings

第一课 问好

Dì yī kè Wèn hǎo

1

LEARNING OBJECTIVES

In this lesson, you will learn to use Chinese to

- Exchange basic greetings;
- Request a person's last name and full name and provide your own;
- Determine whether someone is a teacher or a student;
- Ascertain someone's nationality.

RELATE AND GET READY

In your own culture/community—

1. How do people greet each other when meeting for the first time?
2. Do people say their given name or family name first?
3. How do acquaintances or close friends address each other?

Dialogue I: Exchanging Greetings

你好❶！

你好！

请问❷，你❸贵姓？

我姓①李。你呢②？

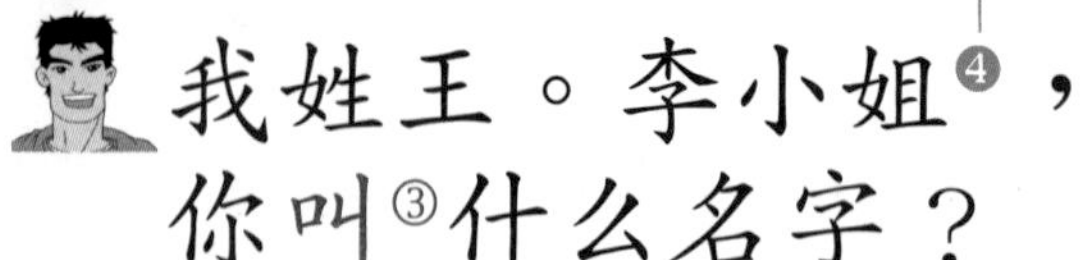
我姓王。李小姐❹，
你叫③什么名字？

我叫李友。王先生，
你叫什么名字？

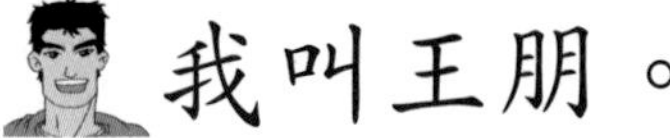
我叫王朋。

LANGUAGE NOTES

❶ 你好！(Nǐ hǎo!) is a common form of greeting. It can be used to address strangers upon first introduction or between old acquaintances. To respond, simply repeat the same greeting.

❷ 请问 (qǐng wèn) is a polite formula to be used to get someone's attention before asking a question or making an inquiry, similar to "excuse me, may I please ask…" in English.

❸ You can replace 你 (nǐ) with its honorific form, 您 (nín), if you wish to be more polite and respectful. See Lesson 6, Dialogue I, Language Note 1.

❹ 小姐 (xiǎojiě) is a word with two third tone syllables. The tone sandhi rule applies, thus making the first third tone 小 (xiǎo) a second tone. The second syllable 姐 (jiě) can also be pronounced in the neutral tone.

Nǐ hǎo❶!

Nǐ hǎo !

Qǐng wèn❷, nǐ❸ guì xìng?

Wǒ xìng① Lǐ. Nǐ ne②?

Wǒ xìng Wáng. Lǐ xiǎojiě❹, nǐ jiào③shénme míngzi?

Wǒ jiào Lǐ Yǒu. Wáng xiānsheng, nǐ jiào shénme míngzi?

Wǒ jiào Wáng Péng.

VOCABULARY

1.	你	nǐ	pr	you
2.	好	hǎo	adj	fine; good; nice; O.K.; it's settled
3.	请	qǐng	v	please (polite form of request); to treat or to invite (somebody)
4.	问	wèn	v	to ask (a question)
5.	贵	guì	adj	honorable; expensive
6.	姓	xìng	v/n	(one's) surname is...; to be surnamed; surname [See Grammar 1.]
7.	我	wǒ	pr	I; me
8.	呢	ne	qp	(question particle) [See Grammar 2.]
9.	小姐	xiǎojiě	n	Miss; young lady
10.	叫	jiào	v	to be called; to call [See Grammar 3.]
11.	什么	shénme	qpr	what

VOCABULARY

12.	名字	míngzi	n	name
13.	先生	xiānsheng	n	Mr.; husband; teacher

Proper Nouns

14.	李友	Lǐ Yǒu	(a personal name)
	李	lǐ	(a surname); plum
15.	王朋	Wáng Péng	(a personal name)
	王	wáng	(a surname); king

Grammar

1. The Verb 姓 (xìng)

姓 (xìng) is both a noun and a transitive verb. When it is used as a verb, it must be followed by an object.

❶ A: 你姓什么？

Nǐ xìng shénme?

(What is your surname? Lit: You are surnamed what?)

B: 我姓李。

Wǒ xìng Lǐ.

(My surname is Li.)

姓 (xìng) is usually negated with 不 (bù). [See Grammar 6.]

❷ **A:** 你姓李吗？

Nǐ xìng Lǐ ma?

(Is your family name Li?)

B: 我不姓李。

Wǒ bú xìng Lǐ.

(My surname is not Li.)

It is incorrect to say: *我不姓。 *Wǒ bú xìng.

However, when 姓 (xìng) is used with 贵 (guì) to form a respectful or polite expression to ask for someone's surname, the proper way to inquire and to respond is as follows:

❸ **A:** 你贵姓？

Nǐ guì xìng?

(What is your surname?) (Lit: Your honorable surname is…?)

Remember to drop the honorific 贵 when you reply:

B: 我姓王。

Wǒ xìng Wáng.

(My surname is Wang.)

It is incorrect to say: *我贵姓王。 *Wǒ guì xìng Wáng.

One may also hear people respond to 你贵姓 (Nǐ guì xìng) by saying 免贵姓王 (Miǎn guì xìng Wáng), 免贵姓李 (Miǎn guì xìng Lǐ). Lit: Dispense with the honorable. [My] surname is Wang/Li.

2. Questions Ending with 呢 (ne)

呢 (ne) often follows a noun or pronoun to form a question when the content of the question is already clear from the context.

❶ **A:** 请问，你贵姓？

Qǐng wèn, nǐ guì xìng?

(What's your family name, please?)

B: 我姓李，你呢？

Wǒ xìng Lǐ, nǐ ne?

(My family name is Li. How about you?)

❷ **A:** 你叫什么名字？

Nǐ jiào shénme míngzi?

(What's your name?)

B: 我叫王朋，你呢？

Wǒ jiào Wáng Péng, nǐ ne?

(My name is Wang Peng. How about you?)

When 呢 (ne) is used in this way, there must be some context. In each of the two examples above, the context is provided by the preceding sentence, 我姓李 (Wǒ xìng Lǐ) in (1), and 我叫王朋 (Wǒ jiào Wáng Péng) in (2).

3. The Verb 叫 (jiào)

The verb 叫 (jiào) has several meanings. It means "to be called" in this lesson. Like 姓 (xìng), it must be followed by an object, which can be either a full name or a given name, but seldom a given name that consists only of one syllable.

❶ **A:** 你叫什么名字？

Nǐ jiào shénme míngzi?

(What is your name?)

B: 我叫王朋。

Wǒ jiào Wáng Péng.

(My name is Wang Peng.)

叫 (jiào) is usually negated with 不 (bù). [See Grammar 6.]

❷ **A:** 你叫李生吗？

Nǐ jiào Lǐ Shēng ma?

(Is your name Li Sheng?)

B: 我不叫李生。

Wǒ bú jiào Lǐ Shēng.

(My name is not Li Sheng.)

From the examples above, we can see that the basic word order in a Chinese sentence runs like this:

Subject + Verb + Object

The word order remains the same in statements and questions. Remember that you don't place the question word at the beginning of a question as you do in English, unless that question word is the subject. (See more on word order in Grammar 3 in Lesson 2 and Grammar 1 in Lesson 4.)

Language Practice

A. Mix and mingle

Walk around the classroom and get to know your classmates:

A: 你好！	**A:** Nǐ hǎo!
B: ______________ 。	**B:** __________.
A: 请问，你贵姓？	**A:** Qǐng wèn, nǐ guì xìng?
B: 我姓______________ 。	**B:** Wǒ xìng __________.
你呢？	Nǐ ne?
A: 我姓______________ ，	**A:** Wǒ xìng __________,
我叫______________ ，	wǒ jiào __________,
你叫什么名字？	nǐ jiào shénme míngzi?
B: 我叫______________ 。	**B:** Wǒ jiào __________.

B. Meeting for the first time/Getting acquainted

Complete the following exchange between two people who have never met before. Do a role play based on the exchange.

A: 你好！	**A:** Nǐ hǎo!
B: ________________ 。	**B:** __________.
A: 我姓________________，	**A:** Wǒ xìng __________,
请问，你贵姓？	qǐng wèn, nǐ guì xìng?
B: ________________ 。	**B:** __________.
A: ________________，	**A:** __________,
你叫什么名字？	nǐ jiào shénme míngzi?
B: 我叫________________ 。	**B:** Wǒ jiào __________.

Dialogue II: Asking about Someone's Nationality

王先生，你是④老师吗⑤？

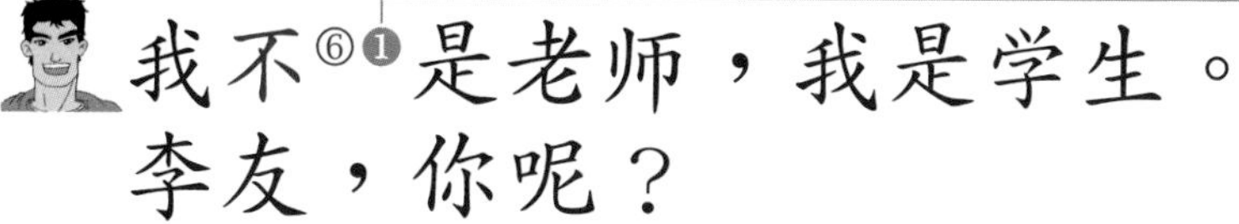

我不⑥❶是老师，我是学生。李友，你呢？

我也⑦是学生。你是中国人吗？

是，我是北京人。你是美国人吗？

是，我是纽约人。

LANGUAGE NOTE

❶ The original tone of 不 is a 4th tone "bù". However, when followed by another 4th tone syllable, 不 changes to 2nd tone, as in 不是 (bú shì).

 Wáng xiānsheng, nǐ shì④ lǎoshī ma⑤?

 Wǒ bú⑥❶ shì lǎoshī, wǒ shì xuésheng. Lǐ Yǒu, nǐ ne?

 Wǒ yě⑦ shì xuésheng. Nǐ shì Zhōngguó rén ma?

 Shì, wǒ shì Běijīng rén. Nǐ shì Měiguó rén ma?

 Shì, wǒ shì Niǔyuē rén.

VOCABULARY

1.	是	shì	v	to be [See Grammar 4.]
2.	老师	lǎoshī	n	teacher
3.	吗	ma	qp	(question particle) [See Grammar 5.]
4.	不	bù	adv	not; no [See Grammar 6.]
5.	学生	xuésheng	n	student
6.	也	yě	adv	too; also [See Grammar 7.]
7.	人	rén	n	people; person

Proper Nouns

8.	中国	Zhōngguó	China
9.	北京	Běijīng	Beijing
10.	美国	Měiguó	America
11.	纽约	Niǔyuē	New York

Grammar

4. The Verb 是 (shì)

In Chinese, 是 (shì) is a verb which can be used to link two units that are in some way equivalent. These two units can be nouns, pronouns, or noun phrases, e.g.,

❶ A: 你是老师吗?

Nǐ shì lǎoshī ma?

(Are you a teacher?)

B: 我是老师。

Wǒ shì lǎoshī.

(I am a teacher.)

❷ 李友是学生。

Lǐ Yǒu shì xuésheng.

(Li You is a student.)

是 (shì) is usually negated with 不 (bù). [See also Grammar 6 below.]

❸ 王朋不是美国人。

Wáng Péng bú shì Měiguó rén.

(Wang Peng is not American.)

5. Questions Ending with 吗 (ma)

When 吗 (ma) is added to the end of a declarative statement, that statement is turned into a question. To answer the question in the affirmative, drop the 吗 (ma) from the end of the question; to answer the question in the negative, drop the 吗 (ma), and insert a negative adverb— usually 不 (bù)—before the verb. [See also Grammar 6 below.]

❶ Question: 你是老师吗？
Nǐ shì lǎoshī ma?
(Are you a teacher?)

Affirmative answer: 我是老师。
Wǒ shì lǎoshī.
(I am a teacher.)

Negative answer: 我不是老师。
Wǒ bú shì lǎoshī.
(I am not a teacher.)

❷ Question: 你姓王吗？
Nǐ xìng Wáng ma?
(Is your family name Wang?)

Affirmative: 我姓王。
Wǒ xìng Wáng.
(My family name is Wang.)

Negative: 我不姓王。
Wǒ bú xìng Wáng.
(My family name is not Wang.)

美中文化研究所理事长兼所长
北京大学教授

王 永 江

北京大学燕北园XX楼XX号
邮编:100091
电话:(010)-6288-XXXX

This is a typical business card. Circle the person's family name. Where is this person located?

6. The Negative Adverb 不 (bù)

In Chinese there are two main negative adverbs. One of the two, 不 (bù), occurs in this lesson.

❶ 我不是北京人。

Wǒ bú shì Běijīng rén.

(I am not from Beijing.)

❷ 李友不是中国人。

Lǐ Yǒu bú shì Zhōngguó rén.

(Li You is not Chinese.)

❸ 老师不姓王。

Lǎoshī bú xìng Wáng.

(The teacher's surname is not Wang.)

❹ 我不叫李中。

Wǒ bú jiào Lǐ Zhōng.

(My name is not Li Zhong.)

7. The Adverb 也 (yě)

The adverb 也 (yě) basically means "too" or "also." In Chinese, adverbs, especially one-syllable adverbs, normally appear after subjects and in front of verbs. They usually cannot precede subjects or follow verbs. The adverb 也 (yě) cannot be put before the subject or at the very end of a sentence.

❶ 我也是学生。

Wǒ yě shì xuésheng.

(I'm a student, too.)

❷ 王朋是学生，李友也是学生。

Wáng Péng shì xuésheng, Lǐ Yǒu yě shì xuésheng.

(Wang Peng is a student. Li You is a student, too.)

❸ 你是中国人，我也是中国人。

Nǐ shì Zhōngguó rén, wǒ yě shì Zhōngguó rén.

(You are Chinese. I am Chinese, too.)

(3a) 你是中国人，*我是中国人也。

Nǐ shì Zhōngguó rén, *wǒ shì Zhōngguó rén yě.

(3b) 你是中国人，*也我是中国人。

Nǐ shì Zhōngguó rén, *yě wǒ shì Zhōngguó rén.

When the adverb 也 (yě) is used together with the negative adverb 不 (bù), 也 (yě) is placed before 不 (bù), e.g.

❹ 王朋不是老师，李友也不是老师。

Wáng Péng bú shì lǎoshī, Lǐ Yǒu yě bú shì lǎoshī.

(Wang Peng is not a teacher. Li You is not a teacher, either.)

❺ 你不是纽约人，我也不是纽约人。

Nǐ bú shì Niǔyuē rén, wǒ yě bú shì Niǔyuē rén.

(You are not from New York. I am not from New York, either.)

Language Practice

C. 是…吗 (shì...ma)

Based on the text of Lesson 1 and your own situation, ask and answer the following questions with a partner.

EXAMPLE 王朋◇学生 — Wáng Péng ◇ xuésheng

A: 王朋是学生吗？ — **A:** Wáng Péng shì xuésheng ma?

B: 王朋是学生。 — **B:** Wáng Péng shì xuésheng.

1. 李友◇美国人 — **1.** Lǐ Yǒu ◇ Měiguó rén
2. 王朋◇中国人 — **2.** Wáng Péng ◇ Zhōngguó rén

3. 李友◇美国学生 — **3.** Lǐ Yǒu ◇ Měiguó xuésheng
4. 王朋◇北京人 — **4.** Wáng Péng ◇ Běijīng rén
5. 李友◇纽约人 — **5.** Lǐ Yǒu ◇ Niǔyuē rén
6. 你◇学生 — **6.** Nǐ ◇ xuésheng

D. 不 (bù)

Based on the text of Lesson 1 and your own situation, ask and answer the following questions with a partner.

EXAMPLE

A: 李小姐叫李朋吗？ — **A:** Lǐ xiǎojiě jiào Lǐ Péng ma?

B: 李小姐不叫李朋。 — **B:** Lǐ xiǎojiě bú jiào Lǐ Péng.

1. 李友是中国人吗？ — **1.** Lǐ Yǒu shì Zhōngguó rén ma?
2. 你是王朋吗? — **2.** Nǐ shì Wáng Péng ma?
3. 王朋是纽约人吗？ — **3.** Wáng Péng shì Niǔyuē rén ma?
4. 王先生叫王友吗？ — **4.** Wáng xiānsheng jiào Wáng Yǒu ma?
5. 你叫李友吗？ — **5.** Nǐ jiào Lǐ Yǒu ma?

E. 也 (yě)

Based on the text of Lesson 1 and your own situation, ask and answer the following questions with a partner.

1. 王朋是中国人，
   你也是中国人吗？ — **1.** Wáng Péng shì Zhōngguó rén, nǐ yě shì Zhōngguó rén ma?
2. 李友是纽约人，
   你也是纽约人吗？ — **2.** Lǐ Yǒu shì Niǔyuē rén, nǐ yě shì Niǔyuē rén ma?

3. 王朋不是老师，你呢？ **3.** Wáng Péng bú shì lǎoshī, nǐ ne?

4. 李友不是中国人，你呢？ **4.** Lǐ Yǒu bú shì Zhōngguó rén, nǐ ne?

5. 王朋姓王，
你也姓王吗？ **5.** Wáng Péng xìng Wáng,
nǐ yě xìng Wáng ma?

F. "I'm American. How about you? Where are you from?"

Walk around the classroom and find out about your classmates' nationality, state, or city origins. Remember that, to say that you are from America, California, or Boston, simply attach the word 人 (rén: person) to the name of the country, state, or city: 我是美国 (Měiguó)/California/Boston 人(rén).

A: 我是美国人，你呢? **A:** Wǒ shì Měiguó rén, nǐ ne?

B: ……。 **B:** ......

A: 你是Kentucky (the state of your current residence)人吗？ **A:** Nǐ shì Kentucky (the state of your current residence) rén ma?

B: 我是…人。/
我不是…人，我是…人。 **B:** Wǒ shì ... rén./
Wǒ bú shì... rén, wǒ shì ...rén.

A: 你是(pick a city in your respondent's home state)人吗？ **A:** Nǐ shì (pick a city in your respondent's home state) rén ma?

B: 我是(Louisville) 人。你呢？ **B:** Wǒ shì (Louisville) rén, nǐ ne?

A: 我是(Portland) 人。 **A:** Wǒ shì (Portland) rén.

HOW ABOUT YOU?

Where are you from?

1.	英国	Yīngguó	pn	Britain; England	
2.	法国	Fǎguó	pn	France	
3.	德国	Déguó	pn	Germany	
4.	日本	Rìběn	pn	Japan	
5.	韩国	Hánguó	pn	South Korea	
6.	加拿大	Jiā'nádà	pn	Canada	
7.	墨西哥	Mòxīgē	pn	Mexico	
8.	印度	Yìndù	pn	India	
9.	越南	Yuènán	pn	Vietnam	
10.	加州	Jiāzhōu	pn	California	
11.	夏威夷	Xiàwēiyí	pn	Hawaii	
12.	上海	Shànghǎi	pn	Shanghai	

If your country/state/city is not listed above, please ask your teacher and make a note here:

我是______________人。

Wǒ shì______________rén.

Culture Highlights

1. Most Chinese family names 姓 (xìng) are monosyllabic. There are, however, a few disyllabic family names such as 欧阳 (Ōuyáng) and 司徒 (Sītú). The number of Chinese family names is fairly limited. According to the most recent census, the most common family names are 李 (Lǐ), 王 (Wáng), 张 (Zhāng), 刘 (Liú), and 陈 (Chén). Family names precede official titles or other forms of address: 王先生 (Wáng xiānsheng, literally, Wang Mister), 李老师 (Lǐ lǎoshī, literally, Li Teacher), etc. When addressing strangers, it is proper to say 先生 (xiānsheng, Mr.) or 小姐 (xiǎojiě, Miss) following their family name.

赵 钱 孙 李
周 吴 郑 王
冯 陈 褚 卫
蒋 沈 韩 杨

These are the first sixteen surnames listed in the *Hundred Surnames*. Do you recognize any of them?

2. Family names 姓 (xìng) are sometimes called 姓氏 (xìngshì). 姓 (xìng) were originally passed down along maternal lines. Indeed, some of the most ancient Chinese family names such as 姬 (Jī), 妫 (Guī), 姒 (Sì), 姚 (Yáo), and 姜 (Jiāng) as well as the character 姓 (xìng) contain the female radical, 女 (nǚ). Aristocratic men and women were born with a 姓 (xìng). However, only aristocratic men would have a 氏 (shì) as a secondary family name. By the Western Han period (207 BCE–8 CE), 姓 (xìng) and 氏 (shì) had become indistinguishable, and even commoners had acquired family names or 姓 (xìng).

3. When talking about Chinese family names, most Chinese people will reference or mention the *Hundred Surnames*, 百家姓 (Bǎi Jiā Xìng). The book records the known family names of the Northern Song Dynasty in the 10th century. The 400-plus family names included in the work are arranged in quatrains with each eighth character rhymed. The book was a popular reading primer recited by schoolchildren.

There are dictionaries to interpret the *Hundred Surnames*. This is the cover of one of those dictionaries.

❹ In Chinese, family names 姓 (xìng) always precede personal or given names 名 (míng). Personal names usually carry auspicious or positive meanings. They can be either monosyllabic, written in one character, or disyllabic, written in two characters. In Chinese culture, a person is seldom referred to by his or her family name alone, especially if the family name is monosyllabic. For example, Wang Peng 王朋 (Wáng Péng), should not be referred to simply as Wang.

❺ When meeting someone for the first time, it is polite to first ask for his or her family name, rather than his/her full name. Then the question 你叫什么名字？(Nǐ jiào shénme míngzi? What is your name?) can be asked to find out his or her given name or full name.

❻ In Chinese culture the use of given names often suggests a much higher degree of intimacy than is the case in the West. If one's given name is monosyllabic, its use is even more limited, usually confined to one's lover or spouse. For example, Wang Peng's girlfriend can address him as Peng, especially in letters, but most people would call him Wang Peng rather than Peng.

Do you know any people with these family names?

毕 **(Bì);** 蔡 **(Cài);** 陈 **(Chén);** 高 **(Gāo);** 黄 **(Huáng);** 李 **(Lǐ);** 林 **(Lín);** 刘 **(Liú);** 罗 **(Luó);** 毛 **(Máo);** 史 **(Shǐ);** 王 **(Wáng);** 吴 **(Wú);** 谢 **(Xiè);** 徐 **(Xú);** 许 **(Xǔ);** 杨 **(Yáng);** 姚 **(Yáo);** 叶 **(Yè);** 张 **(Zhāng);** 郑 **(Zhèng);** 周 **(Zhōu)**

Pronunciation Exercises

1 Practice the following initials:

	b	p	d	t
1.	bǎo	pǎo	dā	tā
2.	bān	pān	dí	tí
3.	bù	pù	duì	tuì
4.	bō	pō	dīng	tīng
5.	bēng	pēng	dēng	tēng

2 Practice the following initials:

	j	q	z	c
1.	jiāo	qiāo	zāi	cāi
2.	jǐng	qǐng	zǎo	cǎo
3.	jīn	qīn	zì	cì
4.	jiè	qiè	zè	cè
5.	jiàn	qiàn	zhè	chè

3 Practice the following initials:

	sh	s	x
1.	shà	sà	xià
2.	shàn	sàn	xiàn
3.	shēn	sēn	xīn
4.	shēng	sēng	xīng

4 Practice the following tones:

1. tiāntiān	**2.** jīnnián	**3.** jīnglǐ	**4.** shēngqì
5. xīngqī	**6.** fādá	**7.** fāzhǎn	**8.** shēngdiào

5 Practice the following tone combinations:

1. nǐ hǎo	**2.** Lǐ Yǒu	**3.** lǎohǔ	**4.** zhǎnlǎn
5. hǎo duō	**6.** nǐ lái	**7.** hǎo shū	**8.** qǐng wèn

6 Practice the following syllables in neutral tones:

1. xiānsheng	**2.** míngzi	**3.** xiáojie	**4.** shénme
5. wǒ de	**6.** nǐ de	**7.** tā de	**8.** shéi de

English Text

Dialogue I

Wang Peng: How do you do?

Li You: How do you do?

Wang Peng: What's your family name, please? (lit. Please, may I ask... your honorable surname is...?)

Li You: My family name is Li. What's yours? (lit. I am surnamed Li, and you?)

Wang Peng: My family name is Wang. Miss Li, what's your name?

Li You: My name is Li You. Mr. Wang, what's your name?

Wang Peng: My name is Wang Peng.

Dialogue II

Li You: Mr. Wang, are you a teacher?

Wang Peng: I'm not a teacher, I'm a student. Li You, how about you?

Li You: I'm a student, too. Are you Chinese?

Wang Peng: Yes, I'm from Beijing (lit. I'm a Beijing-er). Are you American?

Li You: Yes, I'm from New York (lit. I'm a New Yorker).

PROGRESS CHECKLIST

Before proceeding to Lesson 2, be sure that you can complete the following tasks in Chinese:

I am able to

- ✓ Exchange basic greetings;
- ✓ Say my last name and full name;
- ✓ Ask someone's last name and full name;
- ✓ Say if I am a student or not;
- ✓ State my nationality;
- ✓ Ask someone's nationality.

Please review the lesson if any of these tasks seem difficult.

LESSON 2 Family

第二课 家庭

Dì èr kè Jiātíng

LEARNING OBJECTIVES

In this lesson, you will learn to use Chinese to

- Employ basic kinship terms;
- Describe a family photo;
- Ask about someone's profession;
- Say some common professions.

RELATE AND GET READY

In your own culture/community—

1. What is the typical family structure?
2. Does an adult consider his/her parents' house his/her home?
3. Do adults live with their parents?
4. Do people mention their father or mother first when talking about family members?
5. Is it culturally appropriate to ask about people's professions upon first meeting them?

Dialogue I: Looking at a Family Photo

(Wang Peng is in Gao Wenzhong's room and points to a picture on the wall.)

 高文中，那是你的①照片吗？

(They both walk toward the picture and then stand in front of it.)

 是。这是我爸爸，这是我妈妈。

 这❶个②女孩子是谁③？

 她是我姐姐。

 这个男孩子是你弟弟吗？

LANGUAGE NOTES

❶ In colloquial Chinese, 这 can also be pronounced as zhèi and 那 as nèi if followed by a measure word or a numeral and a measure word.

不是，他是我大哥的儿子❷。

你大哥有④女儿吗？

他没有女儿。

❷ "Son" in Chinese is 儿子 (érzi), and 儿子 (érzi, son) cannot be replaced by 男孩子 (nán háizi, boy). "Daughter" is 女儿 (nǚ'ér), and 女儿 (nǚ'ér) cannot be interchanged with 女孩子(nǚ háizi, girl).

(Wang Peng is in Gao Wenzhong's room and points to a picture on the wall.)

Gāo Wénzhōng, nà shì nǐ de① zhàopiàn ma?

(They both walk toward the picture and then stand in front of it.)

Shì. Zhè shì wǒ bàba, zhè shì wǒ māma.

Zhè❶ge② nǚ háizi shì shéi③?

Tā shì wǒ jiějie.

Zhè ge nán háizi shì nǐ dìdi ma?

Bú shì, tā shì wǒ dàgē de érzi❷.

Nǐ dàgē yǒu④ nǚ'ér ma?

Tā méiyǒu nǚ'ér.

VOCABULARY

1.	那	nà	pr	that
2.	的	de	p	(a possessive or descriptive particle) [See Grammar 1.]
3.	照片	zhàopiàn	n	picture; photo
4.	这	zhè	pr	this
5.	爸爸	bàba	n	father, dad
6.	妈妈	māma	n	mother, mom
7.	个	gè/ge	m	(measure word for many common everyday objects) [See Grammar 2.]
8.	女	nǚ	adj	female

VOCABULARY

9.	孩子	háizi	n	child
10.	谁	shéi	qpr	who [See Grammar 3.]
11.	她	tā	pr	she; her
12.	姐姐	jiějie	n	older sister
13.	男	nán	adj	male
14.	弟弟	dìdi	n	younger brother
15.	他	tā	pr	he; him
16.	大哥	dàgē	n	eldest brother
17.	儿子	érzi	n	son
18.	有	yǒu	v	to have; to exist [See Grammar 4.]
19.	女儿	nǚ'ér	n	daughter
20.	没	méi	adv	not

Proper Noun

21.	高文中	Gāo Wénzhōng		(a personal name)
	高	gāo		(a surname) tall; high

The picture on the wall in Gao Wenzhong's room.

Grammar

1. The Particle 的 (de) (I)

To indicate a possessive relationship, the particle 的 appears between the "possessor" and the "possessed." To that extent, it is equivalent to the "'s" structure in English. For example: 老师的名字(lǎoshī de míngzi) = teacher's name. The particle 的 (de) is often omitted in colloquial speech after a personal pronoun and before a kinship term. Therefore, we say "王朋的妈妈" (Wáng Péng de māma, Wang Peng's mother) but "我妈妈" (wǒ māma, my mother). See also Grammar 3 in Lesson 3.

2. Measure Words (I)

In Chinese a numeral is usually not followed immediately by a noun. Rather, a measure word is inserted between the number and the noun, as in (1), (2), and (3) below. Similarly, a measure word is often inserted between a demonstrative pronoun and a noun, as in (4) and (5) below. There are over one hundred measure words in Chinese, but you may hear only two or three dozen in everyday speech. Many nouns are associated with special measure words, which often bear a relationship to the meaning of the given noun.

个 (gè /ge) is the single most common measure word in Chinese. It is also sometimes used as a substitute for other measure words.

❶ 一个人

yí ge rén

(a person)

❷ 一个学生

yí ge xuésheng

(a student)

❸ 一个老师

yí ge lǎoshī

(a teacher)

❹ 这个孩子

zhè ge háizi

(this child)

❺ 那个男学生

nà ge nán xuésheng

(that male student)

3. Question Pronouns

Question pronouns include 谁 (shéi, who), 什么 (shénme, what), 哪 (nǎ/něi, which) [See Lesson 6], 哪儿 (nǎr, where) [See Lesson 5], 几 (jǐ, how many), etc. In a question with a question pronoun, the word order is exactly the same as that in a declarative sentence. Therefore, when learning to form a question with a question pronoun, we can start with a declarative sentence and then replace the part in question with the appropriate question pronoun, e.g.:

❶ 那个女孩子是李友。

Nà ge nǚ háizi shì Lǐ Yǒu.

(That girl is Li You.)

From (1), one can replace 那个女孩子 (Nà ge nǚ háizi) with 谁 (shéi) to form a question if he or she wishes to find out who Li You is:

(1a) 谁是李友？

Shéi shì Lǐ Yǒu?

(Who is Li You?)

Here 谁 (shéi) functions as the subject of the sentence and occupies the same position as 那个女孩子 (Nà ge nǚ háizi) in the corresponding statement.

One can also replace 李友 (Lǐ Yǒu) in (1) with 谁 (shéi) to form a question if he or she wishes to find out who that girl is:

(1b) 那个女孩子是谁？

Nà ge nǚ háizi shì shéi?

(Who is that girl?)

谁 (shéi) functions as the object of the sentence and occupies the same position as 李友 (Lǐ Yǒu).

MORE EXAMPLES:

❷ **A:** 谁是老师？

Shéi shì lǎoshī?

(Who is a teacher?)

B: 李先生是老师。

Lǐ xiānsheng shì lǎoshī.

(Mr. Li is a teacher.)

❸ **A:** 那个女孩子姓什么？

Nà ge nǚ háizi xìng shénme?

(What's that girl's family name?)

B: 那个女孩子姓王。

Nà ge nǚ háizi xìng Wáng.

(That girl's family name is Wang.)

❹ **A:** 谁有姐姐？

Shéi yǒu jiějie?

(Who has older sisters?)

B: 高文中有姐姐。

Gāo Wénzhōng yǒu jiějie.

(Gao Wenzhong has an older sister.)

4. 有 (yǒu) in the Sense of "to Have" or "to Possess"

有 (yǒu) is always negated with 没 (méi) instead of 不 (bù).

EXAMPLES:

❶ **A:** 王先生有弟弟吗？

Wáng xiānsheng yǒu dìdi ma?

(Does Mr. Wang have a younger brother?)

B: 王先生没有弟弟。

Wáng xiānsheng méiyǒu dìdi.

(Mr. Wang doesn't have any younger brothers.)

❷ **A:** 我有三个姐姐，你呢？

Wǒ yǒu sān ge jiějie, nǐ ne?

(I have three older sisters. How about you?)

B: 我没有姐姐。

Wǒ méiyǒu jiějie.

(I don't have any older sisters.)

Language Practice

A. 谁 (shéi, **who**)

Look at the pictures, and work with a partner to find out who they are.

EXAMPLE:

A: 这个人/男孩子是谁？ **A:** Zhè ge rén/nán háizi shì shéi?

B: 这个人/男孩子是王朋。 **B:** Zhè ge rén/nán háizi shì Wáng Péng.

1. 

2. 

B. 有/没有 (yǒu/méiyǒu, **have/do not have**)

Ask and answer the following questions based on the text of Lesson 2 and your own situation.

EXAMPLE:

高大哥◇女儿 Gāo dàgē ◇ nǚ'ér

A: 高大哥有女儿吗？	**A:** Gāo dàgē yǒu nǚ'ér ma?
B: 没有，他没有女儿。	**B:** Méiyǒu, tā méiyǒu nǚ'ér.

1. 高文中 ◇ 姐姐	**1.** Gāo Wénzhōng ◇ jiějie
2. 高大哥 ◇ 儿子	**2.** Gāo dàgē ◇ érzi
3. 你 ◇ 姐姐	**4.** Nǐ ◇ jiějie
4. 你 ◇ 弟弟	**5.** Nǐ ◇ dìdi
5. 你的老师 ◇ 女儿	**6.** Nǐ de lǎoshī ◇ nǚ'ér

C. "Who is this?"

Exchange family pictures and ask about the other person's family members.

A: 这是谁？	**A:** Zhè shì shéi?
B: 这是我____________。	**B:** Zhè shì wǒ ________.

D. Family Picture

Show your family picture to the class and describe the people in the picture.

这是我爸爸，	Zhè shì wǒ bàba,
这是我妈妈，…	zhè shì wǒ māma, ...

Dialogue II: Asking about Someone's Family

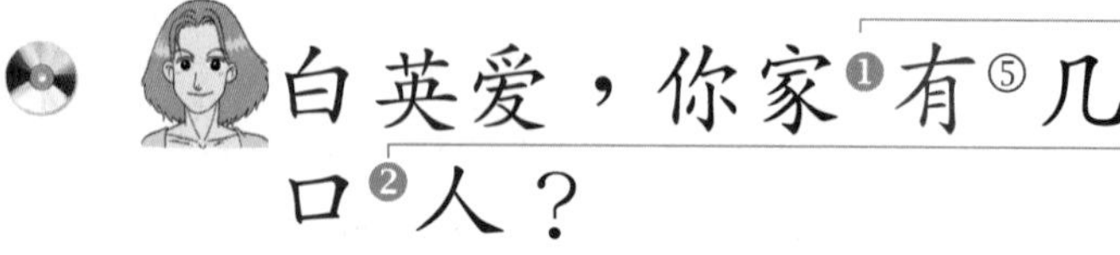

白英爱，你家❶有⑤几口❷人？

我家有六口人。我爸爸、我妈妈、一❸个哥哥、两⑥个妹妹和❹我❺。李友，你家有几口人？

我家有五口人。爸爸、妈妈、大姐、二姐和我。你爸爸妈妈做什么工作？

LANGUAGE NOTES

❶ In Chinese, 家 (jiā) can refer to one's family as well as one's home. So one can point to his or her family picture and say "我家有四口人" (Wǒ jiā yǒu sì kǒu rén; There are four people in my family), and one can also point to his or her house and say "这是我家" (Zhè shì wǒ jiā; This is my home).

❷ 口 (kǒu) is the idiomatic measure word in northern China for the number of family members. In the south, people say 个 (gè /ge) instead.

See next page.

我爸爸是律师，妈妈是英文老师，哥哥、妹妹都⑦是大学生。

我妈妈也是老师，我爸爸是医生。

Bái Yīng'ài, nǐ jiā❶yǒu⑤ jǐ kǒu❷ rén?

Wǒ jiā yǒu liù kǒu rén. Wǒ bàba, wǒ māma, yí❸ ge gēge, liǎng⑥ ge mèimei hé❹ wǒ❺. Lǐ Yǒu, nǐ jiā yǒu jǐ kǒu rén?

Wǒ jiā yǒu wǔ kǒu rén: bàba, māma, dàjiě, èrjiě hé wǒ. Nǐ bàba māma zuò shénme gōngzuò?

Wǒ bàba shì lǜshī, māma shì Yīngwén lǎoshī, gēge, mèimei dōu⑦ shì dàxuéshēng.

Wǒ māma yě shì lǎoshī, wǒ bàba shì yīshēng.

❸ The numeral 一 (yī, one) is pronounced in the first tone (yī) when it stands alone or comes at the end of a phrase or sentence. Otherwise, its pronunciation changes according to the following rules:
(a) Before a fourth-tone syllable, it becomes second tone: 一个 (yí gè).
(b) Before a first-, second- or third-tone syllable, it is pronounced in the fourth tone, e.g., 一张 (yì zhāng, a sheet), 一盘 (yì pán, one plate), 一本 (yì běn, one volume).

❹ Unlike *and*, 和 (hé) cannot link two clauses or two sentences: 我爸爸是老师，*和我妈妈是医生 (Wǒ bàba shì lǎoshī, *hé wǒ māma shì yīshēng).

❺ The pause mark, or series comma, 、 is often used to link two, three or even more parallel words or phrases, e.g., 爸爸、妈妈、两个妹妹和我 (bàba, māma, liǎng ge mèimei hé wǒ; dad, mom, two younger sisters and I). For further discussion of this punctuation mark, see Language Note 1 for Dialogue I in Lesson 4.

VOCABULARY

1.	家	jiā	n	family; home
2.	几	jǐ	nu	how many; some; a few
3.	口	kǒu	m	(measure word for number of family members)
4.	哥哥	gēge	n	older brother
5.	两	liǎng	nu	two; a couple of [See Grammar 6.]

VOCABULARY

6.	妹妹	mèimei	n	younger sister
7.	和	hé	conj	and
8.	大姐	dàjiě	n	eldest sister
9.	二姐	èrjiě	n	second oldest sister
10.	做	zuò	v	to do
11.	工作	gōngzuò	n/v	job; to work
12.	律师	lǜshī	n	lawyer
13.	英文	Yīngwén	n	English (language)
14.	都	dōu	adv	both; all [See Grammar 7.]
15.	大学生	dàxuéshēng	n	college student
	大学	dàxué	n	university; college
16.	医生	yīshēng	n	doctor; physician

Proper Noun

17.	白英爱	Bái Yīng'ài		(a personal name)

Who do you think works in this office?

Grammar

5. 有 (yǒu) in the Sense of "to Exist"

EXAMPLES:

❶ 我家有五个人。

Wǒ jiā yǒu wǔ ge rén.

(There are five people in my family.)

❷ 小高家有两个大学生。

Xiǎo Gāo jiā yǒu liǎng ge dàxuéshēng.

(There are two college students in Little Gao's family.)

6. The Usage of 二 (èr) and 两 (liǎng)

二 (èr) and 两 (liǎng) both mean "two," but they differ in usage. 两 (liǎng) is used in front of common measure words to express a quantity, e.g., 两个人 (liǎng ge rén, two persons). In counting, one uses 二 (èr): "一，二，三，四…" (yī, èr, sān, sì; one, two, three, four...). In compound numerals, 二 (èr) is always used for the 2 on the last two digits, e.g., 二十二 (èrshí'èr, 22); 一百二十五 (yìbǎi èrshí'wǔ, 125). But 二百二十二 (èrbǎi èrshí'èr, 222) can also be said as 两百二十二 (liǎngbǎi èrshí'èr, 222).

7. The Adverb 都 (dōu, both; all)

The word 都 (dōu) indicates inclusiveness. As it always occurs in front of a verb, it is classified as an adverb. However, because it refers to something that has been mentioned earlier in the sentence, or in a preceding sentence, it also has a pronoun-like flavor and it must be used at the end of an enumeration.

EXAMPLES:

❶ 王朋、李友和高文中都是学生。

Wáng Péng, Lǐ Yǒu hé Gāo Wénzhōng dōu shì xuésheng.

(Wang Peng, Li You, and Gao Wenzhong are all students.)

(lit. Wang Peng, Li You, and Gao Wenzhong all are students.)

[都 (dōu) refers back to Wang Peng, Li You and Gao Wenzhong and therefore appears after they are mentioned.]

❷ 王朋和李友都不是律师。

Wáng Péng hé Lǐ Yǒu dōu bú shì lǜshī.

(Neither Wang Peng nor Li You is a lawyer.)

❸ 王朋和白英爱都有妹妹。

Wáng Péng hé Bái Yīng'ài dōu yǒu mèimei.

(Both Wang Peng and Bai Ying'ai have younger sisters.)

(lit. Wang Peng and Bai Ying'ai both have younger sisters.)

❹ 高文中和李友都没有弟弟。

Gāo Wénzhōng hé Lǐ Yǒu dōu méi yǒu dìdi.

(Neither Gao Wenzhong nor Li You has any younger brothers.)

没 (méi) is always used to negate 有 (yǒu). However, to say "not all of ... have," we say 不都有 (bù dōu yǒu) rather than *没都有 (méi dōu yǒu). Whether the negative precedes or follows the word 都 (dōu) makes the difference between partial negation and complete negation.

COMPARE:

a. 他们不都是中国人。(他们：tāmen, they)

(Tāmen bù dōu shì Zhōngguó rén.) (Not all of them are Chinese.)

b. 他们都不是中国人。

(Tāmen dōu bú shì Zhōngguó rén.) (None of them are Chinese.)

c. 他们不都有弟弟。

(Tāmen bù dōu yǒu dìdi.) (Not all of them have younger brothers.)

d. 他们都没有弟弟。

(Tāmen dōu méi yǒu dìdi.) (None of them have any younger brothers.)

Language Practice

E. 有 (yǒu, there is/there are)

Take out your family pictures, ask three of your classmates how many family members they have, and report back to the class.

EXAMPLE: **A:** 请问，你家有几口人？ **A:** Qǐng wèn, nǐ jiā yǒu jǐ kǒu rén?

B: 我家有四口人。 **B:** Wǒ jiā yǒu sì kǒu rén.

Classmate 1 (Chris)

Classmate 2 (Anne)

Classmate 3 (Joe)

F. Question Pronouns 谁 (shéi, who)，几 (jǐ, how many), 什么 (shénme, what)

Based on the texts of Lessons 1 and 2, formulate a question or a response for each of the sentences below using the appropriate question pronoun.

EXAMPLE: **A:** 这是谁？ **A:** Zhè shì shéi?

B: 这是王朋。 **B:** Zhè shì Wáng Péng.

1. A: ____________有儿子？ **1. A:** __________yǒu érzi?

B: 高文中的大哥有儿子。 **B:** Gāo Wénzhōng de dàgē yǒu érzi.

2. A: 李友家有________口人？ 2. A: Lǐ Yǒu jiā yǒu ______ kǒu rén?

B: 李友家有五口人。 B: Lǐ Yǒu jiā yǒu wǔ kǒu rén.

3. A: 白英爱有________个妹妹？ 3. A: Bái Yīng'ài yǒu __ ge mèimei?

B: 白英爱有两个妹妹。 B: Bái Yīng'ài yǒu liǎng ge mèimei.

4. A: 李友的爸爸做________工作？ 4. A: Lǐ Yǒu de bàba zuò __________gōngzuò?

B: 李友的爸爸是医生。 B: Lǐ Yǒu de bàba shì yīshēng.

5. A: 白英爱的妈妈做________工作？ 5. A: Bái Yīng'ài de māma zuò __________gōngzuò?

B: 白英爱的妈妈是英文老师。 B: Bái Yīng'ài de māma shì Yīngwén lǎoshī.

G. Find out Who or What They Are

It's almost Halloween. Your friends put on costumes and props, and you want to know who or what they are. Therefore, you ask them the following questions to find out:

你是________人吗？ or Nǐ shì__________rén ma?

你做什么工作？ Nǐ zuò shénme gōngzuò?

Here are their costumes and props:

1. 2. 3. 4. 5.

H. 都 (dōu, **both; all**)

Based on the information given, rephrase the sentences with 都.

EXAMPLE: 王朋是学生，	Wáng Péng shì xuésheng,
李友也是学生。	Lǐ Yǒu yě shì xuésheng.
→ 王朋和李友	→ Wáng Péng hé Lǐ Yǒu
都是学生。	dōu shì xuésheng.

1. 白英爱的妈妈是老师，
李友的妈妈也是老师。

1. Bái Yīng'ài de māma shì lǎoshī,
Lǐ Yǒu de māma yě shì lǎoshī.

→ ______________________________

2. 李友有姐姐，
高文中也有姐姐。

2. Lǐ Yǒu yǒu jiějie,
Gāo Wénzhōng yě yǒu jiějie.

→ ______________________________

3. 王朋不是纽约人，
高文中也不是纽约人。

3. Wáng Péng bú shì Niǔyuē rén,
Gāo Wénzhōng yě bú shì Niǔyuē rén.

→ ______________________________

4. 王朋没有哥哥，
李友也没有哥哥。

4. Wáng Péng méiyǒu gēge,
Lǐ Yǒu yě méiyǒu gēge.

→ ______________________________

I. 都(dōu, all; both) with 不(bù, not) or 没有 (méiyǒu, not have)

The following chart is about Wang Peng, Li You, Gao Wenzhong, and Bai Ying'ai. It indicates what they do or do not do, and what they have and don't have. Based on the information given, make statements about them using 都(dōu, all; both) with 不(bù, not) or 没有(méiyǒu, not have) appropriately. Note, "✓" means "yes", and "✗" means "no". (他们: tāmen, they)

	学生 xuésheng	律师 lǜshī	弟弟 dìdi	照片 zhàopiàn	姐姐 jiějie
	✓	✗	✗	✓	✗
	✓	✗	✗	✓	✓
	✓	✗	✗	✓	✓
	✓	✗	✗	✓	✗

J. Pair activity

Ask about your partner's family:

A: 你家有几口人？

B: 我家有________口人。

A: 你爸爸/妈妈/哥哥/姐姐/弟弟/妹妹做什么工作？

B: …。

A: Nǐ jiā yǒu jǐ kǒu rén?

B: Wǒ jiā yǒu ______ kǒu rén.

A: Nǐ bàba/māma/gēge/jiějie/dìdi/mèimei zuò shénme gōngzuò?

B: ....

Switch roles.

Report your findings to the class:

Jennifer 家有 ______ 口人。 Jennifer jiā yǒu _____kǒu rén.

她爸爸/妈妈/哥哥/ Tā bàba/māma/gēge/

姐姐/弟弟/妹妹是… jiějie/dìdi/mèimei shì...

HOW ABOUT YOU?

What does everyone in your family do?

e.g. 我爸爸是老师。 Wǒ bàba shì lǎoshī.

What do your family members do? Are they:

1.	商人	shāngrén	merchant; businessperson
2.	军人	jūnrén	soldier; military officer
3.	教授	jiàoshòu	professor
4.	经理	jīnglǐ	manager
5.	工人	gōngrén	worker
6.	工程师	gōngchéngshī	engineer
7.	农民	nóngmín	farmer; peasant
8.	护士	hùshi	nurse

If the professions of your family members are not listed above, please ask your teacher and make a note here:

我爸爸/妈妈/哥哥/姐姐/弟弟/妹妹是 ______________ 。

Wǒ bàba/māma/gēge/jiějie/dìdi/mèimei shì__________.

Culture Highlights

❶ In pairing up kinship terms, the Chinese customarily say the term for the male before that for the female: 爸爸妈妈 (bàba māma, dad and mom), 哥哥姐姐 (gēge jiějie, older brothers and sisters), and 弟弟妹妹 (dìdi mèimei, younger brothers and sisters). People seldom say 妈妈爸爸 (māma bàba, mom and dad), 姐姐哥哥 (jiějie gēge, older sisters and brothers), 妹妹弟弟 (mèimei dìdi, younger sisters and brothers). In pairing up kinship terms for the same gender, the one with seniority is mentioned first: 哥哥弟弟 (gēge dìdi, older and younger brothers), 姐姐妹妹 (jiějie mèimei, older and younger sisters). People seldom say 弟弟哥哥 (dìdi gēge, younger and older brothers) or 妹妹姐姐 (mèimei jiějie, younger and older sisters).

❷ Siblings are 兄弟姐妹 (xiōng dì jiě mèi). 你有兄弟姐妹吗? (Nǐ yǒu xiōng dì jiě mèi ma?) is the way to ask, "Do you have any siblings?" Eldest siblings are called 大哥 (dàgē, eldest brother) and 大姐 (dàjiě, eldest sister); the youngest are 小弟 (xiǎodì, youngest brother) and 小妹 (xiǎomèi, youngest sister). The rest are ranked according to their birth order using numerals, e.g., 二姐 (èrjiě, second eldest sister), 三弟 (sāndì, third oldest younger brother). Younger siblings generally do not refer to their elder brothers and sisters by their names but use the appropriate kinship terms instead.

一家八口人
yì jiā bā kǒu rén

3 On both sides of the Taiwan Strait, the school system is similar to that in the United States. A typical course of education consists of six years of elementary school (小学 xiǎoxué), six years of middle school (中学 zhōngxué), and four years of university (大学 dàxué) or college (学院 xuéyuàn). Middle school is further divided into three years of junior high (初中 chūzhōng) and three years of senior high (高中 gāozhōng). Many children also attend kindergarten before they enter elementary school. Now that you have learned that a college student is called 大学生 (dàxuéshēng) in Chinese, can you guess the words for elementary school students, junior high school students, and senior high school students?

Can you figure out if this is the main gate of an elementary school, a middle school, or a university?

Pronunciation Exercises

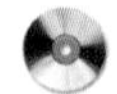

1 Initials:

1.	zhè	chè	shè	rè
2.	zhǎo	chǎo	shǎo	rǎo
3.	zhèn	chèn	shèn	rèn
4.	zhāng	chāng	shāng	rāng

2 The final "e":

1.	gē	dé	zhè	hē
2.	kē	tè	chē	shé
3.	zé	cè	sè	rè

3 Compound Finals:

1.	dōu	duō	tóu	tuó
2.	duī	diū	shuǐ	xuě
3.	shùn	xùn	jiū	zhuī
4.	lüè	nüè	juè	què

4 Tones:

1. chénggōng	**2.** chángcháng	**3.** rénkǒu	**4.** xuéxiào
5. Chángjiāng	**6.** Chángchéng	**7.** míngxiǎn	**8.** chídào

5 The neutral tone:

1. māma	**2.** dìdi	**3.** jiějie	**4.** mèimei
5. bàba	**6.** gēge	**7.** jǐ ge	**8.** zhè ge

English Text

Dialogue I

(*Wang Peng is in Gao Wenzhong's room and points to a picture on the wall.*)

Wang Peng: Gao Wenzhong, is that picture yours?

(*They both walk toward the picture and then stand in front of it.*)

Gao Wenzhong: Yes. This is my dad. This is my mom.

Wang Peng: Who is this girl?

Gao Wenzhong: She is my older sister.

Wang Peng: Is this boy your younger brother?

Gao Wenzhong: No, he is my oldest brother's son.

Wang Peng: Does your oldest brother have any daughters?

Gao Wenzhong: He doesn't have any daughters.

Dialogue II

Li You: Bai Ying'ai, how many people are there in your family?

Bai Ying'ai: There are six people in my family: my dad, my mom, an older brother, two younger sisters and me. Li You, how many people are there in your family?

Li You: There are five people in my family: my dad, my mom, my oldest sister, my second oldest sister, and me. What do your dad and mom do?

Bai Ying'ai: My dad is a lawyer. My mom is an English teacher. My older brother and younger sisters are all college students.

Li You: My mom is also a teacher. My dad is a doctor.

PROGRESS CHECKLIST

Before proceeding to Lesson 3, be sure that you can complete the following tasks in Chinese:

I am able to—

- ☑ Say and write the kinship terms for my family members;
- ☑ Identify different family members in a family photo;
- ☑ Ask someone how many family members he or she has;
- ☑ Ask someone if he or she has any siblings;
- ☑ Mention my family members' professions and my own;
- ☑ Ask someone what he or she does as a profession;
- ☑ Say and write some common professions.

Please review the lesson if any of these tasks seem difficult.

LESSON 3 Dates and Time

第三课 时间

Dì sān kè Shíjiān

3

LEARNING OBJECTIVES

In this lesson, you will learn to use Chinese to

- Tell and speak about time and dates;
- Talk about one's age and birthday;
- Invite someone to dinner;
- Arrange a dinner date.

RELATE AND GET READY

In your own culture/community—

1. Do people write the month before the day or the day before the month?
2. Is it appropriate to ask about people's age and birthday?
3. What do people typically do to celebrate their birthday?

Dialogue I: Taking Someone Out to Eat on His/Her Birthday

(Gao Wenzhong is talking to Bai Ying'ai.)

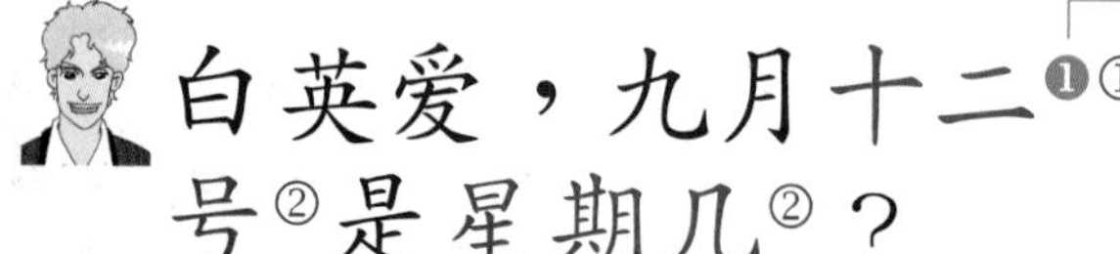
白英爱，九月十二❶①号②是星期几②？

是星期四。

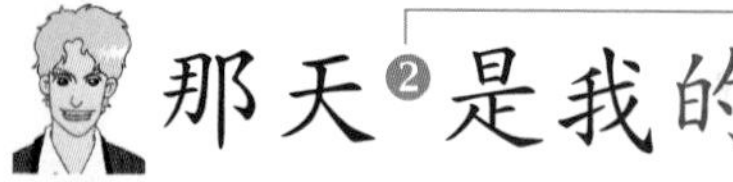
那天❷是我的③生日。

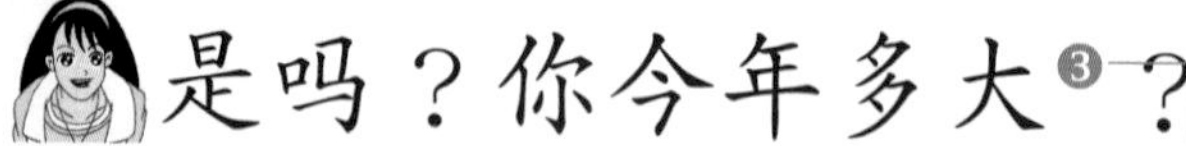
是吗？你今年多大❸？

十八岁❹。

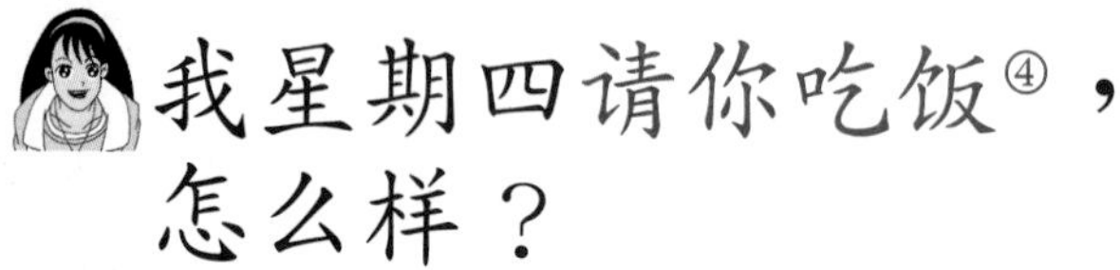
我星期四请你吃饭④，怎么样？

太好了。谢谢，谢谢❺。

LANGUAGE NOTES

❶ Chinese time expressions proceed from the largest to the smallest unit, e.g., 二〇〇九年八月十二日晚上七点 (èr líng líng jiǔ nián bāyuè shí'èr rì wǎnshang qī diǎn, literally, the year 2009, the eighth month, the twelfth day, the evening, seven o'clock).

❷ 天(tiān, day) and 年(nián, year) require no measure word because they are measure words on their own.

See next page.

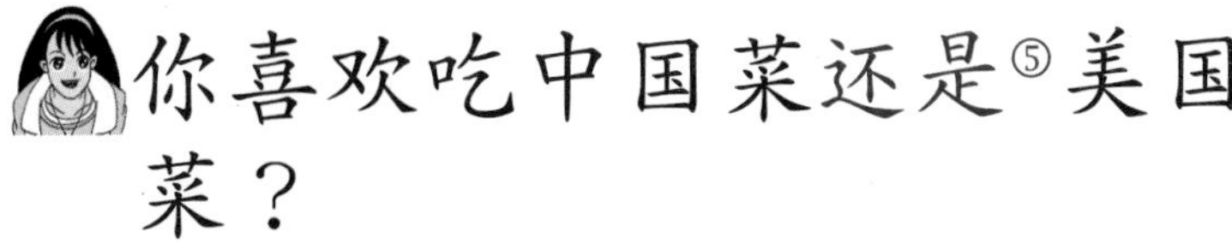
你喜欢吃中国菜还是⑤美国菜？

我是英国人，可是我喜欢吃中国菜。

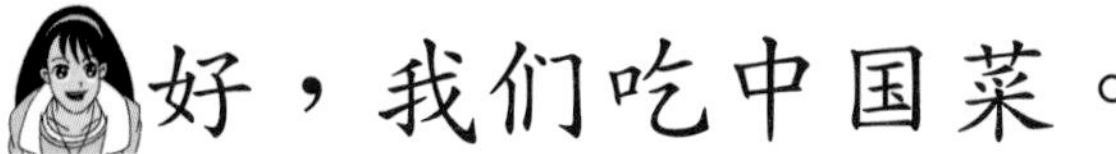
好，我们吃中国菜。

星期四几点？

七点半怎么样？

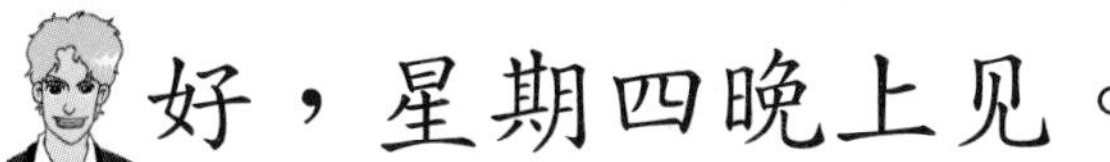
好，星期四晚上见。

再见！

(Gao Wenzhong is talking to Bai Ying'ai.)

Bái Yīng'ài, jiǔyuè shí'èr❶① hào② shì xīngqījǐ②?

Shì xīngqīsì.

Nà tiān❷shì wǒ de③shēngrì.

Shì ma? Nǐ jīnnián duō dà❸?

Shíbā suì❹.

Wǒ xīngqīsì qǐng nǐ chī fàn④, zěnmeyàng?

Tài hǎo le. Xièxie, xièxie❺.

Nǐ xǐhuan chī Zhōngguó cài háishi⑤ Měiguó cài?

Wǒ shì Yīngguó rén, kěshì wǒ xǐhuan chī Zhōngguó cài.

Hǎo, wǒmen chī Zhōngguó cài.

Xīngqīsì jǐ diǎn?

Qī diǎn bàn zěnmeyàng?

Hǎo, xīngqīsì wǎnshang jiàn.

Zàijiàn.

❸ To find out someone's age, we ask, 你今年多大？(Nǐ jīnnián duō dà?). If the person is a child who appears to be under ten, ask instead, 你今年几岁？(Nǐ jīnnián jǐ suì?). To find out an older person's age, it would be more polite to ask, 您多大年纪了？or 您多大岁数了？(Nín duō dà niánjì le? / Nín duō dà suìshù le?).

❹ To give one's age, it is correct to say 我十八岁 (Wǒ shíbā suì, I'm eighteen years old), and the verb 是 is usually not needed. The word 岁 (suì, year of age) can often be dropped. However, if the age is ten or under, the word 岁 cannot be omitted: *我十 (*Wǒ shí) or *我八 (*Wǒ bā). Note that we never say, *我十八年 (*Wǒ shíbā nián).

❺ To express gratitude, one can say 谢谢 (xièxie), or 谢谢，谢谢 (xièxie, xièxie) which is more polite and exuberant.

VOCABULARY

1.	九月	jiǔyuè	n	September
2.	月	yuè	n	month
3.	十二	shí'èr	nu	twelve
4.	号	hào	m	(measure word for number in a series; day of the month)
5.	星期	xīngqī	n	week
6.	星期四	xīngqīsì	n	Thursday
7.	天	tiān	n	day
8.	生日	shēngrì	n	birthday
	生	shēng	v	to give birth to; to be born
	日	rì	n	day; sun
9.	今年	jīnnián	t	this year
	年	nián	n	year
10.	多	duō	adv	how many/much; to what extent; many
11.	大	dà	adj	big; old
12.	十八	shíbā	nu	eighteen
13.	岁	suì	n	year (of age)
14.	吃	chī	v	to eat
15.	饭	fàn	n	meal; (cooked) rice
16.	怎么样	zěnmeyàng	qpr	Is it O.K.? How is that? How does that sound?
17.	太…了	tài...le		too; extremely

VOCABULARY

18.	谢谢	xièxie	v	to thank
19.	喜欢	xǐhuan	v	to like
20.	菜	cài	n	dishes, cuisine
21.	还是	háishi	conj	or [See Grammar 5.]
22.	可是	kěshì	conj	but
23.	我们	wǒmen	pr	we
24.	点	diǎn	m	o'clock (lit. dot, point, thus "points on the clock")
25.	半	bàn	nu	half; half an hour
26.	晚上	wǎnshang	t/n	evening; night
27.	见	jiàn	v	to see
28.	再见	zàijiàn	v	goodbye; see you again
	再	zài	adv	again

Proper Noun

29.	英国	Yīngguó		Britain; England

Grammar

1. Numbers (0, 1–100)

									0 零/〇 líng
1 一 yī	2 二 èr	3 三 sān	4 四 sì	5 五 wǔ	6 六 liù	7 七 qī	8 八 bā	9 九 jiǔ	10 十 shí
11 十一 shíyī	12 十二 shí'èr	13 十三 shísān	14 十四 shísì	15 十五 shíwǔ	16 十六 shíliù	17 十七 shíqī	18 十八 shíbā	19 十九 shíjiǔ	20 二十 èrshí
21 二十一 èrshíyī	22 二十二 èrshí'èr	23 二十三 èrshísān	24 …	25 …	26 …	27 …	28 …	29 二十九 èrshíjiǔ	30 三十 sānshí
…									
91 九十一 jiǔshíyī	92 九十二 jiǔshí'èr	93 九十三 jiǔshísān	94 …	95 …	96 …	97 …	98 …	99 九十九 jiǔshíjiǔ	100 一百 yìbǎi

200 is 二百/两百 (èrbǎi/liǎngbǎi, two hundred).

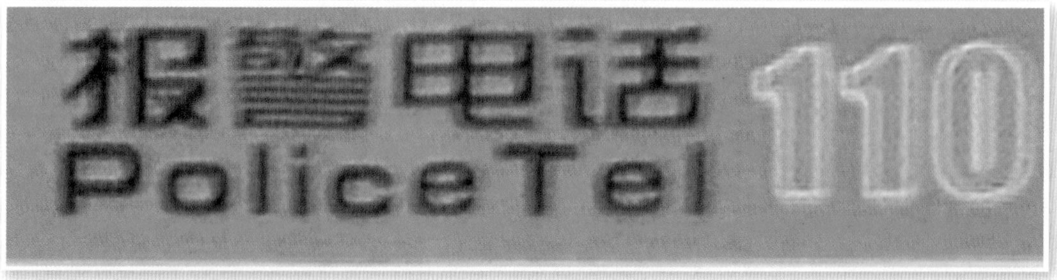

What's the emergency number in China that you can dial if your belongings are stolen? Can you say the number in Chinese?

What's the number to the fire station if you want to report a fire? Can you say it in Chinese?

2. Dates and Time

❶ Days of the week:

In China the week starts on Monday. The expression 星期几 (xīngqījǐ) is used in the question to ask the day of the week. To answer this question, simply replace the word 几 (jǐ, how many) with the number indicating the day of the week, as in 星期四 (xīngqīsì, Thursday), meaning the fourth day of the week. In spoken Chinese the expression 礼拜 (lǐbài, week) is also used. It is more colloquial than 星期 (xīngqī). Therefore, 礼拜四 (lǐbàisì) also means Thursday. Both 星期日 (xīngqīrì) and 星期天 (xīngqītiān) mean Sunday. 星期日 (xīngqīrì) is used more in written Chinese whereas 星期天 (xīngqītiān) is used more in spoken Chinese.

While 星期/礼拜 (xīngqī/lǐbài, week) is commonly used in spoken Chinese, 周 (zhōu, week) is usually used in written Chinese. Monday can also be called 周一 (zhōuyī), Tuesday 周二 (zhōu'èr), etc. Weekend is 周末 (zhōumò) in both spoken and written Chinese, and in written Chinese 周日 (zhōurì) is sometimes used to refer to Sunday, but never *周天 (zhōutiān).

Monday	Tuesday	Wednesday	Thursday	Friday	Saturday	Sunday
星期一 xīngqīyī	星期二 xīngqī'èr	星期三 xīngqīsān	星期四 xīngqīsì	星期五 xīngqīwǔ	星期六 xīngqīliù	星期日 or 星期天 xīngqīrì or xīngqītiān
礼拜一 lǐbàiyī	礼拜二 lǐbài'èr	礼拜三 lǐbàisān	礼拜四 lǐbàisì	礼拜五 lǐbàiwǔ	礼拜六 lǐbàiliù	礼拜日 or 礼拜天 lǐbàirì or lǐbàitiān
周一 zhōuyī	周二 zhōu'èr	周三 zhōusān	周四 zhōusì	周五 zhōuwǔ	周六 zhōuliù	周日 zhōurì

This is a sign outside of a store. Can you figure out on which day the store is closed?

❷ Months:

January:	一月	yīyuè
February:	二月	èryuè
March:	三月	sānyuè
April:	四月	sìyuè
May:	五月	wǔyuè
June:	六月	liùyuè

July:	七月	qīyuè
August:	八月	bāyuè
September:	九月	jiǔyuè
October:	十月	shíyuè
November:	十一月	shíyīyuè
December:	十二月	shí'èryuè

❸ Days of the month:

In spoken Chinese 号 (hào, number) is used to refer to the days of the month. However, in written Chinese 日 (rì, day) is always used.

EXAMPLES: 二月五号 èryuè wǔ hào February 5 (Spoken)

二月五日 èryuè wǔ rì February 5 (Written)

❹ Year:

年 (nián, year) always follows the numbers referring to a year.

EXAMPLES: 一七八六年 yī qī bā liù nián 1786

二〇一五年 èr líng yī wǔ nián 2015

Unlike in English, where the two years given above are read "seventeen eighty-six" and "twenty-fifteen" respectively, years in Chinese are pronounced one digit at a time.

❺ Word order for dates:

To give a date in Chinese, observe the following order:

year	month	day	day of the week
x年 nián	x月 yuè	x号/日 hào/rì	星期x xīngqī

二〇一五年七月二十六号/日星期三

èr líng yī wǔ nián qīyuè èrshíliù hào/rì xīngqīsān

(Wednesday, July 26, 2015)

■2004 年 7 月 13 日■星期二

A date clipped from a Chinese newspaper. Can you read it out loud in Chinese?

6 Telling Time:

These terms are used to tell time: 点/点钟 (diǎn/diǎnzhōng, o'clock), 半 (bàn, half hour), 刻 (kè, quarter hour), and 分 (fēn, minute).

A. HOUR:

两点（钟） liǎng diǎn(zhōng)
十一点（钟） shíyī diǎn(zhōng)

钟 (zhōng) can be omitted from 点钟 (diǎnzhōng).
*二点（钟） (èr diǎn{zhōng}) is not used.

B. MINUTE:

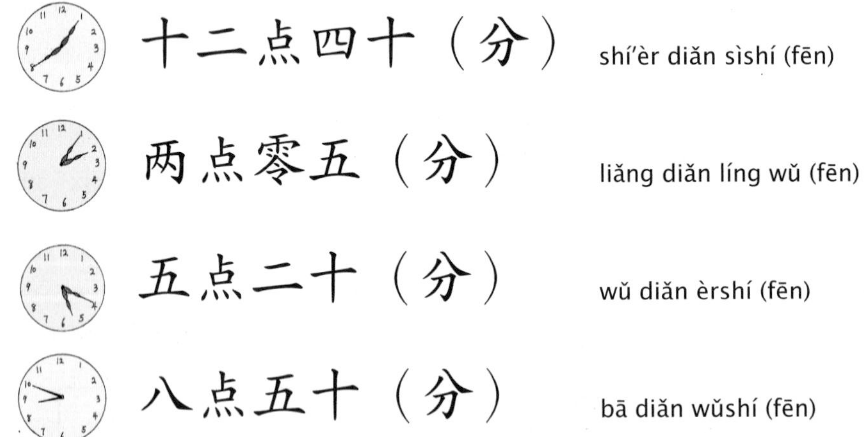

十二点四十（分） shí'èr diǎn sìshí (fēn)
两点零五（分） liǎng diǎn líng wǔ (fēn)
五点二十（分） wǔ diǎn èrshí (fēn)
八点五十（分） bā diǎn wǔshí (fēn)

The term 零/〇 (líng, zero) is usually added before a single-digit number of 分 (fēn, minute), e.g., 两点零五分 (liǎng diǎn líng wǔ fēn). 分 (fēn) can be omitted from the end of the expression if the number for the minutes appears in two syllables. Thus one can say 一点四十 (yī diǎn sìshí) and 两点零五 (liǎng diǎn líng wǔ), but not *两点五 (*liǎng diǎn wǔ) or *一点十 (*yī diǎn shí). Another way of looking at this is that the section related to 分 (fēn, minutes) has to be at least two syllables.

C. QUARTER HOUR:

 两点一刻 liǎng diǎn yí kè

 十一点三刻 shíyī diǎn sān kè

D. HALF HOUR:

 两点半 liǎng diǎn bàn

 十二点半 shí'èr diǎn bàn

*两刻 (liǎng kè, two quarters) is not used.

北京几点？纽约几点？
Běijīng jǐ diǎn? Niǔyuē jǐ diǎn?

E. EVENING TIME:

7:00 p.m.	晚上七点(钟)	wǎnshang qī diǎn (zhōng)
8:05 p.m.	晚上八点零五(分)	wǎnshang bā diǎn líng wǔ (fēn)
9:15 p.m.	晚上九点一刻	wǎnshang jiǔ diǎn yí kè
10:30 p.m.	晚上十点半	wǎnshang shí diǎn bàn

Observe the temporal progression from general to specific, and from largest unit to smallest unit.

3. Pronouns as Modifiers and the Usage of the Particle 的 (de) (II)

When the personal pronouns 我 (wǒ, I), 你 (nǐ, you), and 他 (tā, he) are followed by a term indicating a close personal relationship such as 妈妈 (māma, mother), 弟弟 (dìdi, younger brother), and 家 (jiā, family) the word 的 (de) can be omitted; e.g., 我妈妈 (wǒ māma, my mother), 你弟弟 (nǐ dìdi, your younger brother), 我们家 (wǒmen jiā, our family). Otherwise 的 (de) is generally required; e.g., 我的生日 (wǒ de shēngrì, my birthday), 他的医生 (tā de yīshēng, his doctor).

4. The Sentence Structure of 我请你吃饭 (Wǒ qǐng nǐ chī fàn)

In the sentence 我请你吃饭 (Wǒ qǐng nǐ chī fàn, I will treat you to dinner), 你 (nǐ, you) is the object of the verb 请 (qǐng, to treat) as well as the subject of the second verb 吃 (chī, to eat).

❶ 明天李先生请你吃中国菜。

Míngtiān Lǐ xiānsheng qǐng nǐ chī Zhōngguó cài.

(Mr. Li is inviting you to have Chinese food tomorrow.)

❷ 今天晚上我请你和你妹妹吃美国菜，怎么样？

Jīntiān wǎnshang wǒ qǐng nǐ hé nǐ mèimei chī Měiguó cài, zěnmeyàng?

(How about if I invite you and your younger sister to have American food tonight?)

5. Alternative Questions

The structure (是)…还是… ({shì}... háishi..., ...or...) is used to form an alternative question. If there is another verb used in the predicate, the first 是 (shì) often can be omitted.

❶ 你是中国人，还是美国人？

Nǐ shì Zhōngguó rén, háishi Měiguó rén?

(Are you Chinese or American?)

❷ 你哥哥是老师，还是学生？

Nǐ gēge shì lǎoshī, háishi xuésheng?

(Is your older brother a teacher or a student?)

❸ (是)你请我吃饭，还是他请我吃饭？

(Shì) nǐ qǐng wǒ chī fàn, háishi tā qǐng wǒ chī fàn?

(Who is taking me to dinner, you or he?)

❹ **A:** 他(是)喜欢吃中国菜，还是喜欢吃美国菜？

Tā (shì) xǐhuan chī Zhōngguó cài, háishi xǐhuan chī Měiguó cài?

(Does he like to eat Chinese or American food?)

B: 中国菜、美国菜他都喜欢。

Zhōngguó cài, Měiguó cài tā dōu xǐhuan.

(He likes both Chinese food and American food.)

Language Practice

A. Days of the week

Provide the correct answers based on the calendar provided.

日	一	二	三	四	五	六
				1 十二	2 十三	3 十四
4 十五	5 十六	6 惊蛰	7 十八	8 十九	9 二十	10 廿一
11 廿二	12 廿三	13 廿四	14 廿五	15 廿六	16 廿七	17 廿八
18 廿九	19 二月	20 初二	21 春分	22 初四	23 初五	24 初六
25 初七	26 初八	27 初九	28 初十	29 十一	30 十二	31 十三

EXAMPLE (三月二十一号) (sānyuè èrshíyī hào)

A: 三月二十一号是星期几？ **A:** Sānyuè èrshíyī hào shì xīngqījǐ?

B: 三月二十一号是星期三。 **B:** Sānyuè èrshíyī hào shì xīngqīsān.

1. 三月二十二号 **1.** sānyuè èrshí'èr hào
2. 三月二十三号 **2.** sānyuè èrshísān hào
3. 三月二十四号 **3.** sānyuè èrshísì hào
4. 三月十八号 **4.** sānyuè shíbā hào
5. 三月十九号 **5.** sānyuè shíjiǔ hào
6. 三月二十号 **6.** sānyuè èrshí hào

B. Time

Based on the clues given, ask your partner what time you will meet.

EXAMPLE:

A: 我们几点见？ 

B:  我们七点半见。

A: Wǒmen jǐ diǎn jiàn?

B: Wǒmen qī diǎn bàn jiàn.

C. Birthday

Based on the text, ask and answer the following questions.

EXAMPLE:

A: 高文中的生日(是)几月几号？

B: 高文中的生日(是)九月十二号。

A: Gāo Wénzhōng de shēngrì (shì) jǐ yuè jǐ hào?

B: Gāo Wénzhōng de shēngrì (shì) jiǔyuè shí'èr hào.

HOW ABOUT:

1. 你 — **1.** nǐ
2. 你爸爸 — **2.** nǐ bàba
3. 你妈妈 — **3.** nǐ māma
4. 你们（的）老师 — **4.** nǐmen (de) lǎoshī

D. 还是 (háishi, or)

Ask and answer the following questions based on Lessons 1–3 and your own preferences.

EXAMPLE: 高大哥有儿子还是有女儿？ Gāo dàgē yǒu érzi háishi yǒu nǚ'ér?

→ 高大哥有儿子。 Gāo dàgē yǒu érzi.

1. 王朋是学生◇老师？ **1.** Wáng Péng shì xuésheng ◇ lǎoshī?
2. 高文中今年十八岁◇十九岁？ **2.** Gāo Wénzhōng jīnnián shíbā suì ◇ shíjiǔ suì?
3. 白英爱的爸爸是医生◇律师？ **3.** Bái Yīng'ài de bàba shì yīshēng ◇ lǜshī?
4. 李友是美国人◇英国人？ **4.** Lǐ Yǒu shì Měiguó rén ◇ Yīngguó rén?
5. 你喜欢星期五◇星期六？ **5.** Nǐ xǐhuan xīngqīwǔ ◇ xīngqīliù?
6. 你喜欢吃美国菜◇中国菜？ **6.** Nǐ xǐhuan chī Měiguó cài ◇ Zhōngguó cài?

E. Forming a Birthday Dragon

Let's mobilize the entire class to ask each other's birthdays. After a couple minutes of mingling, you will start to form a line, like a dragon, based on your birthdays. Students whose birthdays are earlier in the year will line up before people whose birthdays are later. Make sure you know how to ask and answer the question, because after the dragon is formed, the teacher will check if everyone is at the right place in the line. The teacher will ask the first student in the line: 你的生日(是)几月几号？(Nǐ de shēngrì {shì} jǐ yuè jǐ hào?). The first student answers, and then he/she asks the second student the same question, the second student answers and asks the third, until the end of the line. Then let's end the activity by singing the "Happy Birthday" song in Chinese.

祝你生日快乐
zhù nǐ shēngrì kuàilè

祝你生日快乐 祝你生日快乐
zhù nǐ shēngrì kuàilè zhù nǐ shēngrì kuàilè

祝你生日快乐 祝你生日快乐
zhù nǐ shēngrì kuàilè zhù nǐ shēngrì kuàilè

F. Family Birthdays

Tell your partner or the class your and your family members' birthdays. Your partner or the rest of the class will take down the information and be ready to answer the teacher's questions:

Chris: 我的生日(是)________月________号，我爸爸的生日（是）________月________号…	**Chris:** Wǒ de shēngrì (shì) ______ yuè ______ hào, wǒ bàba de shēngrì (shì) ______ yuè ______hào...
Teacher: Chris 的生日（是）几月几号？(When is Chris's birthday?)	**Teacher:** Chris de shēngrì (shì) jǐ yuè jǐ hào?
Chris 爸爸的生日（是）几月几号？…	Chris bàba de shēngrì (shì) jǐ yuè jǐ hào?...

G. Find out what types of cuisine your partner likes.

A: 你喜欢吃什么菜？ **A:** Nǐ xǐhuan chī shénme cài?

B: 我喜欢吃________菜。 **B:** Wǒ xǐhuan chī ______ cài.

A: 你喜欢吃________菜吗？ **A:** Nǐ xǐhuan chī ______ cài ma?

B: 我也喜欢吃/
我不喜欢吃________菜。 **B:** Wǒ yě xǐhuan chī/
Wǒ bù xǐhuan chī ______cài.

H. Dinner Invitation

Pick a day and offer to take your partner out to dinner. Your partner will accept your invitation and ask for the time when you two should meet.

A: 星期________我请
你吃饭，怎么样？ **A:** Xīngqī______wǒ qǐng nǐ chī fàn,
zěnmeyàng?

B: ________。 **B:** ______.

星期________几点？ Xīngqī______ jǐ diǎn?

A: ________。 **A:** ______。

Dialogue II: Inviting Someone to Dinner

 白英爱，现在几点？

 五点三刻。

 我六点一刻有事儿。

 你今天很忙❶，明天忙不忙⑥？

 我今天很忙，可是明天不忙。有事儿吗？

 明天我请你吃晚饭，怎么样？

 你为什么请我吃饭？

 因为明天是高文中的生日。

 是吗？好。还⑦请谁？

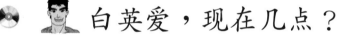

LANGUAGE NOTE

❶ Although usually translated as "very," the Chinese adverb 很 (hěn) is not quite as strong as its English equivalent. Therefore, the sentence 我很忙 (Wǒ hěn máng)—unless the word 很 (hěn) is stressed—is closer to "I am busy" than "I am very busy." (See Grammar 2 in Lesson 5.)

 还请我的同学李友。

 那太好了，我认识李友，她也是我的朋友。明天几点？

 明天晚上七点半。

 好，明天七点半见。

 Bái Yīng'ài, xiànzài jǐ diǎn?

 Wǔ diǎn sān kè.

 Wǒ liù diǎn yí kè yǒu shìr.

 Nǐ jīntiān hěn máng[1], míngtiān máng bu máng[6]?

 Wǒ jīntiān hěn máng, kěshì míngtiān bù máng. Yǒu shìr ma?

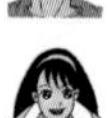 Míngtian wǒ qǐng nǐ chī wǎnfàn, zěnmeyàng?

 Nǐ wèishénme qǐng wǒ chī fàn?

 Yīnwei míngtiān shì Gāo Wénzhōng de shēngrì.

 Shì ma? Hǎo, hái[7] qǐng shéi?

 Hái qǐng wǒ de tóngxué Lǐ Yǒu.

 Nà tài hǎo le! Wǒ rènshi Lǐ Yǒu, tā yě shì wǒ de péngyou. Míngtiān jǐ diǎn?

 Míngtiān wǎnshang qī diǎn bàn.

 Hǎo, míngtiān qī diǎn bàn jiàn.

VOCABULARY

1.	现在	xiànzài	t	now
2.	刻	kè	m	quarter (of an hour)
3.	事（儿）	shì(r)	n	matter; affair; event
4.	今天	jīntiān	t	today
5.	很	hěn	adv	very
6.	忙	máng	adj	busy
7.	明天	míngtiān	t	tomorrow
8.	晚饭	wǎnfàn	n	dinner; supper
9.	为什么	wèishénme	qpr	why
	为	wèi	prep	for
10.	因为	yīnwèi	conj	because
11.	还	hái	adv	also; too; as well [See Grammar 7.]
12.	同学	tóngxué	n	classmate
13.	认识	rènshi	v	to be acquainted with; to recognize
14.	朋友	péngyou	n	friend

Grammar

6. Affirmative + Negative (A-not-A) Questions (I)

Besides adding the question particle 吗 (ma) to a declarative sentence, another common way of forming a question in Chinese is to repeat the verb or adjective in its affirmative and negative form.

EXAMPLES:

❶ A: 你今天忙不忙？

Nǐ jīntiān máng bu máng?

(Are you busy today?)

B: 我今天很忙。

Wǒ jīntiān hěn máng.

(I am busy today.)

❷ A: 你妈妈喜欢不喜欢吃中国菜？

Nǐ māma xǐhuan bu xǐhuan chī Zhōngguó cài?

(Does your mother like to eat Chinese food or not?)

B: 我妈妈不喜欢吃中国菜。

Wǒ māma bù xǐhuan chī Zhōngguó cài.

(My mother doesn't like to eat Chinese food.)

❸ A: 请问，王律师今天有没有事儿？

Qǐng wèn, Wáng lǜshī jīntiān yǒu méi yǒu shìr?

(Excuse me, does Lawyer Wang have anything to do today or not?)

B: 王律师今天没有事儿。

Wáng lǜshī jīntiān méi yǒu shìr.

(Lawyer Wang is free today.)

7. The adverb 还 (hái, also; in addition)

As an adverb, 还 (hái) indicates that the action or situation denoted by the verb involves someone or something else in addition to what has already been mentioned.

EXAMPLES:

❶ 白英爱请高文中和王朋，还请李友。

Bái Yīng'ài qǐng Gāo Wénzhōng hé Wáng Péng, hái qǐng Lǐ Yǒu.

(Bai Ying'ai is inviting Gao Wenzhong and Wang Peng, and Li You, too).

❷ 王朋喜欢吃中国菜，还喜欢吃美国菜。

Wáng Péng xǐhuan chī Zhōngguó cài, hái xǐhuan chī Měiguó cài.

(Wang Peng likes Chinese food, and American food, too).

Language Practice

I. Affirmative + Negative (A-not-A) Questions

Ask your partner the following questions using the appropriate verbs and the A-not-A question form.

EXAMPLE: 王朋 ◇ 是 ◇ 北京人 — Wáng Péng ◇ shì ◇ Běijīng rén

→ 王朋是不是北京人？ — Wáng Péng shì bu shì Běijīng rén?

1. 今天 ◇ 是 ◇ 星期五 — **1.** Jīntiān ◇ shì ◇ xīngqīwǔ

____

2. 高大哥 ◇ 有 ◇ 女儿 — **2.** Gāo dàgē ◇ yǒu ◇ nǚ'ér

____

3. 你◇喜欢◇高文中

3. Nǐ ◇ xǐhuan ◇ Gāo Wénzhōng

____

4. 王朋◇认识◇白英爱

4. Wáng Péng ◇ rènshi ◇ Bái Yīng'ài

____

J. 还 (hái, also; in addition)

EXAMPLE: **A:** 李友认识谁？
(王朋，高文中)

A: Lǐ Yǒu rènshi shéi?
(Wáng Péng, Gāo Wénzhōng)

B: 李友认识王朋，
还认识高文中。

B: Lǐ Yǒu rènshi Wáng Péng,
hái rènshi Gāo Wénzhōng.

1. **A:** 高文中请谁吃饭？
(王医生，白律师)

1. **A:** Gāo Wénzhōng qǐng shéi chī fàn?
(Wáng yīshēng, Bái lǜshī)

B: ______________________________

2. **A:** 王朋喜欢吃什么菜？
(美国菜，中国菜)

2. **A:** Wáng Péng xǐhuan chī shénme cài?
(Měiguó cài, Zhōngguó cài)

B: ______________________________

3. **A:** 白英爱有谁的照片？
(她爸爸的照片，
她妈妈的照片)

3. **A:** Bái Yīng'ài yǒu shéi de zhàopiàn?
(tā bàba de zhàopiàn,
tā māma de zhàopiàn)

B: ______________________________

K. Find out when your partner is busy and when he or she is not busy.

EXAMPLE:

Ask your partner if he or she is busy on Monday.

A: 你星期一忙不忙？	**A:** Nǐ xīngqīyī máng bù máng?
B: 我星期一很忙/不忙。	**B:** Wǒ xīngqīyī hěn máng/bù máng.

How about Tuesday?

A: 星期二呢？你忙不忙？	**A:** Xīngqīèr ne? Nǐ máng bù máng?
B: …	**B:** …

Go through the days of the week.

Report to the class when your partner is and isn't busy:

Joanne 星期一、________、	Joanne xīngqīyī, ______,
________… 很忙，星期二、	______ …hěn máng, xīngqīèr,
________、________… 不忙。	______, ______ …bù máng.

L. Eating out with friends

Pick a day and ask your friend out to dinner:

我星期________请你	Wǒ xīngqī______qǐng nǐ
吃晚饭，怎么样？	chī wǎnfàn, zěnmeyàng?

Your friend happens to be busy on that day, and suggests an alternative time:

星期________，我很忙。	Xīngqī______, wǒ hěn máng.
星期________，怎么样？	Xīngqī______, zěnmeyàng?

Your response:

____

Your friend wants to find out who else will be there, and asks:

你还请谁？ Nǐ hái qǐng shéi?

You tell your friend:

我还请______。 Wǒ hái qǐng __________.

HOW ABOUT YOU?

What special days do you celebrate?

1. 新年 xīnnián New Year
2. 情人节 Qíngrénjié Valentine's Day
3. 母亲节 Mǔqīnjié Mother's Day
4. 父亲节 Fùqīnjié Father's Day
5. 感恩节 Gǎn'ēnjié Thanksgiving

What other special days do you celebrate? If they are not listed above, please ask your teacher and make a note here:

____.

Culture Highlights

1 If you flip open a calendar in China, you will most likely see two different dates for any given day of the year, one date in the traditional lunar system and the other in the international solar system. Typically the date in the lunar system lags about one month or slightly more behind its corresponding date in the solar system. For most years, the Lunar New Year falls in late January or early February.

七月 July

SUN 星期日	MON 星期一	TUE 星期二	WED 星期三	THU 星期四	FRI 星期五	SAT 星期六
十七 1	十八 2	十九 3	二十 4	廿一 5	廿二 6	小暑 7
廿四 8	廿五 9	廿六 10	廿七 11	廿八 12	廿九 13	六月大 14
初二 15	初三 16	初四 17	初五 18	初六 19	初七 20	初八 21
初九 22	大暑 23	十一 24	十二 25	十三 26	十四 27	十五 28
十六 29	十七 30	十八 31				

This is a Chinese calendar. It shows that it's July of the solar system. Can you find the first day of the sixth month of the lunar system?

2 The traditional Chinese manner of counting age, which is still in use among many (mainly older) people on non-official occasions, is based on the number of the calendar years one has lived in, rather than the length of time in actual years that one has lived. For example, a child born in January 2008 can be said to be two years old in January 2009, since he or she has by then lived in two calendar years, 2008 and 2009. But for official purposes, for instance in the census, the child would still be considered one year old. The former is called the child's nominal age (虚岁 xūsuì) and the latter his actual age (实岁 shísuì).

❸ Noodles are the traditional Chinese equivalent of the birthday cake. Because noodles are long, they are considered a symbol of longevity. That is why they are called 长寿面 (chángshòu miàn, longevity noodles). Among the younger generations in urban areas, birthday cakes are also becoming quite common.

长寿面

Pronunciation Exercises

1 The initial r:

1. shēngrì	**2.** rìjì	**3.** rèqíng	**4.** rénmín
5. réngrán	**6.** ránhòu	**7.** ruìlì	**8.** ràngbù

2 Finals:

1.	**ie**	jiè	xiě	qié	tiě
2.	**ue**	jué	xué	quē	qiē*
3.	**uo**	duō	tuō	zuò	cuò
4.	**ou**	dōu	tóu	zǒu	còu
5.	**u**	zhū	chū	zū	cū

3 Two-syllable words:

1. dāndāng	**2.** shōuhuò	**3.** qūchú	**4.** yúnwù
5. jiǎozhà	**6.** chūnqiū	**7.** juébié	**8.** kuìjiù

4 The neutral tone:

1. zhè ge	**2.** nà ge	**3.** wǒmen	**4.** nǐmen
5. wǎnshang	**6.** xièxie	**7.** xǐhuan	**8.** rènshi

5 Tone sandhi [See Sec. D.2 in the Introduction.]:

1. zhǎnlǎn	**2.** lǚguǎn	**3.** yǔsǎn	**4.** qǔshě
5. shǒufǎ	**6.** yǔnxǔ	**7.** xuǎnjǔ	**8.** guǎngchǎng

*qiē is included here to illustrate the contrast between quē and qiē.

English Text

Dialogue I

Gao Wenzhong: Bai Ying'ai, what day is September 12?
Bai Ying'ai: Thursday.
Gao Wenzhong: That (day) is my birthday.
Bai Ying'ai: Really? How old are you this year?
Gao Wenzhong: Eighteen.
Bai Ying'ai: I'll treat you to a meal on Thursday. How's that?
Gao Wenzhong: That would be great. Thank you very much!
Bai Ying'ai: Do you like Chinese food or American food?
Gao Wenzhong: I'm an Englishman, but I like Chinese food.
Bai Ying'ai: All right. We'll have Chinese food.
Gao Wenzhong: Thursday at what time?
Bai Ying'ai: How about seven-thirty?
Gao Wenzhong: All right. See you Thursday evening.
Bai Ying'ai: See you.

Dialogue II

Wang Peng: Bai Ying'ai, what time is it now?
Bai Ying'ai: A quarter to six.
Wang Peng: I have something to do at a quarter after six.
Bai Ying'ai: You are busy today. Are you busy tomorrow?
Wang Peng: I'm busy today, but I won't be tomorrow. Why? (lit., What is it?)
Bai Ying'ai: I'd like to invite you to dinner tomorrow. How about it?
Wang Peng: Why are you inviting me to dinner?
Bai Ying'ai: Because tomorrow is Gao Wenzhong's birthday.
Wang Peng: Really? Great. Who else are you inviting?
Bai Ying'ai: I'm also inviting my classmate Li You.
Wang Peng: That's fantastic. I know Li You. She's also my friend. What time tomorrow?
Bai Ying'ai: Seven-thirty tomorrow evening.
Wang Peng: OK, I'll see you tomorrow at seven-thirty.

PROGRESS CHECKLIST

Before proceeding to Lesson 4, be sure you can complete the following tasks in Chinese:

I am able to

- [x] Say and write dates and times;
- [x] Ask someone's age and birthday;
- [x] Give my age and birthday;
- [x] Name my favorite cuisine;
- [x] Ask about someone's availability and set up a dinner appointment.

Please review the lesson if any of these tasks seem difficult.

LESSON 4 Hobbies

第四课 爱好

Dì sì kè Aìhào

LEARNING OBJECTIVES

In this lesson, you will learn to use Chinese to

- Say and write the terms for basic personal hobbies;
- Ask about someone's hobbies;
- Ask friends out to see a movie;
- Set up plans for the weekend.

RELATE AND GET READY

In your own culture/community—

1. What are people's favorite pastimes?
2. What do people usually do on weekends?

Dialogue I: Talking about Hobbies

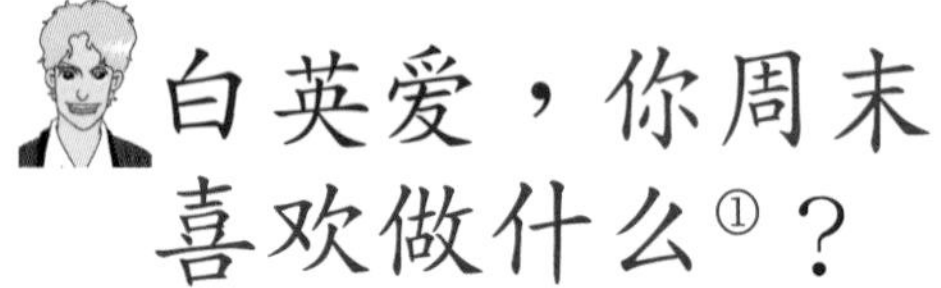

白英爱，你周末喜欢做什么①？

我喜欢打球、看电视❶。你呢？

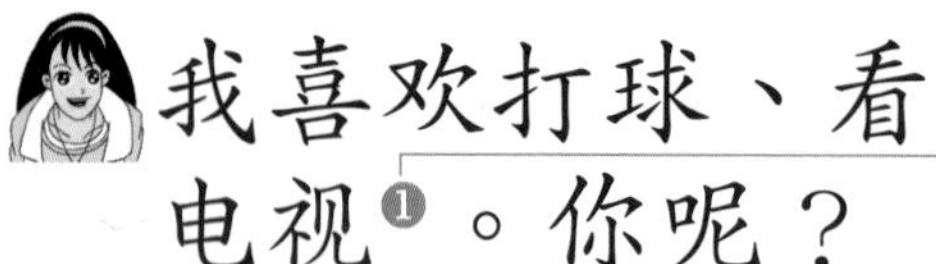

我喜欢唱歌、跳舞，还喜欢听音乐。你也喜欢看书，对不对？

对，有的时候也喜欢看书。

LANGUAGE NOTE

❶ The series comma "、" is very useful in Chinese, as pointed out in Lesson 2, Dialogue 2, Language Note 5. When nouns or pronouns occur in a series, this punctuation mark is used to separate them, while the conjunction 和 (hé) connects the last two items in the series, e.g., 我、你和她 (wǒ、nǐ hé tā, you, she and I); 中国、美国、英国和法国 (Zhōngguó、Měiguó、Yīngguó hé Fǎguó, China, United States, England and France). The series comma can also be used between two or more verbs or adjectives, as for example in 我常常打球、跳舞、看电视 (Wǒ chángcháng dǎ qiú、tiào wǔ、kàn diànshì: I often play ball, dance and watch TV).

你喜欢不喜欢②看电影？

喜欢。我周末常常看电影。

那③我们今天晚上去看④一个外国电影，怎么样？我请客。

为什么你请客？

因为昨天你请我吃饭，所以今天我请你看电影。

那你也请王朋、李友，好吗⑤？

...好。

(Gao Wenzhong is talking to Bai Ying'ai.)

Bái Yīng'ài, nǐ zhōumò xǐhuan zuò shénme①?

Wǒ xǐhuan dǎqiú, kàn diànshì❶. Nǐ ne?

Wǒ xǐhuan chàng gē, tiào wǔ, hái xǐhuan tīng yīnyuè. Nǐ yě xǐhuan kàn shū, duì bu duì?

Duì, yǒude shíhou yě xǐhuan kàn shū.

Nǐ xǐhuan bu xǐhuan② kàn diànyǐng?

Xǐhuan. Wǒ zhōumò chángcháng kàn diànyǐng.

Nà③wǒmen jīntiān wǎnshang qù kàn④yí ge wàiguó diànyǐng, zěnmeyàng? Wǒ qǐng kè.

Wèishénme nǐ qǐng kè?

Yīnwei zuótiān nǐ qǐng wǒ chī fàn, suǒyǐ jīntiān wǒ qǐng nǐ kàn diànyǐng.

Nà nǐ yě qǐng Wáng Péng, Lǐ Yǒu, hǎo ma⑤?

... Hǎo.

VOCABULARY

1.	周末	zhōumò	n	weekend
2.	打球	dǎ qiú	vo	to play ball
	打	dǎ	v	to hit
	球	qiú	n	ball
3.	看	kàn	v	to watch; to look; to read
4.	电视	diànshì	n	television
	电	diàn	n	electricity
	视	shì	n	vision
5.	唱歌(儿)	chàng gē(r)	vo	to sing (a song)
	唱	chàng	v	to sing
	歌	gē	n	song
6.	跳舞	tiào wǔ	vo	to dance
	跳	tiào	v	to jump
	舞	wǔ	n	dance
7.	听	tīng	v	to listen
8.	音乐	yīnyuè	n	music
9.	书	shū	n	book
10.	对	duì	adj	right; correct
11.	有的	yǒude	pr	some
12.	时候	shíhou	n	(a point in) time; moment; (a duration of) time

VOCABULARY

13.	电影	diànyǐng	n	movie
	影	yǐng	n	shadow
14.	常常	chángcháng	adv	often
15.	那	nà	conj	in that case; then
16.	去	qù	v	to go
17.	外国	wàiguó	n	foreign country
18.	请客	qǐng kè	vo	to invite someone (to dinner, coffee, etc.); to play the host
19.	昨天	zuótiān	t	yesterday
20.	所以	suǒyǐ	conj	so

他们喜欢跳舞。
Tāmen xǐhuan tiào wǔ.

他们喜欢打球。
Tāmen xǐhuan dǎ qiú.

Grammar

1. Word Order in Chinese

The basic word order in a Chinese sentence is as follows:

Subject (agent of the action)	Adverbial (time, place, manner, etc.)	Verb	Object (receiver of the action)

Subj.	Adverbial	Verb	Obj.
王朋	周末/常常	听	音乐
Wáng Péng	zhōumò/chángcháng	tīng	yīnyuè

(Wang Peng often listens to music on weekends.)

李友	明天	吃	中国菜
Lǐ Yǒu	míngtiān	chī	Zhōngguó cài

(Li You will have Chinese food tomorrow.)

高文中	昨天下午五点半	去看	外国电影
Gāo Wénzhōng	zuótiān xiàwǔ wǔ diǎn bàn	qù kàn	wàiguó diànyǐng

(Gao Wenzhong went to see a foreign movie at 5:30 yesterday afternoon.)

While this is the most common word order in a Chinese sentence, varying discourse contexts may affect the norm.

2. Affirmative + Negative (A-not-A) Questions (II)

In this type of question there can be no adverbials before the verb other than time words as in (1) and (2). If there is an adverbial—such as 很 (hěn, very), 都 (dōu, all), or 常常 (chángcháng, often)—before the verb, the 吗 type question must be used instead, as in (3), (4), and (5). If there is more than one verb, the question form applies to the first verb, as seen in (6) and (7).

❶ 你明天去不去？

Nǐ míngtiān qù bu qù?

(Are you going tomorrow?)

❷ 她今天晚上看不看电视？

Tā jīntiān wǎnshang kàn bu kàn diànshì?

(Is she going to watch TV tonight?)

❸ 他们都是学生吗？

Tāmen dōu shì xuésheng ma?

(Are they all students?)

(3a) *他们都是不是学生？

*Tāmen dōu shì bu shì xuésheng?

❹ 你常常看电影吗？

Nǐ chángcháng kàn diànyǐng ma?

(Do you often go to the movies?)

(4a) *你常常看不看电影？

*Nǐ chángcháng kàn bu kàn diànyǐng?

❺ 王医生很忙吗？

Wáng yīshēng hěn máng ma?

(Is Dr. Wang very busy?)

(5a) *王医生很忙不忙？

*Wáng yīshēng hěn máng bu máng?

❻ 你想不想跳舞？

Nǐ xiǎng bu xiǎng tiào wǔ?

(Do you want to dance?)

(6a) *你想跳不跳舞？

*Nǐ xiǎng tiào bu tiào wǔ?

❼ 你的同学去不去打球？

Nǐ de tóngxué qù bu qù dǎ qiú?

(7a) *你的同学去打不打球？

*Nǐ de tóngxué qù dǎ bu dǎ qiú?

3. The Conjunction 那(么) (nà {me}, then; in that case)

In a dialogue, immediately following a statement by speaker A, speaker B can often start with 那(么)(nà {me}), which links up the sentences by the two speakers.

❶ A: 今天晚上没事儿。

Jīntiān wǎnshang méi shìr.

(We have nothing to do tonight.)

B: 那我们去看电影，怎么样？

Nàme wǒmen qù kàn diànyǐng, zěnmeyàng?

(In that case, let's go to see a movie. How's that?)

A: 好，我请客。

Hǎo, wǒ qǐng kè.

(Okay, my treat!)

B: 是吗？太好了！

Shì ma? Tài hǎo le.

(Really? Great!)

❷ A: 我今天很忙，不想去吃晚饭。

Wǒ jīntiān hěn máng, bù xiǎng qù chī wǎnfàn.

(I'm very busy today. I don't want to go to dinner.)

B: 那明天呢？

Nà míngtiān ne?

(Then how about tomorrow?)

❸ **A:** 你喜欢不喜欢吃美国菜？

Nǐ xǐhuan bu xǐhuan chī Měiguó cài?

(Do you like to eat American food or not?)

B: 不喜欢。

Bù xǐhuan.

(No, I don't.)

C: 那我们吃中国菜，怎么样？

Nà wǒmen chī Zhōngguó cài, zěnmeyàng?

(Then let's eat Chinese food. How's that?)

D: 我也不喜欢。

Wǒ yě bù xǐhuan.

(I don't like that either.)

今天吃中国菜还是美国菜？
Jīntiān chī Zhōngguó cài háishi Měiguó cài?

4. 去 (qù, to go) + Action

If the performance of an action involves a change of location, then this is the construction we use.

❶ 明天晚上我们去看电影。

Míngtiān wǎnshang wǒmen qù kàn diànyǐng.

(We are going to see a movie tomorrow night.)

❷ 晚上我不去跳舞。

Wǎnshang wǒ bú qù tiào wǔ.

(I will not go dancing tonight.)

❸ 周末我去跳舞，你去不去？

Zhōumò wǒ qù tiào wǔ, nǐ qù bu qù?

(I'll go dancing this weekend. Are you going?)

5. Questions with 好吗 (hǎo ma)

To solicit someone's opinion, we can ask 好吗 (hǎo ma) after stating an idea or suggestion.

❶ 我们去看电影，好吗？

Wǒmen qù kàn diànyǐng, hǎo ma?

(We'll go see a movie, all right?)

❷ 我们今天晚上吃中国菜，好吗？

Wǒmen jīntiān wǎnshang chī Zhōngguó cài, hǎo ma?

(We'll eat Chinese food tonight, all right?)

You will also hear people say 好不好 (hǎo bu hǎo), instead of 好吗 (hǎo ma).

Language Practice

A. Subj + Time + V + Obj

Little Wang has an active lifestyle. The following schedule shows what Little Wang does in the evenings. Look at the schedule, and tell your partner what he does every week.

	Monday	Tuesday	Wednesday	Thursday	Friday	Saturday	Sunday
Little Wang							

EXAMPLE: Monday → 小王星期一晚上看书。 Xiǎo Wáng xīngqīyī wǎnshang kàn shū.

1. Tuesday **2.** Wednesday **3.** Thursday **4.** Friday **5.** weekend

B. 去 + V

Pretend you are Gao Wenzhong, and that you are trying to ask Bai Ying'ai out tomorrow night. You offer several choices for her in case she prefers one to the others. Use …去 + V, 好吗 and the pictures to help yourself come up with the right activities that Bai Ying'ai may like.

EXAMPLE:

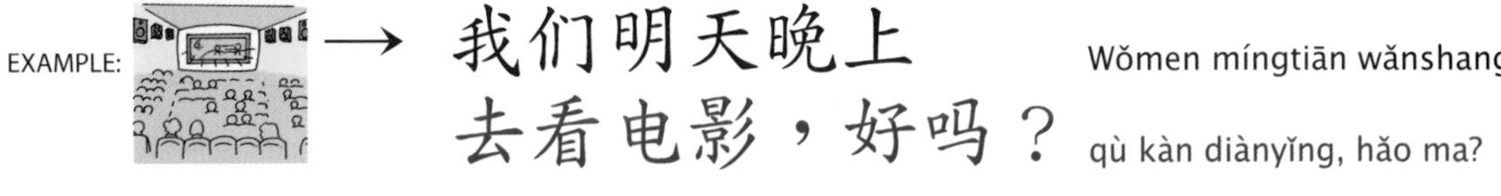

→ 我们明天晚上去看电影，好吗？ Wǒmen míngtiān wǎnshang qù kàn diànyǐng, hǎo ma?

1. 

2. 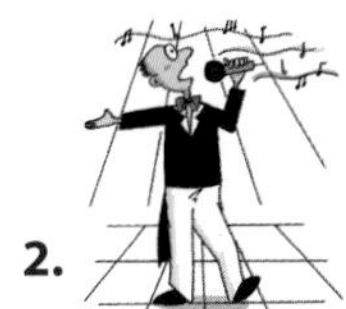

3. 

4. 

C. 因为…所以…(yīnwèi ... suǒyǐ..., because...therefore...)

Let's practice how to explain why you would or would not do something.

EXAMPLE: 你为什么不去看电影？（很忙）

Nǐ wèishénme bú qù kàn diànyǐng? (hěn máng)

→ 因为我很忙，所以我不去看电影。

Yīnwèi wǒ hěn máng, suǒyǐ wǒ bú qù kàn diànyǐng.

1. 你为什么不去打球？（有事儿）
2. 你为什么不去看外国电影？（不喜欢）
3. 你为什么星期五请我吃晚饭？（你的生日）
4. 你为什么不去跳舞？（不喜欢）
5. 你为什么不听音乐？（没有音乐）

1. Nǐ wèishénme bú qù dǎ qiú? (yǒu shìr)
2. Nǐ wèishénme bú qù kàn wàiguó diànyǐng? (bù xǐhuan)
3. Nǐ wèishénme xīngqīwǔ qǐng wǒ chī wǎnfàn? (nǐ de shēngrì)
4. Nǐ wèishénme bú qù tiàowǔ? (bù xǐhuan)
5. Nǐ wèishénme bù tīng yīnyuè? (méiyǒu yīnyuè)

D. "What do you like to do on weekends?"

Find out what your classmates like to do on weekends:

A: 你周末喜欢做什么？

B: 我周末喜欢＿＿＿＿＿＿＿。

A: Nǐ zhōumò xǐhuan zuò shénme?

B: Wǒ zhōumò xǐhuan_______.

Report to the class what your fellow students like to do on weekends.

Be prepared to answer the teacher's questions:

John 周末喜欢做什么？Mary 呢？John 喜欢不喜欢看书？……

John zhōumò xǐhuan zuò shénme? Mary ne? John xǐhuan bù xǐhuan kàn shū?

他们喜欢跳舞。
Tāmen xǐhuan tiào wǔ.

Dialogue II: Would You Like to Play Ball?

(Wang Peng is talking to Gao Wenzhong.)

小高❶，好久不见❷，你好吗❸？

我很好。你怎么样？

我也不错。这个周末你想⑥做什么？想不想去打球？

打球？我不喜欢打球。

那我们去看球，怎么样？

看球？我觉得❹看球也没有意思。

LANGUAGE NOTES

❶ A familiar and affectionate way of addressing a young person is to add 小 (xiǎo, little; small) to the family name, e.g., 小王 (Xiǎo Wáng, Little Wang). Similarly, to address an older acquaintance, 老 (lǎo, old) can be used with the surname, e.g., 老王 (Lǎo Wáng, Old Wang). However, such terms are rarely used to address a relative, or a superior.

❷ Sounds familiar? Now you know where the expression "Long time no see" comes from.

那你这个周末想做什么？

我只想吃饭、睡觉⑤⑦。

算了，我去找别人。

(Wang Peng is talking to Gao Wenzhong.)

Xiǎo Gāo❶, hǎo jiǔ bú jiàn❷, nǐ hǎo ma❸?

Wǒ hěn hǎo. Nǐ zěnmeyàng?

Wǒ yě búcuò. Zhè ge zhōumò nǐ xiǎng⑥zuò shénme? Xiǎng bu xiǎng qù dǎ qiú?

Dǎ qiú? Wǒ bù xǐhuan dǎ qiú.

Nà wǒmen qù kàn qiú, zěnmeyàng?

Kàn qiú? Wǒ juéde❹kàn qiú yě méiyǒu yìsi.

Nà nǐ zhè ge zhōumò xiǎng zuò shénme?

Wǒ zhǐ xiǎng chī fàn, shuì jiào⑤⑦.

Suàn le, wǒ qù zhǎo biérén.

❸ 你好吗？(Nǐ hǎo ma? How are you?) is a question typically asked of people that you already know. The answer is usually "我很好" (Wǒ hěn hǎo, I am fine.)

❹ The position of negatives in Chinese is not always the same as their counterparts in English. An English speaker would say: "I *don't* think going to the movies *is* a lot of fun," but a Chinese speaker would say 我觉得看电影没有意思 (Wǒ juéde kàn diànyǐng méiyou yìsi), which literally means, "I *think* going to the movies *is not* a lot of fun."

❺ The character 觉 is pronounced in two different ways and has two different meanings: jué as in 觉得 (juéde, to feel) and jiào as in 睡觉 (shuì jiào, to sleep).

VOCABULARY

1.	小	xiǎo	adj	small; little
2.	好久	hǎo jiǔ		a long time
	好	hǎo	adv	very
	久	jiǔ	adj	long (of time)
3.	不错	búcuò	adj	pretty good
	错	cuò	adj	wrong

VOCABULARY

4.	想	xiǎng	mv	to want to; would like to; to think [See Grammar 6.]
5.	觉得	juéde	v	to feel; to think
6.	有意思	yǒu yìsi	adj	interesting
	意思	yìsi	n	meaning
7.	只	zhǐ	adv	only
8.	睡觉	shuì jiào	vo	to sleep
	睡	shuì	v	to sleep
	觉	jiào	n	sleep
9.	算了	suàn le		forget it; never mind
10.	找	zhǎo	v	to look for
11.	别人	biérén	n	other people; another person
	别(的)	bié (de)	adj	other

Grammar

6. The Modal Verb 想 (xiǎng, want to; would like to)

想 (xiǎng) has several meanings. In this lesson it is a modal verb indicating a desire to do something. It must be followed by a verb or a clause.

❶ 你想听音乐吗？

Nǐ xiǎng tīng yīnyuè ma?

(Would you like to listen to some music?)

❷ 白老师想打球，可是王老师不想打。

Bái lǎoshī xiǎng dǎ qiú, kěshì Wáng lǎoshī bù xiǎng dǎ.

(Teacher Bai felt like playing ball, but Teacher Wang didn't.)

❸ 你想不想看中国电影？

Nǐ xiǎng bu xiǎng kàn Zhōngguó diànyǐng?

(Do you feel like going to see a Chinese movie?)

❹ 你想不想听外国音乐？

Nǐ xiǎng bu xiǎng tīng wàiguó yīnyuè?

(Do you feel like listening to some foreign music?)

想 (xiǎng) vs. 喜欢 (xǐhuan)

想 (xiǎng) can be translated as "would like to," "to have a desire to." 喜欢 (xǐhuan) is "to like," meaning "be fond of." 想 (xiǎng) and 喜欢 (xǐhuan) are different, and are not interchangeable.

想 (xiǎng) vs. 觉得 (juéde)

Both 想 (xiǎng) and 觉得 (juéde) can be translated as "to think," but the former means "to desire," whereas the latter means "to feel," "to have the opinion," or "to give a comment."

7. Verb+Object as a Detachable Compound

Even though 睡觉 (shuì jiào, to sleep), 唱歌 (chàng gē, to sing), and 跳舞 (tiào wǔ, to dance) are treated each as a word, grammatically speaking, they are all verb-object compounds. When there is an attributive element to modify the object, such as an adjective or a number-measure word combination, it must be inserted between the verb and the noun. Such a compound is called a "detachable compound." It is important to remember that a detachable compound does not take an object. Here are examples:

睡觉 (shuì jiào, to sleep)	→	睡一个好觉	(shuì yí ge hǎo jiào, have a good sleep)
唱歌 (chàng gē, to sing)	→	唱英文歌	(chàng Yīngwén gē, sing an English song)
跳舞 (tiào wǔ, to dance)	→	跳中国舞	(tiào Zhōngguó wǔ, do a Chinese dance)

In later lessons, you will see examples of other elements, like aspect markers, being inserted between the verb and the object in a detachable compound.

Language Practice

E. 想 (xiǎng, **would like to)**

Ask your friend if he or she would like to do the following activities this weekend.

EXAMPLE:   → 你周末想不想打球？
Nǐ zhōumò xiǎng bu xiǎng dǎ qiú?

1. 
2. 
3. 
4. 
5. 

F. 有意思 (yǒu yìsi, **interesting)**

Describe what activity each of the persons is or is not interested in.

EXAMPLE: ✓ 打球 （小高） dǎ qiú (Xiǎo Gāo)

小高觉得打球 Xiǎo Gāo juéde dǎ qiú
很有意思。 hěn yǒu yìsi.

1. ✗ 跳舞（白医生） **1.** tiào wǔ (Bái yīshēng)
2. ✓ 听中国音乐（王律师） **2.** tīng Zhōngguó yīnyuè (Wáng lǜshī)
3. ✓ 看外国电影（李老师） **3.** kàn wàiguó diànyǐng (Lǐ lǎoshī)
4. ✗ 看英文书（王小姐） **4.** kàn Yīngwén shū (Wáng xiǎojiě)
5. ✓ 看电视（高先生） **5.** kàn diànshì (Gāo Xiānsheng)

G. Pair Activity

Find out what your partner would like to do this weekend.

A: 这个周末你想做什么？ **A:** Zhè ge zhōumò nǐ xiǎng zuò shénme?

B: 这个周末我想________。 **B:** Zhè ge zhōumò wǒ xiǎng ________.

Find out if your partner feels like doing something else this weekend.

A: 你想________________吗？ **A:** Nǐ xiǎng ________ma?

B: 我想/不想______________。 **B:** Wǒ xiǎng/bù xiǎng __________.

What types of activities does your partner think are fun?

A: 你觉得（看电影、看书，etc.）有意思吗？ **A:** Nǐ juéde (kàn diànyǐng, kàn shū, etc.) yǒu yìsi ma?

B: 我觉得________________很有意思/没有意思。 **B:** Wǒ juéde ______________ hěn yǒu yìsi/méi yǒu yìsi.

HOW ABOUT YOU?

What's your hobby?

1. 画画儿 huà huàr

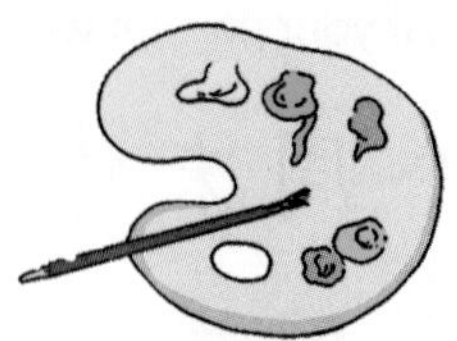

2. 下棋 xià qí

3. 上网聊天儿 shàng wǎng liáo tiānr

4. 玩游戏机 wán yóuxìjī

5. 逛街 guàng jiē

If your hobbies are not listed above, please ask your teacher and make a note here:

我喜欢__________________。 or

我觉得__________________很有意思。

Wǒ xǐhuan ______________. or

Wǒ juéde ______________ hěn yǒu yìsi.

Culture Highlights

1 When Chinese people go out to eat with friends, they rarely split the check at the end of the meal. Usually, someone will insist on picking up the tab by saying: "今天我请客" (Jīntiān wǒ qǐngkè, It's my treat today). The next time someone else will offer to pay. Often more than one person reaches for the bill and there might be a little struggle over who gets to pay.

2 In general, Chinese people don't have the habit of getting a receipt after paying for a meal in a restaurant. But more and more people will ask for an invoice, 发票 (fāpiào), for reimbursement purposes. Here's a copy of an invoice from a restaurant.

北京市服务业、娱乐业、文化体育业专用发票
BEIJING SPECIAL INVOICE FOR SERVICE INDUSTRY, ENTERTAINMENT INDUSTRY AND PHYSICAL CULTURE INDUSTRY
发票联
INVOICE

发票代码 INVOICE CODE 21100077
发票号码 INVOICE NO. 06996489
密码 PASSWORD
信息码 INF. NUMBER 2014070
58077214-04808429-98489025

税务登记号: TAX REGISTRY NO. 11010580179
收款单位: PAYEE 北京　餐饮有限公司
付款单位(个人): PAYER 个人

经营项目 SERVICE ITEM	金额 AMOUNT CHARGED
餐费	185.00

金额合计（人民币大写）TOTAL IN CAPITAL 壹佰捌拾伍元整
机打票号: PRINTING NO. 2014070201069
税控装置防伪码: ANTI-FORGERY CODE 4D71679A09
税控号码 RECEIVER NO. 000154
开票日期: DATE ISSUED 2007-08-01
收款单位(盖章有效) PAYEE(SEAL)
税控装置打印发票手开无效 PRINTED BY RECEIVER, HAND-WRITING INVALID

「机打票号」与「信息码」和「发票号码」必须一致，否则无效
THE PRINTING NUMBER SHOULD COMPLY WITH THE INFORMATION NUMBER AND THE INVOICE NUMBER, OR, THE INVOICE IS ILLEGAL.

奖区 AWARD AREA
1. 刮开奖区覆盖层后显示中奖金额或"谢谢您"。
2. 告知事项：中奖后，在兑奖前不得将发票联和兑奖联撕开，否则，不予以办理兑奖手续。

二 发票联 SECOND INVOICE
58077214-04808429-98489025

Can you tell in which city the invoice was issued?

❸ Playing mahjong 麻将 (májiàng) is one of the most popular pastimes for many Chinese people. The game needs four players and each mahjong set consists of 144 tiles. To win, the players have to draw various tiles to form different combinations, which have all been assigned scores based on pre-set rules. The more difficult the combination, the higher the score is. There are four games in each round, and the players can decide how many rounds they wish to play. Normally, people play either 8 or 12 rounds. Besides mahjong, playing Chinese chess 象棋 (xiàngqí) is another popular pastime in China. The international chess has pieces such as king, queen, rook, knight, and pawn, whereas Chinese chess has commander in chief, general, chariots, horses, and soldiers. Both mahjong and Chinese chess go back centuries. Community centers and clubhouses in China often have a 棋牌室 (qípáishì) or chess and poker room where men and women, especially retirees, meet for chess and mahjong marathons. It is also common to find onlookers gathering around chess players in neighborhood parks.

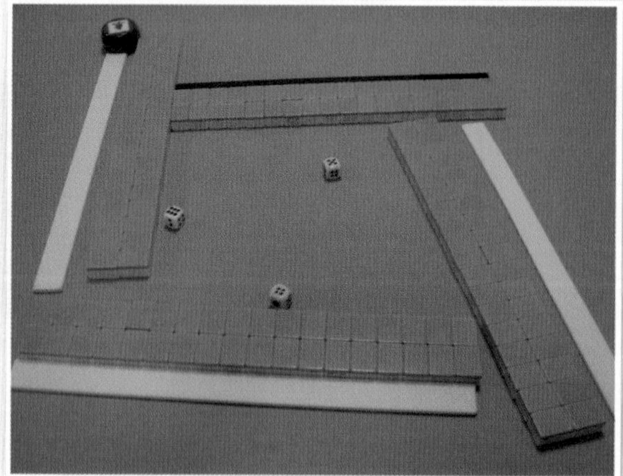

This is how the mahjong tiles are set up before a new game begins.

Each team of Chinese Chess pieces is identified by colors, typically black and red. They are set up as shown. You have learned the character/radical meaning "horse." Can you find where the horses are on the board?

Here are the mahjong tiles. There are some with Chinese numerals on them. Can you identify some of the numbers?

4 Arguably less popular but more prestigious is the game of encirclement 围棋 (wéiqí), better known in the West by its Japanese name Go. It is a deceptively simple game played with counters or stones on a board ruled with 19 vertical and 19 horizontal lines. The objective of the game is to surround and capture the opponent's counters. Every year major corporations sponsor tournaments with master players from China, Japan, and Korea participating and TV stations providing live coverage of important matches.

English Text

Dialogue I

Gao Wenzhong: Bai Ying'ai, what do you like to do on weekends?

Bai Ying'ai: I like to play ball and watch TV. How about you?

Gao Wenzhong: I like to sing, dance, and listen to music. You like to read, right?

Bai Ying'ai: Yes, sometimes I like to read as well.

Gao Wenzhong: Do you like to watch movies?

Bai Ying'ai: Yes, I do. I often watch movies on weekends.

Gao Wenzhong: Then let's go see a foreign movie this evening. OK? My treat.

Bai Ying'ai: Why your treat?

Gao Wenzhong: Because you treated me to dinner yesterday, today I'm treating you to a movie.

Bai Ying'ai: Then invite Wang Peng and Li You as well, OK?

Gao Wenzhong: ...OK.

Dialogue II

(Wang Peng is talking to Gao Wenzhong.)

Wang Peng: Little Gao, long time no see. How are you?

Gao Wenzhong: I'm fine. How about yourself?

Wang Peng: I'm fine, too. What would you like to do this weekend? Would you like to play ball?

Gao Wenzhong: Play ball? I don't like playing ball.

Wang Peng: Then let's watch a ball game. How's that?

Gao Wenzhong: Watch a ball game? I don't think watching a ball game is much fun, either.

Wang Peng: Then what do you want to do this weekend?

Gao Wenzhong: I only want to eat and sleep.

Wang Peng: Never mind. I'll ask somebody else.

PROGRESS CHECKLIST

Before proceeding to Lesson 5, be sure you can complete the following tasks in Chinese:

I am able to

- ☑ Talk about my favorite pastimes and ask about someone else's;
- ☑ Invite someone to a weekend activity;
- ☑ Accept or decline an invitation to a weekend activity;
- ☑ Find someone to do activities with.

Please review the lesson if any of these tasks seem difficult.

LESSON 5

Visiting Friends

第五课 看朋友

Dì wǔ kè Kàn péngyou

LEARNING OBJECTIVES

In this lesson, you will learn to use Chinese to:

- Welcome a visitor;
- Introduce one person to another;
- Compliment someone on his/her house;
- Ask for beverages as a guest at someone else's place;
- Offer beverages to a visitor;
- Briefly describe a visit to a friend's place.

RELATE AND GET READY

In your own culture/community—

1. Is it common to pay a visit to a friend's house without advance notice?
2. Do people bring anything when visiting a friend's home?
3. What are some of the common beverages and foods offered to visitors?

Dialogue: Visiting a Friend's Home

(The doorbell rings.)

谁呀？

是我，王朋，还有李友。

请进，请进，快进来！来，我介绍一下[1]，这是我姐姐，高小音。

小音，你好。认识你很高兴。

认识你们我也很高兴。

你们家很大[2]，也很漂亮。

是吗？❶请坐，请坐。

小音，你在③哪儿❷工作？

我在学校工作。你们想喝点儿①什么？喝茶还是喝咖啡？

我喝茶吧④。

我要一瓶可乐，可以吗？

对不起，我们家没有可乐。

那给我一杯水吧。

LANGUAGE NOTES

❶ Although it takes a question mark, 是吗 (Shì ma?) is not a question here but a mild expression of surprise on hearing something unexpected. Here it indicates one's modesty on receiving a compliment. It could be translated as "Is that so?" "You don't say!" or "Really?"

❷ 哪儿 (nǎr) is a question word meaning "where." Do not confuse it with 那儿 (nàr, there). 这儿 (zhèr) means "here" in Chinese.

(The doorbell rings.)

Shéi ya?

Shì wǒ, Wáng Péng, hái yǒu Lǐ Yǒu.

Qǐng jìn, qǐng jìn, kuài jìn lai! Lái, wǒ jièshào yí xià①, zhè shì wǒ jiějie, Gāo Xiǎoyīn.

Xiǎoyīn, nǐ hǎo. Rènshi nǐ hěn gāoxìng.

Rènshi nǐmen wǒ yě hěn gāoxìng.

Nǐmen jiā hěn dà②, yě hěn piàoliang.

Shì ma? ❶ Qǐng zuò, qǐng zuò.

Xiǎoyīn, nǐ zài③ nǎr❷ gōngzuò?

Wǒ zài xuéxiào gōngzuò. Nǐmen xiǎng hē diǎnr①shénme? Hē chá, háishi hē kāfēi?

Wǒ hē chá ba.④

Wǒ yào yì píng kělè, kěyǐ ma?

Duìbuqǐ, wǒmen jiā méi yǒu kělè.

Nà gěi wǒ yì bēi shuǐ ba.

VOCABULARY

1.	呀	ya	p	(interjectory particle used to soften a question)
2.	进	jìn	v	to enter
3.	快	kuài	adv/adj	fast, quick; quickly
4.	进来	jìn lai	vc	to come in
5.	来	lái	v	to come
6.	介绍	jièshào	v	to introduce
7.	一下	yí xià	n+m	once; a bit [See Grammar 1.]
8.	高兴	gāoxìng	adj	happy, pleased
9.	漂亮	piàoliang	adj	pretty
10.	坐	zuò	v	to sit
11.	在	zài	prep	at; in; on [See Grammar 3.]
12.	哪儿	nǎr	qpr	where
13.	学校	xuéxiào	n	school
14.	喝	hē	v	to drink
15.	点(儿)	diǎn(r)	m	a little, a bit; some [See Grammar 1.]
16.	茶	chá	n	tea
17.	咖啡	kāfēi	n	coffee
18.	吧	ba	p	(a sentence-final particle) [See Grammar 4.]
19.	要	yào	v	to want
20.	瓶	píng	m/n	(measure word for bottles); bottle

VOCABULARY

21.	可乐	kělè	n	[Coke or Pepsi] cola
22.	可以	kěyǐ	mv	can; may
23.	对不起	duìbuqǐ	v	sorry
24.	给	gěi	v	to give
25.	杯	bēi	m	(measure word for cup and glass)
26.	水	shuǐ	n	water

Proper Noun

27.	高小音	Gāo Xiǎoyīn		(a personal name)

Name the beverages in the picture in Chinese.

你要一杯水还是一瓶水？
Nǐ yào yì bēi shuǐ háishi yì píng shuǐ?

Grammar

1. 一下 (yí xià) and (一)点儿 ({yì} diǎnr) Moderating the Tone of Voice

Following a verb, both 一下 (yí xià, lit. "once") and (一)点儿 ({yì} diǎnr "a bit") can soften the tone in a question or an imperative sentence, therefore making it more polite. When used in this way, 一下 (yí xià) modifies the verb, while (一)点儿 ({yì} diǎnr) modifies the object.

❶ 你看一下，这是谁的照片？

Nǐ kàn yí xià, zhè shì shéi de zhàopiàn?

(Take a look. Whose photo is this?)

❷ 你想吃点儿什么？

Nǐ xiǎng chī diǎnr shénme?

(What would you like to eat?)

❸ 你进来一下。

Nǐ jìn lai yí xià.

(Come in for a minute.)

❹ 你喝一点儿茶吧。

Nǐ hē yìdiǎnr chá ba.

(Have a little tea.)

2. Adjectives as Predicates

In Chinese, when an adjective functions as a predicate, it is not preceded by the verb 是 (shì, to be). It is usually modified by 很 (hěn, very), as seen in (1), (2), (3), and (4), or some other adverbial modifier. However, 很 (hěn) is not as strong as "very" in English. When forming a question with an adjective as the predicate, 很 is not used, as seen in (5) and (6).

❶ 我今天很高兴。

Wǒ jīntiān hěn gāoxìng.

(I'm happy today.)

❷ 他妹妹很漂亮。

Tā mèimei hěn piàoliang.

(His younger sister is pretty.)

❸ 那个电影很好。

Nà ge diànyǐng hěn hǎo.

(That movie is good.)

❹ 你们大学很大。

Nǐmen dàxué hěn dà.

(Your university is very large.)

❺ **A:** 你弟弟高吗？

Nǐ dìdi gāo ma?

(Is your younger brother tall?)

B: 他很高。

Tā hěn gāo.

(He is tall.)

❻ **A:** 你家大吗？

Nǐ jiā dà ma?

(Is your house big?)

B: 我家不大，很小。

Wǒ jiā bú dà, hěn xiǎo.

(My house is not big, it's small.)

Chinese adjectives without 很 (hěn) or any sort of modifier before them can often imply comparison or contrast, as seen in (7) and (8) below.

❼ **A:** 姐姐漂亮还是妹妹漂亮？

Jiějie piàoliang háishi mèimei piàoliang?

(Who's prettier, the older sister or the younger sister?)

B: 妹妹漂亮。

Mèimei piàoliang.

(The younger sister is prettier).

❽ 妹妹的中文好，我的中文不好。

Mèimei de Zhōngwén hǎo, wǒ de Zhōngwén bù hǎo.

(My younger sister's Chinese is good. My Chinese is not good.)

3. The Preposition 在 (zài, at; in; on)

Combined with a noun, the preposition 在 (zài) indicates location. When the phrase is placed before a verb, it indicates the location of the action.

❶ **A:** 我的书在哪儿？ **B:** 在那儿。

Wǒ de shū zài nǎr? Zài nàr.

(Where is my book? It's over there.)

❷ **A:** 你在哪儿工作？ **B:** 我在这儿工作。

Nǐ zài nǎr gōngzuò? Wǒ zài zhèr gōngzuò.

(Where do you work? I work here.)

❸ 我在这个大学学中文。

Wǒ zài zhè ge dàxué xué Zhōngwén.

(I study Chinese at this university.)

❹ 我不喜欢在家看电影。

Wǒ bù xǐhuan zài jiā kàn diànyǐng.

(I don't like to watch movies at home.)

4. The Particle 吧 (ba)

吧 (ba) is a sentence-final "suggestion" particle, often used at the end of an imperative sentence to soften the tone.

❶ 你喝咖啡吧。

Nǐ hē kāfēi ba.

(Why don't you have some coffee?)

❷ 请进来吧。

Qǐng jìn lai ba.

(Come in, please.)

❸ 我们跳舞吧。

Wǒmen tiào wǔ ba.

(Let's dance.)

Language Practice

A. 一下 (yí xià)

1. You wish to look at your brother's girlfriend's picture, so you say to your brother…

哥哥，我 ________ 你女朋友的照片，好吗？

Gēge, wǒ ______ nǐ nǚpéngyou de zhàopiàn, hǎo ma?

2. You'd like your friend, Little Bai, to introduce you to Ms. Li, so you say…

小白，我想认识李小姐。请你 ________ 。

Xiǎo Bái, wǒ xiǎng rènshi Lǐ xiǎojiě. Qǐng nǐ ______.

3. You are at the doctor's office for your appointment; the nurse tells you the doctor is busy, and asks you to sit down for a bit. So she says…

对不起，医生现在 有事儿，请你 ________ 。

Duìbuqǐ, yīshēng xiànzài yǒu shìr, qǐng nǐ ______.

4. Your roommate has bought a CD, and suggests that you listen to it, so she says…

这个音乐不错。 你 ________ 。

Zhège yīnyuè búcuò. Nǐ ______.

5. Your teacher wants to talk to you about something after class and asks you to come with him, so he says…

我有事儿找你。 你 ________ 。

Wǒ yǒu shìr zhǎo nǐ. Nǐ ______.

B. Adjectives as Predicates

高文中的家◇漂亮

Gāo Wénzhōng de jiā ◇ piàoliang

EXAMPLE: If people ask your opinion of Gao Wenzhong's house,

高文中的家漂亮吗？

Gāo Wénzhōng de jiā piàoliang ma?

and you think Gao Wenzhong's house is beautifully decorated, you can say…

高文中的家很漂亮。

Gāo Wénzhōng de jiā hěn piàoliang.

But, if you don't think Gao's house is beautifully decorated, you can say…

高文中的家不漂亮。

Gāo Wénzhōng de jiā bú piàoliang.

Work with a partner. Find out from each other what you think about your doctor, school, teacher, classmates, and textbook.

1. 你的医生◇忙

1. Nǐ de yīshēng ◇ máng

2. 你的学校◇大

2. Nǐ de xuéxiào ◇ dà

3. 你的同学◇高兴 — 3. Nǐ de tóngxué ◇ gāoxìng

4. 你的老师◇好 — 4. Nǐ de lǎoshī ◇ hǎo

5. 你的书◇有意思 — 5. Nǐ de shū ◇ yǒu yìsi

C. 在 (zài)

1. Look at the pictures given, and tell where Wang Peng and Li You are, and what they are doing there.

EXAMPLE:  王朋和李友在图书馆 (túshūguǎn, library) 看书。

Wáng Péng hé Lǐ Yǒu zài túshūguǎn kàn shū.

1.   2.   3.  

2. Everyone has a different routine and favorite places. Now let's find out where these people do their activities.

EXAMPLE:

小高在哪儿工作？ Xiǎo Gāo zài nǎr gōngzuò? 

小高在学校工作。 Xiǎo Gāo zài xuéxiào gōngzuò.

1. 李医生在哪儿听音乐？ Lǐ yīshēng zài nǎr tīng yīnyuè? 

2. 王朋在哪儿打球？ Wáng Péng zài nǎr dǎ qiú?

3. 李友在哪儿看电影？ Lǐ Yǒu zài nǎr kàn diànyǐng?   

4. 小白在哪儿睡觉？ Xiǎo Bái zài nǎr shuì jiào?

D. 点儿 (diǎnr)

Imagine the main characters of the text all come to your house as your guests: you now try to offer them something to drink, to eat, or to do. Use the pictures as clues and work with a partner.

EXAMPLE:

高文中，你想喝点儿什么？
Gāo Wénzhōng, nǐ xiǎng hē diǎnr shénme?

1.  

2.  

3.  

E. Do you all know each other in your class?

Mobilize the entire class and form a big circle. Taking turns, introduce the person on your right to the person on your left.

1: 我介绍一下， 这是________。	**1:** Wǒ jièshào yí xià, zhè shì ______.
2: 认识你很高兴。 我介绍一下，这是________。	**2:** Rènshi nǐ hěn gāoxìng. Wǒ jièshào yí xià, zhè shì ______.
3: 认识你很高兴。 我介绍一下，这是________。	**3:** Rènshi nǐ hěn gāoxìng. Wǒ jièshào yí xià, zhè shì ______.

F. Group Activity

In groups of three, one acts as a host and asks the two guests what they would like to drink:

A: 你/你们想喝点儿什么？ — **A:** Nǐ/Nǐmen xiǎng hē diǎnr shénme?

B: 我喝＿＿＿＿＿＿吧。 — **B:** Wǒ hē ＿＿＿＿ ba.

C: 我喝＿＿＿＿＿＿吧。 — **C:** Wǒ hē ＿＿＿＿ ba.

Apologize to one of your guests that you don't have the beverage and offer an alternative:

A: 对不起，没有＿＿＿＿＿＿。＿＿＿＿＿＿，可以吗？ — **A:** Duìbuqǐ, méiyǒu ＿＿＿＿. ＿＿＿＿, kěyǐ ma?

The guest accepts or asks for something else:

B or **C:** 那给我一杯/一瓶＿＿＿＿吧。 — **B** or **C:** Nà gěi wǒ yì bēi/yì píng ＿＿＿＿ ba.

G. Survey the class

First pair up and ask your partner these questions. Then report your findings to the class.

你喜欢喝什么？ — Nǐ xǐhuan hē shénme?

你喜欢喝可乐还是咖啡？ — Nǐ xǐhuan hē kělè háishi kāfēi?

你喜欢喝茶吗？ — Nǐ xǐhuan hē chá ma?

你喜欢喝水还是喝茶？ — Nǐ xǐhuan hē shuǐ háishi hē chá?

The most popular beverage in the class is ＿＿＿＿＿.

你想喝什么？

Nǐ xiǎng hē shénme?

Narrative: At a Friend's House

昨天晚上，王朋和李友去高文中家玩儿。在高文中家，他们认识了⑤ 高文中的姐姐。她叫高小音，在学校的图书馆工作。她请王朋喝❶茶，王朋喝了两杯。李友不喝茶，只喝了一杯水。他们一起聊天儿、看电视。王朋和李友晚上十二点才⑥回家。

LANGUAGE NOTE

❶ Unlike its English counterpart, 喝 (hē) always functions as a transitive verb. In other words, unless it's clear from the context, the beverage has to be specified. Therefore, 他常常喝 (Tā chángcháng hē) is not a complete sentence unless when the beverage is understood, e.g.:

A: 他常常喝咖啡吗？

(Tā chángcháng hē kāfēi ma?)

Does he often drink coffee?

B: 他常常喝。

(Tā chángcháng hē.)

He often does.

Zuótiān wǎnshang, Wáng Péng hé Lǐ Yǒu qù Gāo Wénzhōng jiā wánr. Zài Gāo Wénzhōng jiā, tāmen rènshi le⑤ Gāo Wénzhōng de jiějie. Tā jiào Gāo Xiǎoyīn, zài xuéxiào de túshūguǎn gōngzuò. Tā qǐng Wáng Péng hē❶ chá, Wáng Péng hē le liǎng bēi. Lǐ Yǒu bù hē chá, zhǐ hē le yì bēi shuǐ. Tāmen yìqǐ liáo tiānr, kàn diànshì. Wáng Péng hé Lǐ Yǒu wǎnshang shí'èr diǎn cái⑤ huí jiā.

她在哪儿看书？

Tā zài nǎr kàn shū?

VOCABULARY

1.	玩(儿)	wán(r)	v	to have fun; to play
2.	了	le	p	(a dynamic particle) [See Grammar 5.]
3.	图书馆	túshūguǎn	n	library
4.	一起	yìqǐ	adv	together
5.	聊天(儿)	liáo tiān(r)	vo	to chat
	聊	liáo	v	to chat
	天	tiān	n	sky
6.	才	cái	adv	not until, only then [See Grammar 6.]
7.	回家	huí jiā	vo	to go home
	回	huí	v	to return

Grammar

5. The Particle 了 (le) (I)

The dynamic particle 了 (le) signifies: 1) the occurrence or completion of an action or event, or 2) the emergence of a situation. The action, event, or situation usually pertains to the past, but sometimes it can refer to the future. Therefore 了 (le) is not a past tense marker, and the use of 了 (le) should not be taken as an equivalent to the past tense in English. In this lesson, 了 (le) indicates the occurrence or completion of an action or event. It is usually used after a verb. But sometimes it appears after a verb and the object of the verb in interrogative and declarative sentences.

❶ 今天妈妈喝了三杯水。

Jīntiān Māma hē le sān bēi shuǐ.

(Mom had three glasses of water today.)

(occurrence or completion of an action, in the past)

❷ 星期一小高请我喝了一瓶可乐。

Xīngqīyī Xiǎo Gāo qǐng wǒ hē le yì píng kělè.

(On Monday Little Gao bought me a bottle of cola.)

(occurrence or completion of an event, in the past)

❸ **A:** 昨天晚上你去打球了吗？

Zuótiān wǎnshang nǐ qù dǎ qiú le ma?

(Yesterday evening did you go play ball?)

(occurrence or completion of an event, in the past, an interrogative sentence)

B: 昨天晚上我去打球了。

Zuótiān wǎnshang wǒ qù dǎ qiú le.

(Yesterday evening I went to play ball.)

(occurrence or completion of an event, in the past)

❹ 明天我吃了晚饭去看电影。

Míngtiān wǒ chī le wǎnfàn qù kàn diànyǐng.

(Tomorrow I'll go see a movie after I have eaten dinner.)

(occurrence or completion of an action in the first part of the sentence, in the future)

There is often a specific time phrase in a sentence with the dynamic particle 了 (le) — such as 今天 (jīntiān, today) in (1), 星期一 (xīngqīyī, Monday) in (2), or 昨天晚上 (zuótiān wǎnshang, last night) in (3).

When 了 (le) is used between the verb and the object, the object is usually preceded by a modifier. The following—numeral + measure word—is the most common type of modifier for the object:

三杯 (sān bēi, three cups / three glasses) in (1)

一瓶 (yì píng, one bottle) in (2)

If there are other phrases or sentences following the object of the first clause, then the object does not need a modifier. See example (4) above. This V 了 O+V(O) structure can be used to depict a sequence of two actions, and it doesn't matter whether the two actions take place in the past or in the future.

If the object following 了 (le) is a proper noun, as "Harry Potter" in (5) below, it does not need a modifier, either.

5 我昨天看了《哈利•波特》，那个电影很好。

Wǒ zuótiān kàn le «Hālì Bōtè». Nà ge diànyǐng hěn hǎo.

(I saw *Harry Potter* yesterday. That movie was good.)

To say that an action did not take place in the past, use 没(有) (méi {yǒu}) instead of 不…了 (bù...le) or 没有…了 (méiyǒu...le).

FOR EXAMPLE:

6 昨天我没有听音乐。

Zuótiān wǒ méiyǒu tīng yīnyuè.

(I didn't listen to music yesterday.)

(6a) *昨天我不听音乐了。

*Zuótiān wǒ bù tīng yīnyuè le.

(6b) *昨天我没有听音乐了。

*Zuótiān wǒ méiyǒu tīng yīnyuè le.

Interrogative forms:

❼ **A:** 你吃饭了吗？ or 你吃饭了没有？

Nǐ chī fàn le ma? or Nǐ chī fàn le méiyǒu?

(Did you eat?)

B: 我没吃。

Wǒ méi chī.

(No, I didn't.)

❽ **A:** 你喝了几杯水？

Nǐ hē le jǐ bēi shuǐ?

(How many glasses of water did you drink?)

B: 我喝了一杯水。

Wǒ hē le yì bēi shuǐ.

(I drank one glass of water.)

A sign on a bubble tea shop, a reminder to passersby to drop in and get their daily cup of bubble tea.

6. The Adverb 才 (cái, not until)

The adverb 才 (cái, not until) indicates that the occurrence of an action or situation is later than the speaker may have expected. That lateness is perceived by the speaker, and is not necessarily objective, as seen in (2) and (3). 才 (cái) never takes the particle 了 (le), whether or not it pertains to an action or situation in the past.

❶ 我请他六点吃晚饭，他六点半才来。

Wǒ qǐng tā liù diǎn chī wǎnfàn, tā liù diǎn bàn cái lái.

(I invited him out to dinner at six o'clock. He didn't come till six-thirty.)

❷ 小高常常晚上十二点才回家。

Xiǎo Gāo chángcháng wǎnshang shí'èr diǎn cái huí jiā.

(Little Gao often doesn't go home until midnight.)

❸ 她晚上很晚才睡觉。

Tā wǎnshang hěn wǎn cái shuì jiào.

(She goes to bed very late in the evening.)

Language Practice

H. 了 (le)

Little Gao has so much energy! He can do so much in one day: dancing, singing, studying, eating, and working. Look at the following pictures, and recap what he did yesterday.

EXAMPLE:  x4 

小高昨天喝了四杯咖啡。 Xiǎo Gāo zuótiān hē le sì bēi kāfēi.

1.  x1
2.  x3
3.  x2
4.  x4

I. 才 (cái)

Imagine you are a very disciplined and time-conscious person. You do everything according to a set schedule. Your roommate, on the other hand, is a slow mover. Now you are comparing your daily routine with your roommate's, and you have found s/he does everything later than you do.

EXAMPLE:  7:00 vs. 8:00

我七点喝咖啡，她八点才喝（咖啡）。

Wǒ qī diǎn hē kāfēi, tā bā diǎn cái hē (kāfēi).

1.  9:00 vs. 9:30
2.  2:15 vs. 2:45
3.  6:00 vs. 7:15
4.  8:00 vs. 8:30
5.  9:30 vs. 12:00

J. Find out what your partner did last night.

你昨天晚上去朋友家玩儿了吗？ Nǐ zuótiān wǎnshang qù péngyou jiā wánr le ma?

If the answer is negative, then ask

你昨天晚上去哪儿了？ Nǐ zuótiān wǎnshang qù nǎr le?

你喝什么了？ Nǐ hē shénme le?

你喝了几杯/几瓶？ Nǐ hē le jǐ bēi/jǐ píng?

After gathering the information, report to the class what your partner did last night:

Mark 昨天晚上去朋友家玩了/没有去朋友家玩儿… Mark zuótiān wǎnshang qù péngyou jiā wánr le/méiyǒu qù péngyou jiā wánr...

K. It was Little Wang's birthday yesterday.

Recap what Little Wang did on his birthday according to the three pictures provided. Don't forget to mention the time in each picture!

HOW ABOUT YOU?

What's your favorite beverage?

1.	可口可乐	Kěkǒukělè	pn	Coca-Cola
2.	百事可乐	Bǎishìkělè	pn	Pepsi-Cola
3.	雪碧	Xuěbì	pn	Sprite
4.	汽水(儿)	qìshuǐ(r)	n	soft drink; soda pop
5.	矿泉水	kuàngquánshuǐ	n	mineral water
6.	果汁	guǒzhī	n	fruit juice

If your favorite beverage is not listed above, please ask your teacher and make a note here:

我喜欢喝 ________。

Wǒ xǐhuan hē ________.

Culture Highlights

1. 认识你很高兴 (rènshi nǐ hěn gāoxìng) or 很高兴认识你 (hěn gāoxìng rènshi nǐ) is a translation of "I'm very happy to meet you". It may, therefore, sound rather Western to some native Chinese speakers. However, as the traditional Chinese equivalent polite forms have long since become obsolete, this expression is becoming more common.

A modern upscale tea house, 茶馆儿 (cháguǎnr), awaits its customers.

2. Generally speaking, privacy is a somewhat less sacrosanct concept in Chinese culture than it is in the West. One would not necessarily be considered an intruder if one drops by a friend's place with no warning. Nor are topics such as age, marital status, and salary necessarily considered off limits in a polite conversation. For those who believe in the traditional Chinese notion of friendship or personal loyalty, sharing such personal information is an important gesture of trust. But there was a more practical reason in modern times until recently: when people had very limited living spaces, everyone was literally very close to everyone else, and privacy became too expensive a luxury. All this, however, is changing. The much improved housing conditions have offered more private spaces to most people, especially the urbanites. In a legal sense, the Chinese citizens are becoming more aware of each other's "privacy rights" (yǐnsī quán).

他们喝茶聊天儿。

Tāmen hē chá liáo tiānr.

你想喝什么茶？

Nǐ xiǎng hē shénme chá?

3. Tea, 茶 (chá), can probably be called the national drink of China. It depends on whom

you ask, but in general, Chinese tea may be classified into the following categories according to the different methods by which it is processed: green tea, black tea, Wulong tea, compressed tea, and scented tea. Chrysanthemum tea, 菊花茶 (júhuā chá), is a species of scented tea, whereas Longjing tea, 龙井茶 (lóngjǐng chá), belongs to the green tea family. Although tea is the most popular beverage in China, the number of coffee drinkers has been on the rise in recent years, as evidenced by the varieties of coffee on supermarket shelves and the surge of coffee shops, such as Starbucks, 星巴克 (Xīngbākè), in many Chinese cities.

This is a beverage menu of a restaurant. What kind of tea can you order?

English Text

Dialogue

Gao Wenzhong: Who is it?

Wang Peng: It's me, Wang Peng. Li You is here, too.

Gao Wenzhong: Please come in. Please come in. Let me introduce you to one another. This is my sister, Gao Xiaoyin.

Wang Peng and Li You: How do you do, Xiaoyin! Pleased to meet you.

Gao Xiaoyin: Pleased to meet you, too.

Li You: Your home is very big, and very beautiful, too.

Gao Wenzhong: Is that so? Have a seat, please.

Wang Peng: Xiaoyin, where do you work?

Gao Xiaoyin: I work at a school. What would you like to drink? Would you like to drink tea or coffee?

Wang Peng: I'll have tea.

Li You: I'd like to have a bottle of cola, is that OK?.

Gao Xiaoyin: I'm sorry. We don't have cola.

Li You: Then please give me a glass of water.

Narrative

Last night Wang Peng and Li You went to Gao Wenzhong's house for a visit. At Gao Wenzhong's house they met Gao Wenzhong's older sister. Her name is Gao Xiaoyin. She works at a school library. She offered tea to Wang Peng. Wang Peng had two cups. Li You doesn't drink tea. She only had a glass of water. They chatted and watched TV together. Wang Peng and Li You did not get home until twelve o'clock.

PROGRESS CHECKLIST

Before proceeding to Lesson 6, be sure that you can complete the following tasks in Chinese:

I am able to—

- [x] Introduce one person to another;
- [x] Greet guests when they visit my house;
- [x] Offer guests beverages to drink;
- [x] As a guest, ask the host/hostess for a beverage;
- [x] Ask about a friend's availability and set up a dinner appointment.

Please review the lesson if any of these tasks seem difficult.

That's How the Chinese Say It!

A Review of Functional Expressions from Lessons 1–5

After gauging your progress and before moving on to the next phase, let's take a break and see how some of the functional expressions that you have encountered in the previous lessons really work!

I. 算了 (**suàn le,** forget it; never mind) (Lesson 4)

You can say this to someone when you sense that you've put him or her in an awkward position or when someone has made a mistake but you don't wish to pursue the matter. You can also say this when you are dissatisfied with what someone is doing and want him or her to stop.

❶ A: 明天我们去打球，怎么样？

Míngtiān wǒmen qù dǎ qiú, zěnmeyàng?

(We'll go play ball tomorrow, all right?)

B: 明天我很忙。

Míngtiān wǒ hěn máng.

(I'm busy tomorrow.)

A: 那算了。

Nà suàn le.

(All right then, never mind.)

❷ A: 你今年多大？

Nǐ jīnnián duō dà?

(How old are you this year?)

B: 你为什么问我多大？

Nǐ wèishénme wèn wǒ duō dà?

(Why are you asking me how old I am?)

A: 算了，我不问了。

Suàn le, wǒ bú wèn le.

(Never mind. I won't ask any more.)

❸ 算了，算了，你回家吧，我来做。

Suàn le, suàn le, nǐ huí jiā ba, wǒ lái zuò.

(Forget about it. You can go home. I'll take over.)

II. 谁呀 (shéi ya, who is it?)(Lesson 5)

When you hear a knock on the door, this is what you usually say.

❶ A: (Knocking on the door.)

B: 谁呀？

Shéi ya?

(Who is it?)

A: 是我，李友。

Shì wǒ, Lǐ Yǒu.

(It's me, Li You.)

B: 请进。

Qǐng jìn.

(Please come in.)

❷ A: (Knocking on the door.)

B: 谁呀？

Shéi ya?

(Who is it?)

A: 我，小王。

Wǒ, Xiǎo Wáng.

(It's me, Little Wang.)

B: 进来。

Jìn lai.

(Come in.)

III. 是吗 (shì ma, really; is that so?) (Lesson 5)

You say this when you hear something unexpected.

❶ A: 你的英文老师不是美国人。

Nǐ de Yīngwén lǎoshī bú shì Měiguó rén.

(Your English teacher is not American.)

B: 是吗？他是哪国人？

Shì ma? Tā shì nǎ guó rén?

(Is that so? What country is he from?)

A: 他是英国人。

Tā shì Yīngguó rén.

(He is British.)

❷ A: 学校的图书馆很漂亮。

Xuéxiào de túshūguǎn hěn piàoliang.

(The school library is very pretty.)

B: 是吗？我明天去看看。

Shì ma? Wǒ míngtiān qù kàn kan.

(Really? I'll go take a look tomorrow.)

Any other useful expressions you would like to learn?

Please ask your teacher and make a note here:

___

___

___

Making Appointments

6

LESSON 6

第六课　约时间

Dì liù kè　Yuē shíjiān

LEARNING OBJECTIVES

In this lesson, you will learn to use Chinese to

- Answer a phone call and initiate a phone conversation;
- Set up an appointment with a teacher on the phone;
- Ask for a favor;
- Ask someone to return your call.

RELATE AND GET READY

In your own culture/community—

1. What does one say first when answering a phone call?
2. Do people state their names when answering the phone?
3. How do students address their teachers?
4. What do you say to ask a favor?

Dialogue I: Calling One's Teacher

（李友给[1]常老师打电话）

喂？

喂，请问，常老师在吗？

我就是。您[❶]是哪位？

老师，您好。我是李友。

李友，有事儿吗？

老师，今天下午您有时间[❷]吗？我想问[❸]您几个问题。

LANGUAGE NOTES

❶ The personal pronoun 您 (nín) is often used to address an older person or someone of a higher social rank. It is common for strangers to address each other with 您 and then switch to 你 (nǐ) as they become more familiar with each other.

❷ "To have free time" is 有时间 (yǒu shíjiān) or 有空儿 (yǒu kòngr), never 有时候 (yǒu shíhou).

❸ Both 问 (wèn) and 请 (qǐng) could be "to ask" in English. The verb 问 (wèn) means "to inquire," e.g., 我问她一个问题 (Wǒ wèn tā yí ge wèntí, I ask her a question). To mean "to invite" or "to request", say 请 (qǐng), e.g., 我请她跳舞 (Wǒ qǐng tā tiào wǔ, I invite her to dance).

对不起，今天下午我要②开会。

明天呢？

明天上午我有两节❹课，下午三点要给二年级考试。

您什么时候❺有空儿？

明天四点以后❻才有空儿。

要是❼您方便，四点半我到您的办公室去，行吗？

四点半，没问题❽。我在办公室等你。

谢谢您。

别③客气。

(Lǐ Yǒu gěi ①Cháng lǎoshī dǎ diànhuà)

Wéi?

Wéi, qǐng wèn, Cháng lǎoshī zài ma?

Wǒ jiù shì. Nín❶ shì nǎ wèi?

Lǎoshī, nín hǎo. Wǒ shì Lǐ Yǒu.

Lǐ Yǒu, yǒu shìr ma?

Lǎoshī, jīntiān xiàwǔ nín yǒu shíjiān❷ ma? Wǒ xiǎng wèn❸ nín jǐ ge wèntí.

Duìbuqǐ, jīntiān xiàwǔ wǒ yào② kāi huì.

Míngtiān ne?

❹ The measure word for academic courses is 门 (mén). Compare: 三门课 (sān mén kè, three courses), 三节课 (sān jié kè, three class periods) and 三课 (sān kè, three lessons).

❺ 几点 (jǐ diǎn) is to ask for a specific time, as in "what time is it?" The general question word for "when" is 什么时候 (shénme shíhou), not 什么时间 (shénme shíjiān).

❻ In English, we say "after four o'clock." The word "after" appears before the time expression "four o'clock." The Chinese equivalent is 四点以后 (sìdiǎn yǐhòu). Note the difference in word order. Likewise, we say "before Monday," but 星期一以前 (xīngqīyī yǐqián) in Chinese.

❼ 要是 (yàoshi, if) is a conjunction to introduce a contingent or hypothetical action or situation. It's not the "whether if" in English.

❽ 没问题 (méi wèntí) here means "no problem." It is used to assure someone that a promise will be fulfilled or a favor will be done. But when people thank you and say 谢谢 (xièxie), you cannot respond with 没问题 (méi wèntí).

Míngtiān shàngwǔ wǒ yǒu liǎng jié[4] kè, xiàwǔ sān diǎn yào gěi èr niánjí kǎo shì.

Nín shénme shíhou[5] yǒu kòngr?

Míngtiān sì diǎn yǐhòu[6] cái yǒu kòngr.

Yàoshi[7] nín fāngbiàn, sì diǎn bàn wǒ dào nín de bàngōngshì qù, xíng ma?

Sì diǎn bàn, méi wèntí[8]. Wǒ zài bàngōngshì děng nǐ.

Xièxie nín.

Bié[3] kèqi.

VOCABULARY

1.	给	gěi	prep	to; for [See Grammar 1.]
2.	打电话	dǎ diànhuà	vo	to make a phone call
	电话	diànhuà	n	telephone
3.	喂	wéi/wèi	interj	(on telephone) Hello!; Hey!
4.	在	zài	v	to be present; to be at (a place)
5.	就	jiù	adv	precisely; exactly
6.	您	nín	pr	you (honorific for 你)
7.	哪	nǎ/něi	qpr	which
8.	位	wèi	m	(polite measure word for people)
9.	下午	xiàwǔ	t	afternoon
10.	时间	shíjiān	n	time
11.	问题	wèntí	n	question; problem
12.	要	yào	mv	will, be going to; to want to, to have a desire to [See Grammar 2.]

VOCABULARY

13.	开会	kāi huì	vo	to have a meeting
	开	kāi	v	to open; to hold (a meeting, party, etc.)
	会	huì	n	meeting
14.	上午	shàngwǔ	t	morning
15.	节	jié	m	(measure word for class periods)
16.	课	kè	n	class; course; lesson
17.	年级	niánjí	n	grade in school
18.	考试	kǎo shì	vo/n	to give or take a test; test
	考	kǎo	v	to give or take a test
	试	shì	n/v	test; to try; to experiment
19.	以后	yǐhòu	t	after; from now on, later on
20.	空(儿)	kòng(r)	n	free time
21.	要是	yàoshi	conj	if
22.	方便	fāngbiàn	adj	convenient
23.	到	dào	v	to go to; to arrive
24.	办公室	bàngōngshì	n	office
25.	行	xíng	v	all right; O.K.
26.	等	děng	v	to wait; to wait for
27.	别	bié	adv	don't [See Grammar 3.]
28.	客气	kèqi	adj	polite

Proper Noun

29.	常老师	Cháng lǎoshī		Teacher Chang

Grammar

1. The Preposition 给 (gěi)

给 (gěi) can be a verb or a preposition. In Chinese, prepositions are generally combined with nouns or pronouns to form prepositional phrases, which appear before verbs as adverbials.

❶ 他给我打了一个电话。

Tā gěi wǒ dǎ le yí ge diànhuà.

(He gave me a call.)

❷ 他是谁？请你给我们介绍一下。

Tā shì shéi? Qǐng nǐ gěi wǒmen jièshào yí xià.

(Who is he? Please introduce us.)

❸ 你有你姐姐的照片吗？给我看一下，行吗？

Nǐ yǒu nǐ jiějie de zhàopiàn ma? Gěi wǒ kàn yí xià, xíng ma?

(Do you have a picture of your older sister? Can you let me have a look?)

2. The Modal Verb 要 (yào, will; be going to) (I)

The modal verb 要 (yào) has several meanings. In this lesson, 要 (yào) indicates a future action, particularly a scheduled event or an activity that one is committed to. The negative form is expressed by adding 不 (bù) and deleting 要 (yào).

❶ 下午我们要考试。

Xiàwǔ wǒmen yào kǎo shì.

(In the afternoon we are going to have a test.)

❷ 今天晚上妹妹要去看电影。

Jīntiān wǎnshang mèimei yào qù kàn diànyǐng.

(This evening my younger sister is going to see a movie.)

❸ A: 明天我要去小白家玩儿。你呢？

Míngtiān wǒ yào qù Xiǎo Bái jiā wánr, nǐ ne?

(Tomorrow I'm going to visit Little Bai. How about you?)

B: 明天我不去小白家玩儿，我要开会。

Míngtiān wǒ bú qù Xiǎo Bái jiā wánr, wǒ yào kāi huì.

(Tomorrow I'm not going to visit Little Bai. I am going to a meeting.)

3. The Adverb 别 (bié, don't)

别 (bié, don't) is used to advise someone to refrain or stop someone from doing something. Depending on the context, it can be used to form a polite formula, a gentle reminder, or a serious admonition:

❶ 别客气。

Bié kèqi.

(No need to be so polite.)

❷ 你别说。

Nǐ bié shuō.

(Don't tell/say anything.)

❸ 别进来！

Bié jìn lai!

(Don't come in!)

❹ 那个电影没有意思，你别看。

Nà ge diànyǐng méi yǒu yìsi, nǐ bié kàn.

(That movie is boring. Don't go see it.)

Language Practice

A. 给 (gěi) as a preposition

Little Gao is very nice to his friends. If you and your classmates are his friends, you will often find him doing the following:

EXAMPLE: 介绍朋友 — jièshào péngyou

→ 小高常常给我们介绍朋友。 → Xiǎo Gāo chángcháng gěi wǒmen jièshào péngyou.

a. 1. 打电话 — dǎ diànhuà

2. 介绍新电影 — jièshào xīn diànyǐng

b. 1. 看他爸爸妈妈的照片 — kàn tā bàba māma de zhàopiàn

2. 听中国音乐 — tīng Zhōngguó yīnyuè

3. 喝英国茶 — hē Yīngguó chá

B. 要 (yào) indicating a future commitment

Li You has the coming few days all planned out. What will Li You be doing? Take turns with a partner forming questions and answers based on the information provided below.

EXAMPLE: 明天◇去跳舞 — míngtiān ◇ qù tiào wǔ

A: 李友明天做什么？ — A: Lǐ Yǒu míngtiān zuò shénme?

B: 李友明天要去跳舞。 — B: Lǐ Yǒu míngtiān yào qù tiào wǔ.

1. 今天晚上◇请朋友喝咖啡 — jīntiān wǎnshang ◇ qǐng péngyou hē kāfēi

2. 明天上午◇去同学家练习中文 — míngtiān shàngwǔ ◇ qù tóngxué jiā liànxí Zhōngwén

3. 明天下午◇
去老师的办公室问问题

4. 这个星期五◇
去学校看电影

5. 这个周末◇
给小高介绍一个朋友

3. míngtiān xiàwǔ ◇
qù lǎoshī de bàngōngshì wèn wèntí

4. zhè ge xīngqīwǔ ◇
qù xuéxiào kàn diànyǐng

5. zhè ge zhōumò ◇
gěi Xiǎo Gāo jièshào yí ge péngyou

C. 要是 (yàoshi, if)

Use the following chart to practice how to be flexible and accommodating.

EXAMPLE: suggestion based on **personal preference**:

要是你不喜欢唱歌，
我们跳舞，怎么样？

Yàoshi nǐ bù xǐhuan chàng gē,
wǒmen tiào wǔ, zěnmeyàng?

Give suggestions based on: 1) desire, 2) personal interest, 3) personal preference, and 4) availability.

Yes/No	EXAMPLE: preference (不)喜欢 (bù) xǐhuan	1. desire (不)想 (bù) xiǎng	2. interest 觉得…(没)有意思 juéde (méi) yǒu yìsi	3. preference (不)喜欢 (bù) xǐhuan	4. availability (没)有空儿 (méi) yǒu kòngr
✗				 tea	Today
✓				 Cofe	Tomorrow

D. Pair Activity

Ask each other:

要是你有时间，
你想去哪儿玩儿？

Yàoshi nǐ yǒu shíjiān,
nǐ xiǎng qù nǎr wánr?

要是朋友请你吃饭，
你想吃什么菜？

Yàoshi péngyou qǐng nǐ chī fàn,
nǐ xiǎng chī shénme cài?

要是同学请你看电影，
你想看什么电影？

Yàoshi tóngxué qǐng nǐ kàn diànyǐng,
nǐ xiǎng kàn shénme diànyǐng?

E. Pair Activity: "Hello, is Jason there?"

Call your partner. Find out first if your partner is there.

A: You　　B: Your partner　　C: Your partner's brother

A: 喂，请问，
________ 在吗？

A: Wéi, qǐng wèn,
________ zài ma?

B: 我就是。/

C: ________ 不在。

B: Wǒ jiù shì. /

C: ________ bú zài.

Ask the caller to identify him/herself.

B/C: 您是哪位？

B/C: Nín shì nǎ wèi?

A: 我是________。

A: Wǒ shì ________.

Find out the reason for the call:

B/C: ________，
你好！有事儿吗？

B/C: ________,
Nǐ hǎo! Yǒu shìr ma?

If it's convenient, you'd like to go to your friend's place this evening to watch TV.

A: ...

It happens that your partner and his brother are scheduled to play a ball game and are not available this evening. But they are free tomorrow night if it's okay with you.

B/C: ...

The new proposed night works for you. Accept it and set a time before saying goodbye and hanging up the phone.

A: ...

Dialogue II: Calling a Friend for Help

  喂，请问，王朋在吗？

 我就是。你是李友吧[1]？

 王朋，我下个星期[4]要考中文，你帮我准备一下，跟我练习说中文，好吗？

 好啊，但是你得[5]请我喝咖啡。

 喝咖啡，没问题。那我什么时候跟你见面？你今天晚上有空儿吗？

 今天晚上白英爱请我吃饭。

LANGUAGE NOTE

❶ Compare the two particles 吧 (ba) and 吗 (ma):

你是李友吧？

(Nǐ shì Lǐ Yǒu ba?)

You are Li You, aren't you?

(I think you're Li You. Am I right?)

你是李友吗？

(Nǐ shì Lǐ Yǒu ma?)

Are you Li You?

(I am not quite sure.)

是吗？白英爱请你吃饭？

对。我回来⑥以后给你打电话。

好，我等你的电话。

Wéi, qǐng wèn, Wáng Péng zài ma?

Wǒ jiù shì. Nǐ shì Lǐ Yǒu ba❶?

Wáng Péng, wǒ xià ge xīngqī④yào kǎo Zhōngwén, nǐ bāng wǒ zhǔnbèi yí xià, gēn wǒ liànxí shuō Zhōngwén, hǎo ma?

Hǎo a, dànshì nǐ děi⑤ qǐng wǒ hē kāfēi.

Hē kāfēi, méi wèntí. Nà wǒ shénme shíhou gēn nǐ jiàn miàn? Nǐ jīntiān wǎnshang yǒu kòngr ma?

Jīntiān wǎnshang Bái Yīng'ài qǐng wǒ chī fàn.

Shì ma? Bái Yīng'ài qǐng nǐ chī fàn?

Duì. Wǒ huí lai⑥ yǐhòu gěi nǐ dǎ diànhuà.

Hǎo, wǒ děng nǐ de diànhuà.

可口汤

酸辣鸡蛋汤------------------------------12元

柿茄木须汤------------------------------10元

玉米粳------------------------------------16元

凤片纯菜汤------------------------------15元

清汤三鲜---------------------------------28元

白英爱和王朋吃中国菜还是美国菜？
Bái Yīng'ài hé Wáng Péng chī Zhōngguó cài háishi Měiguó cài?

VOCABULARY

1.	下个	xià ge		next one
	下	xià		below; next
2.	中文	Zhōngwén	n	Chinese language
	文	wén	n	language; script; written language
3.	帮	bāng	v	to help
4.	准备	zhǔnbèi	v	to prepare
5.	练习	liànxí	v	to practice
6.	说	shuō	v	to say; to speak
7.	啊	a	p	(a sentence-final particle of exclamation, interrogation, etc.)
8.	但是	dànshì	conj	but
9.	得	děi	av	must; to have to
10.	跟	gēn	prep	with
11.	见面	jiàn miàn	vo	to meet up; to meet with
	面		n	face
12.	回来	huí lai	vc	to come back

Grammar

4. Time Expressions

下个星期 (xià ge xīngqī, next week) literally means "the week below." By the same token, 上个星期 (shàng ge xīngqī, last week) literally means "the week above." The measure word 个 can be omitted: 下个星期=下星期; 上个星期=上星期. "Last/next month" is 上个月/下个月 (shàng ge yuè/xià ge yuè). However, we don't say *上月/下月.

To help you remember, envision a calendar. Next week/month is below (下, xià) this week/month; last week/month is above (上, shàng) this week/month.

Time Expressions Involving Month and Week

上上个月	shàng shàng ge yuè the month before last	上上(个)星期	shàng shàng (ge) xīngqī the week before last
上个月	shàng ge yuè last month	上(个)星期	shàng (ge) xīngqī last week
这个月	zhè ge yuè this month	这(个)星期	zhè (ge) xīngqī this week
下个月	xià ge yuè next month	下(个)星期	xià (ge) xīngqī next week
下下个月	xià xià ge yuè the month after next	下下(个)星期	xià xià (ge) xīngqī the week after next

The above expressions with 月 (yuè, month) and 星期 (xīngqī, week) form two parallel series. "One week" is 一个星期 (yí ge xīngqī), therefore "one week later" is 一个星期以后 (yí ge xīngqī yǐhòu). "One month" is 一个月 (yí ge yuè), not 一月 (yīyuè, January). "One month later" is 一个月以后 (yí ge yuè yǐhòu).

Additional Time Expressions Involving Year and Day

大前天	dàqiántiān three days ago	大前年	dàqiánnián three years ago
前天	qiántiān the day before yesterday	前年	qiánnián the year before last
昨天	zuótiān yesterday	去年	qùnián last year
今天	jīntiān today	今年	jīnnián this year
明天	míngtiān tomorrow	明年	míngnián next year
后天	hòutiān the day after tomorrow	后年	hòunián the year after next
大后天	dàhòutiān three days from today	大后年	dàhòunián three years from now

The above expressions with 天 (tiān, day) and 年 (nián, year) form two parallel series except for 昨天 (zuótiān, yesterday) and 去年 (qùnián, last year).

5. The Modal Verb 得 (děi, must)

The modal verb 得 (děi) means "need to" or "must".

❶ 我现在得去开会，没空儿跟你聊天儿。

Wǒ xiànzài děi qù kāi huì, méi kòngr gēn nǐ liáo tiānr.

(I need to go to a meeting right now, and have no time to chat with you.)

❷ 我有事儿，得去学校。

Wǒ yǒu shìr, děi qù xuéxiào.

(I've some business [to attend to]. I must go to school.)

The negative form of 得 (děi, must) is 不用 (búyòng, need not) or 不必 (búbì, need not), not *不得 (bù děi). Therefore, the correct way to say "You don't have to go to the library" in Chinese is A, not B:

A. 你不用去图书馆。 or 你不必去图书馆。

Nǐ búyòng qù túshūguǎn. Nǐ búbì qù túshūguǎn.

B. *你不得去图书馆。

*Nǐ bù děi qù túshūguǎn.

6. Directional Complements (I)

来/去 (lái/qù, to come/go) can serve as a directional complement after such verbs as 进 (jìn, to enter) and 回 (huí, to return). 来 (lái, to come) signifies movement toward the speaker, while 去 (qù, to go) signifies movement away from the speaker.

❶ [A is at home, speaking on the phone to B, who is away from home.]

A: 你什么时候回来？

Nǐ shénme shíhou huí lai?

(When are you coming back?)

B: 我六点回去。

Wǒ liù diǎn huí qu.

(I'm going back at six.)

❷ [A is outside, and B is inside. A knocks on the door, and B tells A to come in.]

B: 进来。

Jìn lai.

(Come in.)

[Both A and B are outside. A tells B to go inside.]

A: 进去。

Jìn qu.

(Go in.)

Language Practice

F. A 跟 B + V(O) (A gēn B + V(O), A does something with B)

Look at the portraits of the characters and the words given, and practice saying who does what with whom.

EXAMPLE:  ◇  ◇ 说中文 shuō Zhōngwén

→ 常老师跟李友说中文。 Cháng lǎoshī gēn Lǐ Yǒu shuō Zhōngwén.

1.  ◇ ◇ 聊天儿 liáo tiānr
2.  ◇ ◇ 跳舞 tiào wǔ
3.  ◇ ◇ 说英文 shuō Yīngwén
4.  ◇ ◇ 见面吃晚饭 jiàn miàn chī wǎnfàn

G. 别 (bié, don't) and 得 (děi, must)

Use the following key words to practice how to persuade or urge someone not to do something because he or she has to do something else.

EXAMPLE: ✗ 聊天儿  看书 ✗ liáo tiānr ✓ kàn shū

→ 你别聊天儿，你得看书。 → Nǐ bié liáo tiānr, nǐ děi kàn shū.

1. ✗ 喝茶 ✓ 睡觉 — 1. ✗ hē chá ✓ shuì jiào
2. ✗ 看电视 ✓ 给老师打电话 — 2. ✗ kàn diànshì ✓ gěi lǎoshī dǎ diànhuà
3. ✗ 睡觉 ✓ 去考试 — 3. ✗ shuì jiào ✓ qù kǎo shì
4. ✗ 打球 ✓ 练习说中文 — 4. ✗ dǎ qiú ✓ liànxí shuō Zhōngwén

5. ✗ 去朋友家玩儿　　5. ✗ qù péngyou jiā wánr
✓ 去学校工作　　✓ qù xuéxiào gōngzuò

H. A 跟 B 见面 (A gēn B jiàn miàn, A meets with B)

Among the characters in the text, indicate whom you would or would not like to meet with.

EXAMPLE: → 我（不）想跟王朋见面。　　Wǒ (bù) xiǎng gēn Wáng Péng jiàn miàn.

1. 
2.
3. 
4. 
5. 

I. With a partner

Take out your day planner, and take turns asking each other questions:

你这个星期天上午（要）做什么？　　Nǐ zhè ge xīngqītiān shàngwǔ (yào) zuò shénme?

你下个星期三下午（要）做什么？　　Nǐ xià ge xīngqīsān xiàwǔ (yào) zuò shénme?

你下个星期五晚上（要）做什么？　　Nǐ xià ge xīngqīwǔ wǎnshang (yào) zuò shénme?

J. What does your friend have to do if he or she wants you to help him/her?

study Chinese	practice playing ball
practice singing	practice dancing

"If I help you…, you have to …"

要是我帮你________________，你得______________。　　Yàoshi wǒ bāng nǐ______________, nǐ děi _________.

K. Role Play: My girlfriend/boyfriend is not home.

A: the caller B: the mother of the caller's boyfriend/girlfriend

A is calling his/her girlfriend/boyfriend to go out on a date. But A is surprised that B answers the phone…

A: 您好！请问___________ ___________在吗？	**A:** Nín hǎo! Qǐng wèn ________ ________ zài ma?
B: 不在。你是哪位？	**B:** Bú zài. Nǐ shì nǎ wèi?
A: 我是__________________。	**A:** Wǒ shì ______________.
B: 你找________________ 有事儿吗？	**B:** Nǐ zhǎo __________ yǒu shìr ma?

A then tells B the reason for the call…

A: 我明天晚上想请他/她__________________。	**A:** Wǒ míngtiān wǎngshang xiǎng qǐng tā ______________.

B seems to know her daughter/son's schedule very well…

B: 他/她明天晚上要_____________，没空儿。	**B:** Tā míngtiān wǎngshang yào ______________, méi kòngr.

A is disappointed, but does not give up, and proposes a different time…

A: 那他/她________________ 有时间吗？	**A:** Nà tā______________ yǒu shíjiān ma?

B gives the same answer with a different activity that the daughter/son is committed to…

B: 他/她__________________ 要______________________， 没时间。	**B:** Tā ______________ yào ______________, méi shíjiān.

A thinks that he or she had better ask B to tell the daughter/son to call him/her back…

A: 那请他/她回来以后 __________________, 我等他/她的电话。	**A:** Nà qǐng tā huí lai yǐhòu __________, wǒ děng tā de diànhuà.

Though a bit reluctant, B promises she will do that, then hangs up the phone.

B: 好，再见。	**B:** Hǎo, zàijiàn.

A tries to thank B and says goodbye before the click.

A: 谢谢您！再见。	**A:** Xièxie nín! Zàijiàn.

HOW ABOUT YOU?

What languages do you speak?

1.	法文	Fǎwén	pn	the French language
2.	日文	Rìwén	pn	the Japanese language
3.	德文	Déwén	pn	the German language
4.	韩文	Hánwén	pn	the Korean language
5.	俄文	Éwén	pn	the Russian language
6.	西班牙文	Xībānyáwén	pn	the Spanish language
7.	意大利文	Yìdàlìwén	pn	the Italian language
8.	葡萄牙文	Pútáoyáwén	pn	the Portuguese language
9.	希腊文	Xīlàwén	pn	the Greek language
10.	拉丁文	Lādīngwén	pn	the Latin language

If a language you speak is not listed above, please ask your teacher and make a note here: ____________________________________.

Culture Highlights

1. About Chinese phone etiquette: The receiver of the call usually does not identify herself immediately on picking up the phone, as some people like to do in some other cultures. Instead, she would only say 喂 (wéi/wèi) and let the caller initiate the conversation.

2. To make a long distance call in China, dial 0 first, then the area code followed by the phone number. Here are the area codes for two of the most important cities in China:

   Beijing: 10

   Shanghai: 21

   To call a cell phone number, however, you don't need to dial 0 first. It seems that almost every adult in China has a cell phone, 手机 (shǒujī), and they are not afraid to use it! China is now the largest cell phone market in the world. The cost of telephone communication in China can be significantly reduced by using calling cards, 电话卡 (diànhuà kǎ). There are various types of calling cards, which are available in neighborhood convenience stores.

❸ Both 中文 (Zhōngwén) and 汉语 (Hànyǔ) mean "the Chinese language." 汉 is the name of the predominant ethnic group in China, and 汉语 literally means "the language of the Han people." Therefore, Chinese citizens of non-Han ethnic backgrounds will most likely refer to the Chinese language as 汉语 rather than 中文. There is also a difference in nuance between 语 (yǔ, speech) and 文 (wén, writing), but for most purposes 汉语 (Hànyǔ) and 中文 (Zhōngwén) are generally considered synonymous.

This is a billboard for one of the major telecommunication companies in China. Can you figure out what services the company provides?

As seen here, there are so many choices when purchasing calling cards.

English Text

Dialogue I

(Li You is on the phone with Teacher Chang.)

Teacher Chang: Hello?

Li You: Hello, is Teacher Chang there?

Teacher Chang: This is she. Who is this, please?

Li You: Teacher, how are you? This is Li You.

Teacher Chang: Hi, Li You. What's going on?

Li You: Teacher, are you free this afternoon? I'd like to ask you a few questions.

Teacher Chang: I'm sorry. This afternoon I have to go to a meeting.

Li You: What about tomorrow?

Teacher Chang: Tomorrow morning I have two classes. Tomorrow afternoon at three o'clock I have to give an exam to the second-year class.

Li You: When will you be free?

Teacher Chang: I won't be free until after four o'clock tomorrow.

Li You: If it's convenient for you, I'll go to your office at four-thirty. Is that all right?

Teacher Chang: Four-thirty? No problem. I'll wait for you in my office.

Li You: Thank you.

Teacher Chang: You're welcome.

Dialogue II

Li You: Hello, is Wang Peng there?

Wang Peng: This is he. Is this Li You?

Li You: Hi, Wang Peng. Next week I have a Chinese exam. Could you help me prepare and practice speaking Chinese with me?

Wang Peng: Sure, but you must take me out for coffee.

Li You: Take you out for coffee? No problem. So, when can I see you? Are you free this evening?

Wang Peng: This evening Bai Ying'ai is taking me out to dinner.

Li You: Is that so? Bai Ying'ai is taking you out to dinner?

Wang Peng: That's right. I will call you when I get back.

Li You: O.K. I'll wait for your call.

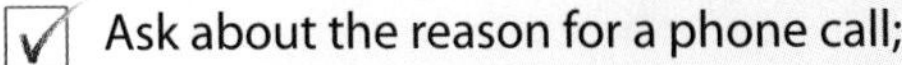

PROGRESS CHECKLIST

Before proceeding to Lesson 7, be sure you can complete the following tasks in Chinese:

I am able to

- ☑ Ask about the reason for a phone call;
- ☑ Ask for a favor politely;
- ☑ Set up an appointment on the phone;
- ☑ Negotiate to find a common time that everyone can meet ;
- ☑ Request that my call be returned.

Please review the lesson if any of these tasks seem difficult.

LESSON 7 Studying Chinese

第七课 学中文

Dì qī kè Xué Zhōngwén

LEARNING OBJECTIVES

In this lesson, you will learn to use Chinese to

- Comment on one's performance in an exam;
- Comment on one's character writing;
- Talk about one's experience in learning Chinese vocabulary and grammar;
- Talk about one's study habits;
- Remark on typical scenes from one's language class.

RELATE AND GET READY

In your own culture/community,

1. How do people convey that they have done well in a course of study?
2. How do people convey that they have done poorly in a course of study?
3. What are considered good study habits for a foreign language student?

Dialogue I: How Did You Do on the Exam?

（王朋跟李友说话）

李友，你上个星期考试考得①怎么样？

因为你帮我复习，所以考得不错。但是我写中国字写得太②慢了！

是吗？以后我跟你一起练习写字，好不好❶？

那太好了！我们现在就③写，怎么样？

好，给我一枝笔④、一张纸。写什么字？

LANGUAGE NOTES

❶ Like 行吗 (xíng ma) and 好吗 (hǎo ma), the expression 好不好 (hǎo bu hǎo, is it OK?) can also be used to seek someone's approval of a proposal.

你教我怎么写“懂”字吧。

好吧。

你写字写得真②好，真快。

哪里，哪里❷。你明天有中文课吗？我帮你预习。

明天我们学第七⑤课。第七课的语法很容易，我都懂，可是生词太多，汉字也有一点儿⑥难。

没问题，我帮你。

❷ 哪里 (nǎli), which literally means "where," is a polite reply to a compliment. In recent times, however, 哪里 (nǎli) has become somewhat old-fashioned. Many people will respond to a compliment by saying 是吗 (shì ma, is that so). Some young people in urban areas will also acknowledge a compliment by saying 谢谢 (xièxie, thanks) instead.

(Wáng Péng gēn Lǐ Yǒu shuō huà.)

Lǐ Yǒu, nǐ shàng ge xīngqī kǎo shì kǎo de① zěnmeyàng?

Yīnwèi nǐ bāng wǒ fùxí, suǒyǐ kǎo de búcuò. Dànshì wǒ xiě Zhōngguó zì xiě de tài② màn le!

Shì ma? Yǐhòu wǒ gēn nǐ yìqǐ liànxí xiě zì, hǎo bu hǎo❶?

Nà tài hǎo le! Wǒmen xiànzài jiù③ xiě, zěnmeyàng?

Hǎo, gěi wǒ yì zhī bǐ④, yì zhāng zhǐ. Xiě shénme zì?

Nǐ jiāo wǒ zěnme xiě "dǒng" zì ba.

Hǎo ba.

Nǐ xiě zì xiě de zhēn② hǎo, zhēn kuài.

Nǎli, nǎli. ❷ Nǐ míngtiān yǒu Zhōngwén kè ma? Wǒ bāng nǐ yùxí.

Míngtiān wǒmen xué dì qī⑤kè. Dì qī kè de yǔfǎ hěn róngyì, wǒ dōu dǒng, kěshì shēngcí tài duō, Hànzì yě yǒuyìdiǎnr⑥nán.

Méi wèntí, wǒ bāng nǐ.

VOCABULARY

1.	说话	shuō huà	vo	to talk
	话	huà	n	word; speech
2.	上个	shàng ge		the previous one
3.	得	de	p	(a structural particle) [See Grammar 1.]
4.	复习	fùxí	v	to review
5.	写	xiě	v	to write
6.	字	zì	n	character
7.	慢	màn	adj	slow
8.	枝	zhī	m	(measure word for long, thin, inflexible objects such as pens, rifles, etc.)
9.	笔	bǐ	n	pen
10.	张	zhāng	m	(measure word for flat objects, paper, pictures, etc.)
11.	纸	zhǐ	n	paper
12.	教	jiāo	v	to teach
13.	怎么	zěnme	qpr	how; how come
14.	懂	dǒng	v	to understand
15.	真	zhēn	adv	really [See Grammar 2.]
16.	哪里	nǎli	pr	where
17.	预习	yùxí	v	to preview
18.	学	xué	v	to study; to learn
19.	第	dì	prefix	(prefix for ordinal numbers) [See Grammar 5.]

VOCABULARY

20.	语法	yǔfǎ	n	grammar
21.	容易	róngyì	adj	easy
22.	生词	shēngcí	n	new words; vocabulary
23.	多	duō	adj	many; much
24.	汉字	Hànzì	n	Chinese characters
25.	难	nán	adj	difficult

Grammar

1. Descriptive Complements (I)

The particle 得 (de) can be used after a verb or an adjective. This lesson mainly deals with 得 (de) as it appears after a verb. What follows 得 (de) in the construction introduced in this lesson is called a descriptive complement, which can be an adjective, an adverb, or a verb phrase. In this lesson, the words that function as descriptive complements are all adjectives. These complements serve as comments on the actions expressed by the verbs that precede 得 (de).

❶ 他写字写得很好。

Tā xiě zì xiě de hěn hǎo.

(He writes characters well.)

[很好 (hěn hǎo, very well) is a comment on the action 写 (xiě, to write).]

❷ 他昨天睡觉睡得很晚。

Tā zuótiān shuì jiào shuì de hěn wǎn.

(He went to bed late last night.)

[很晚 (hěn wǎn, very late) is a comment on the action 睡觉 (shuì jiào, to sleep).]

❸ 妹妹歌唱得很好。

Mèimei gē chàng de hěn hǎo.

(My younger sister sings beautifully.)

[很好 (hěn hǎo, very well) is a comment on the action 唱 (chàng, to sing).]

If the complement is an adjective, it is usually preceded by 很 (hěn, very), as is the case when an adjective is used as a predicate. If the verb is followed by an object, the verb has to be repeated before it can be followed by the "得 (de) + Complement" structure, e.g., 写字写得 (xiě zì xiě de) in (1). By repeating the verb, the "verb + object" combination preceding it becomes a "topic" and the complement that follows serves as a comment on it. (See Grammar 1 in Lesson 10.) The first verb can be omitted if the meaning is clear from the context, as in (3).

2. The Adverbs 太 (tài, too) and 真 (zhēn, really)

When adverbs 太 (tài, too) and 真 (zhēn, really) are used in exclamatory sentences, they convey in most cases not new factual information but the speaker's approval, disapproval, etc. If the speaker wants to make a more "objective" statement or description, other intensifiers such as 很 (hěn, very), or 特别 (tèbié, especially) are often used in place of 太 (tài, too) or 真 (zhēn, really).

❶ **A:** 他写字写得怎么样？

Tā xiě zì xiě de zěnmeyàng?

(How well does he write characters?)

One would normally answer:

B: 他写字写得很好。

Tā xiě zì xiě de hěn hǎo.

(He writes characters very well.)

rather than:

B1: 他写字写得真好。

Tā xiě zì xiě de zhēn hǎo.

Compare B1 with C below:

C: 小李，你写字写得真好！
你可以教我吗？

Xiǎo Lǐ, nǐ xiě zì xiě de zhēn hǎo! Nǐ kěyǐ jiāo wǒ ma?

(Little Li, you write characters really well! Could you teach me?)

When 太 (tài, too) is used in an exclamatory sentence, 了 (le) usually appears at the end of the sentence:

❶ 这个电影太有意思了！

Zhège diànyǐng tài yǒu yìsi le!

(This movie is really interesting!)

❷ 我的语法太不好了！ 我得多练习。

Wǒ de yǔfǎ tài bù hǎo le! Wǒ děi duō liànxí.

(My grammar really is awful! I have to practice more.)

❸ 你跳舞跳得太好了。

Nǐ tiào wǔ tiào de tài hǎo le!

(You really dance beautifully!)

3. The Adverb 就 (jiù) (I)

The adverb 就 (jiù) is used before a verb to suggest the earliness, briefness, or quickness of the action.

❶ 他明天七点就得上课。

Tā míngtiān qī diǎn jiù děi shàng kè.

(He has to go to class [as early as] at 7:00am tomorrow.)

❷ 我们八点看电影，他七点半就来了。

Wǒmen bā diǎn kàn diànyǐng, tā qī diǎn bàn jiù lái le.

(We [were supposed to] see the movie at 8:00, but he came [as early as] 7:30.)

就 (jiù) and 才 (cái) compared

[See also Grammar 6 in Lesson 5.]

The adverb 就 (jiù) suggests the earliness or promptness of an action in the speaker's judgment. The adverb 才 (cái) is the opposite. It suggests the tardiness or lateness of an action as perceived by the speaker.

❶ **A:** 八点上课，小白七点就来了。

Bā diǎn shàng kè, Xiǎo Bái qī diǎn jiù lái le.

(Class started at 8:00, but Little Bai came [as early as] 7:00.)

B: 八点上课，小张八点半才来。

Bā diǎn shàng kè, Xiǎo Zhāng bā diǎn bàn cái lái.

(Class started at 8:00, but Little Zhang didn't come until 8:30.)

❷ **A:** 我昨天五点就回家了。

Wǒ zuótiān wǔ diǎn jiù huí jiā le.

(Yesterday I went home when it was only 5:00.) (The speaker thought 5:00 was early.)

B: 我昨天五点才回家。

Wǒ zuótiān wǔ diǎn cái huí jiā.

(Yesterday I didn't go home until 5:00.) (The speaker thought 5:00 was late.)

When commenting on a past action, 就 (jiù) is always used with 了 (le) to indicate promptness, but 才 (cái) is never used with 了.

4. Double Objects

Some verbs can take two objects. The object representing a person, persons, or an animate entity precedes the one representing an inanimate thing.

❶ 老师教我们生词和语法。

Lǎoshī jiāo wǒmen shēngcí hé yǔfǎ.

(The teacher teaches us vocabulary and grammar.)

❷ 大哥给了我一瓶水。

Dà gē gěi le wǒ yì píng shuǐ.

(My big brother gave me a bottle of water.)

❸ 你教我汉字，可以吗？

Nǐ jiāo wǒ Hànzì, kěyǐ ma?

(Will you teach me Chinese characters, please?)

❹ 我想问你一个问题。

Wǒ xiǎng wèn nǐ yí ge wèntí.

(I'd like to ask you a question.)

5. Ordinal Numbers

Ordinal numbers in Chinese are formed by placing 第 (dì) before cardinal numbers, e.g., 第一 (dì yī, the first), 第二杯茶 (dì èr bēi chá, the second cup of tea), 第三个月 (dì sān ge yuè, the third month). However, 第 (dì) is not used in names of months: 一月，二月，三月 (yīyuè, èryuè, sānyuè, January, February, March). Neither is it used to indicate the birth order of siblings: 大哥，二哥，三哥 (dàgē, èrgē, sāngē, oldest brother, second oldest brother, third oldest brother); 大姐，二姐，三姐 (dàjiě, èrjiě, sānjiě, oldest sister second oldest sister, third oldest sister).

6. 有（一）点儿 (yǒu{yì}diǎnr, somewhat, rather; a little bit)

The phrase 有一点儿 (yǒuyìdiǎnr) precedes adjectives or verbs. It often carries a negative tone. The 一 (yī) in the phrase is optional.

❶ 我觉得中文有(一)点儿难。

Wǒ juéde Zhōngwén yǒu(yì)diǎnr nán.

(I think Chinese is a little bit difficult.)

*我觉得中文有(一)点儿容易。

* Wǒ juéde Zhōngwén yǒu(yì)diǎnr róngyì.

*(I think Chinese is a little bit easy.)

❷ 我觉得这一课生词有点儿多。

Wǒ juéde zhè yí kè shēngcí yǒudiǎnr duō.

(I think there are a few too many new words in this lesson.)

[The speaker is complaining about it.]

However, when the sentence suggests a change of the situation, the phrase 有一点儿 (yǒuyìdiǎnr) can carry a positive tone, e.g.:

❸ 我以前不喜欢他，现在有(一)点儿喜欢他了。

Wǒ yǐqián bù xǐhuan tā, xiànzài yǒu(yì)diǎnr xǐhuan tā le.

(I used to dislike him, but now I somewhat like him.)

[以前 yǐqián = previously or before. See Lesson 8.]

Take care not to confuse 有一点儿 (yǒuyìdiǎnr, a little), which is an adverbial used to modify adjectives, with 一点儿 (yì diǎnr, a little), which usually modifies nouns. In the above sentences, 有一点儿 (yǒuyìdiǎnr) cannot be replaced by 一点儿 (yì diǎnr). Compare:

❹ 给我一点儿咖啡。

Gěi wǒ yì diǎnr kāfēi.

(Give me a little coffee.)

❺ 给我一点儿时间。

Gěi wǒ yì diǎnr shíjiān.

(Give me a little time.)

❻ 我有一点儿忙。

Wǒ yǒuyìdiǎnr máng.

(I am kind of busy.)

*我一点儿忙。

Wǒ yì diǎnr máng.

❼ 她有一点儿不高兴。

Tā yǒuyìdiǎnr bù gāoxìng.

(She is a little bit unhappy.)

*她一点儿不高兴。

*Tā yì diǎnr bù gāoxìng.

Language Practice

A. Verb + 得 (de) + Complement

Describe how Little Wang does things based on the key words given. Pay attention to the structure of the verbs involved.

EXAMPLE: 考试 (VO) 好	kǎo shì (VO) hǎo
→ 小王常常考试考得很好。	→ Xiǎo Wáng chángcháng kǎo shì kǎo de hěn hǎo.
1. 睡觉 (VO) 晚	1. shuì jiào (VO) wǎn
2. 喝咖啡 (VO) 多	2. hē kāfēi (VO) duō
3. 写字 (VO) 快	3. xiě zì (VO) kuài
4. 预习 (V) 不错	4. yùxí (V) búcuò
5. 工作 (V) 好	5. gōngzuò (V) hǎo

B. 太…了 (tài...le, too) and 真 (zhēn, really)

There are things around you that amaze you. Practice how to mark your comments using exclamatory sentences.

EXAMPLE: 汉字◇有意思	Hànzì ◇ yǒu yìsi
→ 汉字太有意思了！or 汉字真有意思！	→ Hànzì tài yǒu yìsi le! or Hànzì zhēn yǒu yìsi!
1. 老师家◇漂亮	1. lǎoshī jiā ◇ piàoliang
2. 考试◇容易	2. kǎo shì ◇ róngyì
3. 语法◇难	3. yǔfǎ ◇ nán
4. 同学的中文◇好	4. tóngxué de Zhōngwén ◇ hǎo
5. 我写字◇慢	5. wǒ xiě zì ◇ màn

C. 有一点儿 (yǒuyìdiǎnr, a little bit) + adjective

Instead of making a big fuss over your Chinese class, how about toning down your complaints a little and rephrasing with 有一点儿 (yǒuyìdiǎnr, a little bit) + adjective?

EXAMPLE: 语法 ◇ 难	yǔfǎ ◇ nán
→ 语法有一点儿难。	→ Yǔfǎ yǒuyìdiǎnr nán.
1. 第七课的生词 ◇ 多	1. dì qī kè de shēngcí ◇ duō
2. 我们的考试 ◇ 难	2. wǒmen de kǎo shì ◇ nán
3. 中文课 ◇ 早 (zǎo, early)	3. Zhōngwén kè ◇ zǎo (early)
4. 汉字 ◇ 难	4. Hànzì ◇ nán
5. 老师说话 ◇ 快	5. lǎoshī shuō huà ◇ kuài

D. Compare your relative strengths with a partner.

EXAMPLE: 

A: 你唱歌唱得怎么样？	A: Nǐ chàng gē chàng de zěnmeyàng?
B: 我唱歌唱得 ________，你呢？	B: Wǒ chàng gē chàng de ________, nǐ ne?
A: ________________	A: ________________

1. 

2. 

3. 

E. Q & A

Suppose you want to talk to your Chinese conversation partner about your Chinese study. To get ready for the conversation, you anticipate some of your partner's questions and give your answers.

EXAMPLE: 学中文 — xué Zhōngwén

→ **Q:** 你学中文学得怎么样？ — **Q:** Nǐ xué Zhōngwén xué de zěnmeyàng?

A: 我学中文学得 ________ 。 — **A:** Wǒ xué Zhōngwén xué de ________.

1. 说中文 — shuō Zhōngwén
2. 写汉字 — xiě Hànzì
3. 预习生词 — yùxí shēngcí
4. 复习语法 — fùxí yǔfǎ

Dialogue II: Preparing for a Chinese Class

（李友跟白英爱说话）

白英爱，你平常来得很早，今天怎么⑦这么晚？

我昨天预习中文，早上❶四点才③睡觉，你也睡得很晚吗？

我昨天十点就③睡了。因为王朋帮我练习中文，所以我功课做得很快。

有个中国朋友真好。

（上中文课）

大家早❷，现在我们开始上课。第七课你们都预习了吗？

LANGUAGE NOTES

❶ Both 早上 (zǎoshang) and 上午 (shàngwǔ) are usually translated as "morning," but the two Chinese words are not interchangeable. 早上 (zǎoshang) refers to early morning; and 上午 (shàngwǔ) to the latter part of the morning or to the first half of the day (until noon).

❷ 早 (zǎo, Good morning!) is heard quite often in Chinese cities. Other morning greetings, such as 早上好 (zǎoshang hǎo) and 早安 (zǎo'ān), still sound rather formal to many Chinese people.

预习了。

李友，请你念课文。…念得很好。你昨天晚上听录音了吧？

我没听。

但是她的朋友昨天晚上帮她学习了。

你的朋友是中国人吗？

是。

他是一个男的⑧，很帅❸，很酷，叫王朋。⑨

❸ 帅 (shuài) is used to describe a handsome—usually young—man. To describe an attractive woman one uses the word 漂亮 (piàoliang, pretty). The term 好看 (hǎokàn, good-looking) is gender-neutral, and can be used for people of either sex and in any age group.

(Lǐ Yǒu gēn Bái Yīng'ài shuō huà.)

Bái Yīng'ài, nǐ píngcháng lái de hěn zǎo, jīntiān zěnme⑦ zhème wǎn?

Wǒ zuótiān yùxí Zhōngwén, zǎoshang❶ sì diǎn cái③ shuì jiào, nǐ yě shuì de hěn wǎn ma?

Wǒ zuótiān shí diǎn jiù③ shuì le. Yīnwèi Wáng Péng bāng wǒ liànxí Zhōngwén, suǒyǐ wǒ gōngkè zuò de hěn kuài.

Yǒu ge Zhōngguó péngyou zhēn hǎo.

(Shàng Zhōngwén kè)

Dàjiā zǎo❷, xiànzài wǒmen kāishǐ shàng kè. Dì qī kè nǐmen dōu yùxí le ma?

Yùxí le.

Lǐ Yǒu, qǐng nǐ niàn kèwén. ... Niàn de hěn hǎo. Nǐ zuótiān wǎnshang tīng lùyīn le ba?

Wǒ méi tīng.

Dànshì tā de péngyou zuótiān wǎnshang bāng tā xuéxí le.

Nǐ de péngyou shì Zhōngguó rén ma?

Shì.

Tā shì yí ge nán de⑧, hěn shuài❸, hěn kù, jiào Wáng Péng.⑨

VOCABULARY

1.	平常	píngcháng	adv	usually
2.	早	zǎo	adj	early
3.	这么	zhème	pr	so; this (late, etc.)
4.	晚	wǎn	adj	late
5.	早上	zǎoshang	t	morning
6.	功课	gōngkè	n	homework; schoolwork
7.	大家	dàjiā	pr	everybody
8.	上课	shàng kè	vo	to go to a class; to start a class; to be in class
9.	开始	kāishǐ	v/n	to begin, to start; beginning
10.	念	niàn	v	to read aloud
11.	课文	kèwén	n	text of a lesson
12.	录音	lùyīn	n/vo	sound recording; to record
13.	学习	xuéxí	v	to study; to learn
14.	帅	shuài	adj	handsome
15.	酷	kù	adj	cool

Grammar

7. 怎么 (zěnme, how; how come) in Questions

怎么 (zěnme, how; how come) is an interrogative pronoun. It is often used to ask about the manner of an action as in (1), and sometimes the reason or the cause of an action, as in (2) and (3) below.

❶ 请你教我怎么写"懂"这个字。

Qǐng nǐ jiāo wǒ zěnme xiě "dǒng" zhè ge zì.

(Please teach me how to write the character "dong.")

❷ 你怎么才来？

Nǐ zěnme cái lái?

(How come you've just arrived?)

❸ 你怎么没去看电影？

Nǐ zěnme méi qù kàn diànyǐng?

(Why didn't you go to the movie?)

Both 怎么 (zěnme, how come) and 为什么 (wèishénme, why) are used to ask about the cause of or reason for something. However, 怎么 (zěnme, how come) conveys the speaker's bewilderment or surprise whereas 为什么 (wèishénme, why) does not.

8. The 的 (de) Structure (I)

[See also Grammar 3 in Lesson 9.] We have a 的 (de) structure when an adjective is followed by the structural particle 的 (de). Grammatically, a 的 (de) structure is equivalent to a noun. When Bai Ying'ai says, "他是一个男的 (Tā shì yí ge nán de)," it is clear from the context that she means a male (one). Another example:

我写了十个字，五个难的，五个容易的。

Wǒ xiě le shí ge zì, wǔ ge nán de, wǔ ge róngyì de.

(I wrote ten characters, five difficult ones and five easy ones.)

9. The Use of Nouns and Pronouns in Continuous Discourse

If a noun serves as the unchanged subject in a continuous discourse, its later appearances in the ensuing clauses or sentences generally should be substituted by an appropriate pronoun or simply omitted. The pronoun, in turn, can also be omitted after its first appearance.

❶ 小白很喜欢学中文。(她)晚上预习课文、复习语法、练习写汉字，常常很晚才睡觉。

Xiǎo Bái hěn xǐhuan xué Zhōngwén. (Tā) wǎnshang yùxí kèwén, fùxí yǔfǎ, liànxí xiě Hànzì, chángcháng hěn wǎn cái shuì jiào.

(Little Bai likes to study Chinese very much. At night, she previews the text, reviews the grammar, and practices writing the characters. Often she doesn't go to bed until very late.)

If we keep repeating the subject as seen in (2) or the pronoun as in (3), we will end up with a bunch of choppy, seemingly unrelated sentences:

❷ 小白很喜欢学中文。小白晚上预习课文，小白复习语法、小白练习写汉字。小白常常很晚才睡觉。

Xiǎo Bái hěn xǐhuan xué Zhōngwén. Xiǎo Bái wǎnshang yùxí kèwén, Xiǎo Bái fùxí yǔfǎ, Xiǎo Bái liànxí xiě Hànzì. Xiǎo Bái chángcháng hěn wǎn cái shuì jiào.

❸ 小白很喜欢学中文。她晚上预习课文，她复习语法、她练习写汉字。她常常很晚才睡觉。

Xiǎo Bái hěn xǐhuan xué Zhōngwén. Tā wǎnshang yùxí kèwén, tā fùxí yǔfǎ, tā liànxí xiě Hànzì. Tā chángcháng hěn wǎn cái shuì jiào.

Language Practice

E. 怎么 (zěnme, **how come)**

Use the words given, and practice how to ask your partner why he/she is not behaving as expected. It is quite unlike him/her.

EXAMPLE: 来学校◇早 vs. 晚 — lái xuéxiào ◇ zǎo vs. wǎn

→ 你平常来学校来得很早，今天怎么这么晚？ → Nǐ píngcháng lái xuéxiào lái de hěn zǎo, jīntiān zěnme zhème wǎn?

1. 预习生词◇好 vs. 不好 — **1.** yùxí shēngcí ◇ hǎo vs. bù hǎo
2. 念课文◇快 vs. 慢 — **2.** niàn kèwén ◇ kuài vs. màn
3. 考试◇不错 vs. 不好 — **3.** kǎo shì ◇ búcuò vs. bù hǎo
4. 写字◇漂亮 vs. 难看 (nánkàn, ugly) — **4.** xiě zì ◇ piàoliang vs. nánkàn (ugly)

F. 才 vs. 就 (cái **vs.** jiù)

Choose 才 (cái) or 就 (jiù) to indicate whether something takes place later or sooner than expected.

EXAMPLES:

a. 妈妈 6:00pm 回家 vs. 昨天晚上 6:30pm — **a.** māma 6:00pm huí jiā vs. zuótiān wǎnshang 6:30pm

→ 妈妈平常晚上六点回家，昨天晚上六点半才回家。 → Māma píngcháng wǎnshang liùdiǎn huí jiā, zuótiān wǎnshang liùdiǎn bàn cái huí jiā.

b. 7:45am 吃早饭 vs. 今天早上 7:30am

→ 高文中平常七点三刻吃早饭，今天早上七点半就吃早饭了。

b. 7:45am chī zǎofàn vs. jīntiān zǎoshang 7:30am

Gāo Wénzhōng píngcháng qī diǎn sān kè chī zǎofàn, jīntiān zǎoshang qī diǎn bàn jiù chī zǎofàn le.

1. 8:00am 去上课 vs. 昨天 8:15am

1. 8:00am qù shàng kè vs. zuótiān 8:15am

2. 9:00am 去学校工作 vs. 昨天 8:50am

2. 9:00am qù xuéxiào gōngzuò vs. zuótiān 8:50am

3. 9:00pm 开始做功课 vs. 上个星期五 8:00pm

3. 9:00pm kāishǐ zuò gōngkè vs. shàng ge xīngqīwǔ 8:00pm

4. 星期三 给学生考试 vs. 上个星期星期四

4. xīngqīsān gěi xuésheng kǎo shì vs. shàng ge xīngqī xīngqīsì

5. 星期二 复习生词语法 vs. 上个星期星期一

5. xīngqīèr fùxí shēngcí yǔfǎ vs. shàng ge xīngqī xīngqīyī

G. 真 (zhēn, really)

Practice how to praise or disapprove of something or someone using the words given.

EXAMPLE: 这个学校 ◇ 好。 — Zhè ge xuéxiào ◇ hǎo

→ 这个学校真好。 — → Zhè ge xuéxiào zhēn hǎo.

1. 李小姐 ◇ 漂亮 — Lǐ xiǎojiě ◇ piàoliang
2. 跳舞 ◇ 有意思 — tiào wǔ ◇ yǒu yìsi
3. 王朋 ◇ 帅 — Wáng Péng ◇ shuài
4. 汉字 ◇ 难 — Hànzì ◇ nán
5. 这一课的语法 ◇ 多 — Zhè yí kè de yǔfǎ ◇ duō

H. Pair Activity

You find your friend's behavior rather inexplicable, so you ask:

今天是你妈妈的生日，
你怎么不/没……

Jīntiān shì nǐ māma de shēngrì,
nǐ zěnme bù/méi......

明天你有考试，
你怎么不……

Míngtiān nǐ yǒu kǎoshì,
nǐ zěnme bù......

I. Pair Activity

Here is Gao Wenzhong's usual schedule and a list of what actually happened yesterday:

The usual schedule	**What happened yesterday**
9:00 study Chinese	8:45 studied Chinese
10:00 listen to the audio	9:30 listened to recordings
10:30 go to school	10:15 went to school
12:00 go home	12:30 returned home
13:00 have lunch	13:15 had lunch

Student A asks Student B a question about each of Gao Wenzhong's daily routines:

EXAMPLE: **A:** 高文中平常几点开始学习中文？ Gāo Wénzhōng píngcháng jǐdiǎn kāishǐ xuéxí Zhōngwén?

Student B answers each question according to the usual schedule, and then explains yesterday's deviation from that schedule:

B: 他平常上午九点开始学习中文。 Tā píngcháng shàngwǔ jiǔdiǎn kāishǐ xuéxí Zhōngwén.

可是他昨天上午八点三刻就开始学习中文了。 Kěshì tā zuótiān shàngwǔ bā diǎn sān kè jiù kāishǐ xuéxí Zhōngwén le.

1. listen to the audio **2.** go to school **3.** go home **4.** have lunch

HOW ABOUT YOU?

What's in your study?

Traditionally, paper, ink sticks, writing brushes, and ink stones are known as the four "treasures" of the scholar's study.

What treasures lie in your study?

1.	铅笔	qiānbǐ	n	pencil
2.	钢笔	gāngbǐ	n	fountain pen
3.	毛笔	máobǐ	n	writing brush
4.	圆珠笔	yuánzhūbǐ	n	ballpoint pen
5.	本子	běnzi	n	notebook
6.	练习本	liànxíběn	n	exercise book
7.	课本	kèběn	n	textbook
8.	字典	zìdiǎn	n	dictionary

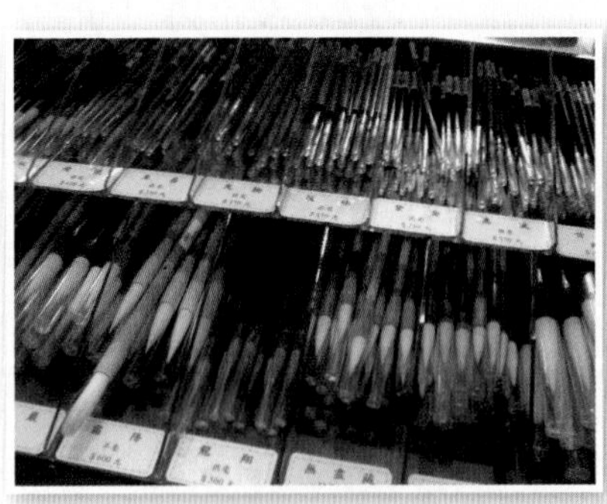

If there are items in your study that are not listed above, please ask your and make a note here: _______________.

Culture Highlights

❶ In the 1950s, as part of the campaign to raise the nation's literacy rate, the government of the People's Republic of China set out to simplify some of the more complex characters, or 汉字 (Hànzì). That accounts for the bifurcation of 简体字 (jiǎntǐzì, simplified characters) and 繁体字 (fántǐzì, traditional characters, or, literally, complex characters.) Currently, simplified characters are used in mainland China and Singapore. However, people in Taiwan, Hong Kong, and many Chinese diasporas still write traditional characters. Many of the simplified characters were actually not new inventions. They had been used at different times in China's long history, and a few of them even have a longer history than their *fantizi* counterparts. The additional burden on Chinese learners caused by this bifurcation is actually not as onerous as it may appear. After all, many of the characters were not affected.

❷ Traditionally, the Chinese wrote vertically from top to bottom, and from right to left. Store signs and placards, however, were often inscribed horizontally, typically from right to left. Now almost everyone in China writes horizontally from left to right. But the traditional way of writing is still kept alive in calligraphy.

This is a store sign which was commissioned more than one hundred years ago. It is read from right to left, and it's the name of the person who established the store. Can you recognize his family name?

Should this sign be read from the left to the right or from the right to the left?

3 For many centuries the Chinese wrote with a 毛笔 (máobǐ), or "writing brush," as it is called in English. But nowadays people have switched to more convenient Western-style writing instruments such as 铅笔 (qiānbǐ, pencils), 钢笔 (gāngbǐ, fountain pens), and 圆珠笔 (yuánzhūbǐ, ballpoint pens), which are also known in Taiwan as 原子笔 (yuánzǐbǐ). The traditional 毛笔 (máobǐ) is now used almost exclusively in calligraphy.

4 The term 文房四宝 (wénfáng sìbǎo, "Four Treasures of the Studio") is often used to refer to traditional Chinese stationery, which usually includes 笔 (bǐ, writing brushes), 墨 (mò, ink sticks), 纸 (zhǐ, paper), and 砚 (yàn, ink stones). The traditional paper for writing and painting is known as 宣纸 (xuānzhǐ), named after its most famous place of production, 宣城 (Xuānchéng) in Anhui Province. Ink is made by grinding an ink stick on an ink stone with water. Two of the most famous kinds of ink stones are called 端砚 (duānyàn) and 歙砚 (shèyàn) from Guangdong and Anhui respectively. Many are carved. Ink sticks are typically made from burnt pinewood with a binding agent and an aromatic substance. Antique ink sticks and ink stones are highly prized collectibles.

This is a window display of a store specializing in ink stones.

English Text

Dialogue I

(Wang Peng is talking with Li You.)

Wang Peng: How did you do on last week's exam?

Li You: Because you helped me review, I did pretty well, but I am too slow at writing the Chinese characters.

Wang Peng: Really? I'll practice writing characters with you from now on. How's that?

Li You: That would be great! Let's do it right now, OK?

Wang Peng: OK. Give me a pen and a piece of paper. What character should we write?

Li You: Why don't you teach me how to write the character "dǒng" (to understand)?

Wang Peng: Fine.

Li You: You write characters really well, and very fast, too.

Wang Peng: You flatter me. Do you have Chinese class tomorrow? I'll help you prepare for it.

Li You: Tomorrow we'll study Lesson Seven. The grammar for Lesson Seven is easy; I can understand all of it. But there are too many new words, and the Chinese characters are a bit difficult.

Wang Peng: No problem. I'll help you.

Dialogue II

(Li You is talking with Bai Ying'ai.)

Li You: Bai Ying'ai, you usually come very early. How come you got here so late today?

Bai Ying'ai: Yesterday I was preparing for Chinese. I didn't go to bed till four o'clock in the morning. Did you go to bed very late, too?

Li You: No, yesterday I went to bed at ten. Because Wang Peng helped me practice Chinese, I finished my homework very quickly.

Bai Ying'ai: It's so great to have a Chinese friend.

(In Chinese class)

Teacher Chang: Good morning, everyone. Let's begin. Have you all prepared for Lesson Seven?

Students: Yes, we have.

Teacher Chang: Li You, would you please read the text aloud? ...You read very well. Did you listen to the tape recording last night?

Li You: No, I didn't.

Bai Ying'ai: But her friend helped her study yesterday evening.

Teacher Chang: Is your friend Chinese?

Li You: Yes.

Bai Ying'ai: It's a he. He's handsome and cool. His name is Wang Peng.

PROGRESS CHECKLIST

Before proceeding to Lesson 8, be sure you can complete the following tasks in Chinese:

I am able to—

- ☑ Describe how well or badly I did on a test;
- ☑ Describe the way one reads, writes, and speaks Chinese;
- ☑ Ask someone to help me with my Chinese;
- ☑ Explain how I prepare for my Chinese class;
- ☑ Describe my experiences in learning Chinese.

Please review the lesson if any of these tasks seem difficult.

LESSON 8

第八课

Dì bā kè

School Life

学校生活

Xuéxiào shēnghuó

8

LEARNING OBJECTIVES

In this lesson, you will learn to use Chinese to

- Describe the routine of a student's life on campus;
- Write a simple diary entry;
- Write a brief letter in the proper format;
- Express your modesty in terms of your foreign language ability;
- Invite friends to go on an outing.

RELATE AND GET READY

In your own culture/community—

1. Is there a fixed format for diary entries?
2. Do people follow a certain format in writing a letter?
3. Are expressions of modesty considered culturally appropriate?

A Diary: A Typical School Day

An Entry from Li You's Diary

李友的一篇日记

十一月三日　星期二

今天我很忙，很累。早上七点半起床①，洗了澡以后就②吃早饭。我一边吃饭，一边③听录音。九点到教室去上课④。

第一节课是中文，老师教我们发音、生词和语法，也教我们写字，还给了⑤ 我们一篇新课文⑥，这篇课文很有意思。第二节是电脑❶课，很难。

LANGUAGE NOTE

❶ The usual colloquial term for a computer is 电脑 (diànnǎo), literally, "electric brain." A more formal term, especially in mainland China, is 电子计算机 (diànzǐ jìsuànjī) or "electronic computing machine," or simply 计算机 (jìsuànjī). But in Taiwan 计算机 (jìsuànjī) means a calculator. In mainland China, a calculator is called 计算器 (jìsuànqì).

中午我和同学们一起到餐厅去吃午饭。我们一边吃，一边练习说中文。下午我到图书馆去上网。四点王朋来找我打球。五点三刻吃晚饭。七点半我去白英爱的宿舍跟她聊天(儿)。到那儿的时候，她正在⑦做功课。我八点半回家。睡觉以前，高文中给我打了一个电话，告诉我明天要考试，我说我已经知道了。

Lǐ Yǒu de yì piān rìjì

Shíyīyuè sānrì, xīngqīèr

Jīntiān wǒ hěn máng, hěn lèi. Zǎoshang qī diǎn bàn qǐ chuáng①, xǐ le zǎo yǐhòu jiù② chī zǎofàn. Wǒ yìbiān chī fàn, yìbiān③ tīng lùyīn. Jiǔ diǎn dào jiàoshì qù shàng kè④.

Dì yī jié kè shì Zhōngwén, lǎoshī jiāo wǒmen fāyīn, shēngcí hé yǔfǎ, yě jiāo wǒmen xiě zì, hái gěi le⑤ wǒmen yì piān xīn kèwén⑥, zhè piān kèwén hěn yǒu yìsi. Dì èr jié shì diànnǎo❶ kè, hěn nán.

Zhōngwǔ wǒ hé tóngxué men yìqǐ dào cāntīng qù chī wǔfàn. Wǒmen yìbiān chī, yìbiān liànxí shuō Zhōngwén. Xiàwǔ wǒ dào túshūguǎn qù shàng wǎng. Sì diǎn Wáng Péng lái zhǎo wǒ dǎ qiú. Wǔ diǎn sān kè chī wǎnfàn. Qī diǎn bàn wǒ qù Bái Yīng'ài de sùshè gēn tā liáo tiān(r). Dào nàr de shíhou, tā zhèngzài⑦zuò gōngkè. Wǒ bā diǎn bàn huí jiā. Shuì jiào yǐqián, Gāo Wénzhōng gěi wǒ dǎ le yí ge diànhuà, gàosu wǒ míngtiān yào kǎoshì, wǒ shuō wǒ yǐjīng zhīdao le.

VOCABULARY

1.	篇	piān	m	(measure word for essays, articles, etc.)
2.	日记	rìjì	n	diary
3.	累	lèi	adj	tired
4.	起床	qǐ chuáng	vo	to get up
	床	chuáng	n	bed

VOCABULARY

5.	洗澡	xǐ zǎo	vo	to take a bath/shower
6.	早饭	zǎofàn	n	breakfast
7.	一边	yìbiān	adv	simultaneously; at the same time [See Grammar 3.]
8.	教室	jiàoshì	n	classroom
9.	发音	fāyīn	n	pronunciation
10.	新	xīn	adj	new
11.	电脑	diànnǎo	n	computer
	脑	nǎo	n	brain
12.	中午	zhōngwǔ	n	noon
13.	餐厅	cāntīng	n	dining room, cafeteria
14.	午饭	wǔfàn	n	lunch, midday meal
15.	上网	shàng wǎng	vo	to go online; to surf the internet
16.	宿舍	sùshè	n	dormitory
17.	那儿	nàr	pr	there
18.	正在	zhèngzài	adv	in the middle of (doing something) [See Grammar 7.]
19.	以前	yǐqián	t	before
20.	告诉	gàosu	v	to tell
21.	已经	yǐjīng	adv	already
22.	知道	zhīdao	v	to know

同学们在餐厅吃午饭。
Tóngxué men zài cāntīng chī wǔfàn.

学生已经起床去上课了。
Xuésheng yǐjīng qǐ chuáng qù shàng kè le.

Grammar

1. The Position of Time-When Expressions

Time-when expressions come before the verb. They often appear after the subject. However, they sometimes precede the subject under certain discourse conditions. In this lesson, we focus on practicing the ones positioned after the subject.

❶ 我们十点上课。
Wǒmen shí diǎn shàng kè.
(We start the class at ten.)

❷ 我们几点去？
Wǒmen jǐ diǎn qù?
(What time are we going?)

❸ 你什么时候睡觉？
Nǐ shénme shíhou shuì jiào?
(What time do you go to bed?)

❹ 他明天上午八点来。
Tā míngtiān shàngwǔ bā diǎn lái.
(He will come at eight tomorrow morning.)

This is a sign outside a student cafeteria. What is the sign for? Can you answer the following questions after reading the sign?

学生什么时候吃早饭？什么时候吃午饭？什么时候吃晚饭？

Xuésheng shénme shíhou chī zǎofàn? Shénme shíhou chī wǔfàn? Shénme shíhou chī wǎnfàn?

2. The Adverb 就 (jiù) (II)

[See also Grammar 3 in Lesson 7.]

The adverb 就 (jiù) connecting two verbs or verb phrases indicates that the second action happens as soon as the first one is completed.

❶ 他今天早上起床以后就听中文录音了。

Tā jīntiān zǎoshang qǐ chuáng yǐhòu jiù tīng Zhōngwén lùyīn le.

(He listened to the Chinese recordings right after he got up this morning.)

❷ 王朋写了信以后就去睡觉了。

Wáng Péng xiě le xìn yǐhòu jiù qù shuì jiào le.

(Wang Peng went to bed right after he had finished writing the letter.)

❸ 我做了功课以后就去朋友家玩儿。

Wǒ zuò le gōngkè yǐhòu jiù qù péngyou jiā wánr.

(I will go to my friend's for a visit right after I finish my homework.)

3. 一边…一边… (yìbiān...yìbiān...)

This structure denotes the simultaneity of two ongoing actions. In general, the word or phrase for the action that started earlier follows the first 一边 (yìbiān), while that for the action that started later follows the second 一边 (yìbiān).

❶ 我们一边吃饭，一边练习说中文。

Wǒmen yìbiān chī fàn, yìbiān liànxí shuō Zhōngwén.

(We practiced speaking Chinese while having dinner.)

❷ 他常常一边吃饭一边看电视。

Tā chángcháng yìbiān chī fàn yìbiān kàn diànshì.

(He often eats and watches TV at the same time.)

Generally, the verb that follows the first 一边 (yìbiān) indicates the principal action for the moment, while the one that follows the second 一边 (yìbiān) denotes an accompanying action.

❸ 我一边洗澡一边唱歌。

Wǒ yìbiān xǐ zǎo, yìbiān chàng gē.

(I sang while taking a shower.)

❹ 我妹妹喜欢一边看书一边听音乐。

Wǒ mèimei xǐhuan yìbiān kàn shū, yìbiān tīng yīnyuè.

(My younger sister loves listening to music while she reads.)

4. Series of Verbs/Verb Phrases

A number of verbs or verb phrases can be used in succession to represent a series of actions. The sequential order of these verbs or verb phrases usually coincides with the temporal order of the actions.

❶ 他常常去高小音家吃饭。

Tā chángcháng qù Gāo Xiǎoyīn jiā chī fàn.

(He often goes to eat at Gao Xiaoyin's place.)

❷ 下午我要到图书馆去看书。

Xiàwǔ wǒ yào dào túshūguǎn qù kàn shū.

(This afternoon I will go to the library to read.)

❸ 我明天想找同学去打球。

Wǒ míngtiān xiǎng zhǎo tóngxué qù dǎ qiú.

(I'd like to find some classmates to play ball with me tomorrow.)

❹ 你明天来我家吃晚饭吧。

Nǐ míngtiān lái wǒ jiā chī wǎnfàn ba.

(Come and have dinner at my house tomorrow.)

5. The Particle 了 (le) (II)

[See also Lesson 5 Grammar 5 and Lesson 11 Grammar 2.]

If a statement enumerates a series of realized actions or events, 了 (le) usually appears at the end of the series, rather than after each of the verbs.

昨天第一节课是中文。老师教我们发音、生词和语法，也教我们写字，还给了我们一篇新课文。那篇课文很有意思。

Zuótiān dì yī jié kè shì Zhōngwén. Lǎoshī jiāo wǒmen fāyīn, shēngcí hé yǔfǎ, yě jiāo wǒmen xiě zì, hái gěi le wǒmen yì piān xīn kèwén. Nà piān kèwén hěn yǒu yìsi.

(Yesterday the first class was Chinese. Our teacher taught us pronunciation, vocabulary, and grammar, taught us how to write characters, and gave us a new text. That text was very interesting.)

6. The Particle 的 (III)

When a disyllabic or polysyllabic adjective modifies a noun, the particle 的 (de) is usually inserted between the adjective and the noun, e.g. 漂亮的学校 (piàoliang de xuéxiào, beautiful schools), 容易的汉字 (róngyì de Hànzì, easy characters), 有意思的电影 (yǒu yìsi de diànyǐng, interesting movies). However, with monosyllabic adjectives, 的 (de) is often omitted, e.g., 新课文 (xīn kèwén, new lesson texts), 新电脑 (xīn diànnǎo, new computers), 大教室 (dà jiàoshì, big classrooms); 好老师 (hǎo lǎoshī, good teachers). If the adjective is preceded by 很 (hěn), however, 的 (de) cannot be dropped, e.g., 很新的电脑 (hěn xīn de diànnǎo, very new computers); 很大的教室 (hěn dà de jiàoshì, very big classrooms); 很好的老师 (hěn hǎo de lǎoshī, very good teachers).

7. The Adverb 正在 (zhèngzài, be doing...)

The adverb 正在 (zhèngzài) denotes an ongoing or progressive action at a certain point of time. It is more emphatic than 在 (zài) when it serves the same function.

❶ **A:** 李友，你在做什么？

Lǐ Yǒu, nǐ zài zuò shénme?

(Li You, what are you doing?)

B: 我在练习写汉字。

Wǒ zài liànxí xiě Hànzì.

(I'm practicing writing Chinese characters.)

❷ 我们现在正在上课，你别打电话。

Wǒmen xiànzài zhèngzài shàng kè, nǐ bié dǎ diànhuà.

(We are having a class right now. Don't make phone calls.)

❸ 我昨天到他宿舍的时候，他正在练习发音。

Wǒ zuótiān dào tā sùshè de shíhou, tā zhèngzài liànxí fāyǐn.

(When I got to his dorm yesterday, he was in the middle of practicing pronunciation.)

❹ **A:** 你知道不知道王老师在哪儿？

Nǐ zhīdao bù zhīdào Wáng lǎoshī zài nǎr?

(Do you know where Teacher Wang is?)

B: 他正在办公室开会。

Tā zhèngzài bàngōngshì kāi huì.

(He is having a meeting in his office.)

Language Practice

A. Time Expression + V

The following is a record of what Little Gao did yesterday. Practice how to recap what happened using the appropriate time expressions.

EXAMPLE: 小高早上八点起床。 Xiǎo Gāo zǎoshang bā diǎn qǐ chuáng.

	8:00am	
1.		
2.	8:30am	
3.	9:15am	
4.	12:00pm	
5.		

B. 一边…一边… (yìbiān...yìbiān...)

Look at the pictures given, and practice how to describe two simultaneous actions.

EXAMPLE: 他们  Tāmen

→ 他们一边聊天儿，一边喝茶。 Tāmen yìbiān liáo tiānr, yìbiān hē chá.

1. 王小姐  Wáng xiǎojiě
2. 高先生  Gāo xiānsheng
3. 小李  Xiǎo Lǐ
4. 小白  Xiǎo Bái

C. Subject + Verb 1 + Verb 2

Turn the following words into sentences.

EXAMPLE: 王朋 ◇ 小高家 ◇ 吃饭 Wáng Péng ◇ Xiǎo Gāo jiā ◇ chī fàn

→ 王朋到小高家去吃饭。 Wáng Péng dào Xiǎo Gāo jiā qù chī fàn.

or 王朋去小高家吃饭。 or Wáng Péng qù Xiǎo Gāo jiā chī fàn.

1. 我弟弟 ◇ 图书馆 ◇ 看书 Wǒ dìdi ◇ túshūguǎn ◇ kàn shū
2. 他 ◇ 教室 ◇ 练习发音 Tā ◇ jiàoshì ◇ liànxí fāyīn
3. 李友 ◇ 同学的宿舍 ◇ 聊天儿 Lǐ Yǒu ◇ tóngxué de sùshè ◇ liáo tiānr
4. 小白 ◇ 学校 ◇ 听录音 Xiǎo Bái ◇ xuéxiào ◇ tīng lùyīn

5. 小王◇老师的办公室◇问问题 | 5. Xiǎo Wáng ◇ lǎoshī de bàngōngshì ◇ wèn wèntí

D. Verb + Object 1 + Object 2

D1: What does your teacher teach you in your Chinese class?

EXAMPLE: 学生◇生词 | xuésheng ◇ shēngcí

→ 老师教学生生词。 → Lǎoshī jiāo xuésheng shēngcí.

1. 学生◇汉字 | xuésheng ◇ Hànzì
2. 大家◇语法 | dàjiā ◇ yǔfǎ
3. 我们◇中文发音 | wǒmen ◇ Zhōngwén fāyīn
4. 大家◇课文 | dàjiā ◇ kèwén

D2: What kinds of questions do the students often ask their teachers in a language classroom?

EXAMPLE: 发音 | fāyīn

→ 学生常常问老师发音的问题。 | Xuésheng chángcháng wèn lǎoshī fāyīn de wèntí.

1. 生词 | shēngcí
2. 语法 | yǔfǎ
3. 课文 | kèwén
4. 汉字 | Hànzì

E. 正在… (zhèngzài …)

Practice with your partner how to ask and describe what they are doing based on the pictures provided.

EXAMPLE:  

→ **A:** 他正在做什么？ | **A:** Tā zhèngzài zuò shénme?

B: 他正在睡觉。 | **B:** Tā zhèngzài shuì jiào.

1. 
2. 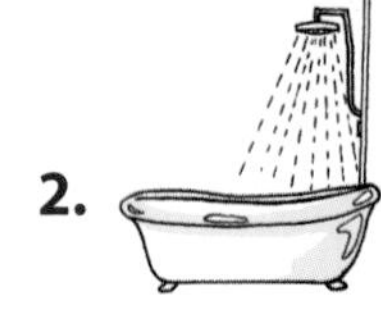
3. 
4. 

F. Pair Activity

Find out your partner's daily routine:

你平常几点起床？ Nǐ píngcháng jǐ diǎn qǐ chuáng?

你平常几点吃早饭？ Nǐ píngcháng jǐ diǎn chī zǎofàn?

你平常几点去上课？ Nǐ píngcháng jǐ diǎn qù shàng kè?

你平常几点吃午饭？ Nǐ píngcháng jǐ diǎn chī wǔfàn?

你平常几点吃晚饭？ Nǐ píngcháng jǐ diǎn chī wǎnfàn?

你平常什么时候洗澡？ Nǐ píngcháng shénme shíhou xǐ zǎo?

起床以后洗还是睡觉以前洗？ Qǐ chuáng yǐhòu xǐ háishi shuì jiào yǐqián xǐ?

G. Pair Activity

Take a look at Tom's daily schedule and ask each other the following questions:

12:30	have lunch
1:30	go online
2:00	study Chinese
3:00	go to the library
4:00	play basketball with friends
5:00	shower
6:30	have dinner

Tom吃了午饭以后就做什么？ Tom chī le wǔfàn yǐhòu jiù zuò shénme?

Tom学了中文以后就做什么？ Tom xué le Zhōngwén yǐhòu jiù zuò shénme?

Tom跟朋友打了球以后就做什么？ Tom gēn péngyou dǎ le qiú yǐhòu jiù zuò shénme?

A Letter: Talking about Studying Chinese

A Letter

一封信

(The teacher asked the students to write their friends a letter in Chinese as a homework assignment. Here's what Li You wrote to Gao Xiaoyin.)

小音：

你好！好久不见，最近怎么样？

这个学期我很忙，除了专业课以外，还[8]得学中文。我们的中文课很有意思。因为我们的中文老师只会[9]说中文，不会说英文，所以上课的时候我们只说中文，不说英文。开始我觉得很难，后来[1]，王朋常常帮我练习中文，就[10] 觉得不难了[2]。

LANGUAGE NOTES

[1] 后来 (hòulái) is usually translated as "later," but it pertains only to an action or situation in the past.

[2] This sentence-final particle 了 usually indicates a change of status or the realization of a new situation. For more examples, please see Grammar 2 in Lesson 11 (Level 1 Part 2).

你喜欢听音乐吗？下个星期六，我们学校有一个音乐会，希望你能⑨来。我用中文写信写得很不好，请别笑我。祝

好

你的朋友
李友
十一月十八日

Yì fēng xìn

(The teacher asked the students to write their friends a letter in Chinese as a homework assignment. Here's what Li You wrote to Gao Xiaoyin.)

Xiǎoyīn:

Nǐ hǎo! Hǎo jiǔ bú jiàn, zuìjìn zěnmeyàng?

Zhè ge xuéqī wǒ hěn máng, chúle zhuānyè kè yǐwài, hái⑧ děi xué Zhōngwén. Wǒmen de Zhōngwén kè hěn yǒu yìsi. Yīnwèi wǒmen de Zhōngwén lǎoshī zhǐ huì⑨shuō Zhōngwén, bú huì shuō Yīngwén, suǒyǐ shàng kè de shíhou wǒmen zhǐ shuō Zhōngwén, bù shuō Yīngwén. Kāishǐ wǒ juéde hěn nán, hòulái❶, Wáng Péng chángcháng bāng wǒ liànxí Zhōngwén, jiù⑩ juéde bù nán le❷.

Nǐ xǐhuan tīng yīnyuè ma? Xià ge xīngqīliù, wǒmen xuéxiào yǒu yí ge yīnyuèhuì, xīwàng nǐ néng⑨ lái. Wǒ yòng Zhōngwén xiě xìn xiě de hěn bù hǎo, qǐng bié xiào wǒ. Zhù

Hǎo

Nǐ de péngyou
Lǐ Yǒu
Shíyīyuè shíbā rì

VOCABULARY

1.	封	fēng	m	(measure word for letters)
2.	信	xìn	n	letter (correspondence)
3.	最近	zuìjìn	t	recently
	最	zuì	adv	(of superlative degree; most, -est)
	近	jìn	adj	close; near
4.	学期	xuéqī	n	school term; semester/quarter
5.	除了…以外	chúle...yǐwài	conj	in addition to; besides [See Grammar 8.]
6.	专业	zhuānyè	n	major (in college); specialty
7.	会	huì	av	can; know how to [See Grammar 9.]
8.	后来	hòulái	t	later
9.	音乐会	yīnyuèhuì	n	concert
10.	希望	xīwàng	v/n	to hope; hope
11.	能	néng	av	can; to be able to [See Grammar 9.]
12.	用	yòng	v	to use
13.	笑	xiào	v	to laugh at; to laugh; to smile
14.	祝	zhù	v	to wish (well)

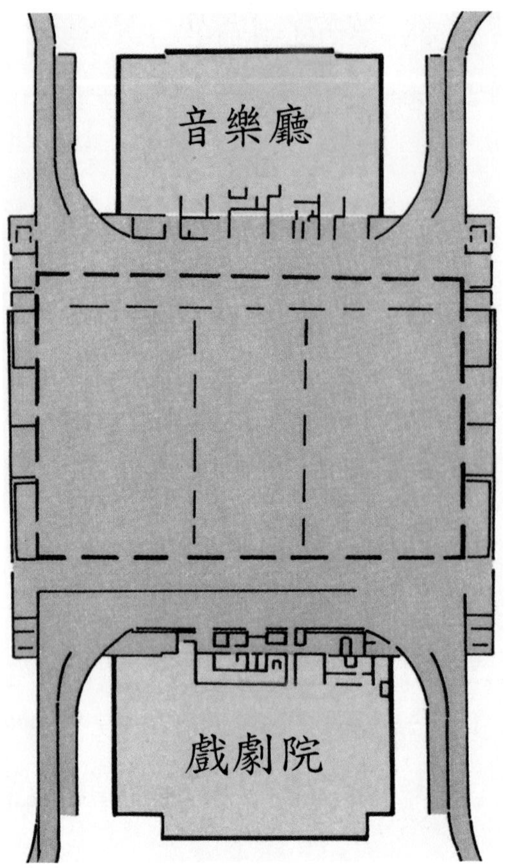

This is a floor plan of a performing arts facility. Circle the concert hall.

Grammar

8. 除了…以外，还… (chúle...yǐwài, hái... **in addition to..., also...**)

❶ 我除了学中文以外，还学专业课。

Wǒ chúle xué Zhōngwén yǐwài, hái xué zhuānyè kè.

(Besides Chinese, I also take courses in my major.)

❷ 上个周末我们除了看电影以外，还听音乐了。

Shàng ge zhōumò wǒmen chúle kàn diànyǐng yǐwài, hái tīng yīnyuè le.

(Last weekend, besides seeing a movie, we also listened to music.)

❸ 他除了喜欢听音乐以外，还喜欢打球。

Tā chúle xǐhuan tīng yīnyuè yǐwài, hái xǐhuan dǎ qiú.

(In addition to listening to music, he also likes to play ball.)

The activities in each of the three sentences above are performed by the same subject. But if activities are done by different subjects, the adverb 也 has to be used.

❹ 除了小王以外，小李也喜欢唱歌、跳舞。

Chúle Xiǎo Wáng yǐwài, Xiǎo Lǐ yě xǐhuan chàng gē, tiào wǔ.

(In addition to Little Wang, Little Li also likes singing and dancing.)

9. 能 (néng) and 会 (huì) (I) Compared

Both 能 (néng) and 会 (huì) have several meanings. The basic meaning of 能 (néng) is "to be capable of (the action named by the following verb)." It can also be an indication of whether one's own abilities or circumstances allow the execution of an action. Additional meanings will be introduced in later lessons.

❶ 我能喝十杯咖啡。

Wǒ néng hē shí bēi kāfēi.

(I can drink ten cups of coffee.)

❷ 今天下午我要开会，不能去听音乐会。

Jīntiān xiàwǔ wǒ yào kāi huì, bù néng qù tīng yīnyuèhuì.

(I have a meeting this afternoon. I cannot go to the concert.)

❸ 我们不能在图书馆聊天儿。

Wǒmen bù néng zài túshūguǎn liáo tiānr.

(We cannot chat in the library.)

会 (huì), as used in this lesson, means having the skill to do something through learning or instruction.

❹ 李友会说中文。

Lǐ Yǒu huì shuō Zhōngwén.

(Li You can speak Chinese.)

5 小白会唱很多美国歌。

Xiǎo Bái huì chàng hěn duō Měiguó gē.

(Little Bai can sing many American songs.)

6 我不会上网，请你教我。

Wǒ bú huì shàng wǎng. Qǐng nǐ jiāo wǒ.

(I don't know how to use the Internet. Please teach me how.)

10. The Adverb 就 (jiù) (III)

The adverb 就 (jiù) can heighten the close relationship between two actions or situations. In this usage, the action or situation indicated by the verb or adjective that follows 就 (jiù) is usually contingent upon the action or situation denoted by the verb or adjective in a preceding clause. The relationship is often causal, as seen in (1) and (2), or conditional, as (3) and (4).

1 （因为）小高喜欢吃中国菜，（所以）我们就吃中国菜。

(Yīnwèi) Xiǎo Gāo xǐhuan chī Zhōngguó cài, (suǒyǐ) wǒmen jiù chī Zhōngguó cài.

(Little Gao preferred Chinese food, so we went for Chinese food.)

2 （因为）小王的专业是电脑，（所以）我就请他教我怎么上网。

(Yīnwèi) Xiǎo Wáng de zhuānyè shì diànnǎo, (suǒyǐ) wǒ jiù qǐng tā jiāo wǒ zěnme shàng wǎng.

(Little Wang's major is computer science, so I asked him to teach me how to use the Internet.)

3 要是同学帮我复习，我考试就考得很好。

Yàoshi tóngxué bāng wǒ fùxí, wǒ kǎoshì jiù kǎo de hěn hǎo.

(If my classmates help me review, I will do well on my test.)

4 要是你不能来，我就去你那儿。

Yàoshi nǐ bù néng lái, wǒ jiù qù nǐ nàr.

(If you can't come over, I will go to your place.)

❺ 写汉字，开始觉得难，常常练习，就觉得容易。

Xiě Hànzì, kāishǐ juéde nán, chángcháng liànxí, jiù juéde róngyì.

(When [you] first learn to write Chinese characters, [you] would find it difficult. If [you] practice often, [you] would find it easy.)

Language Practice

H. 除了…以外，还… (chúle ... yǐwài, hái...)

Use the words given to describe what Mr. Bai does.

EXAMPLE: 上音乐课◇上电脑课 — shàng yīnyuè kè ◇ shàng diànnǎo kè

→ 白先生除了上音乐课以外，还上电脑课。 → Bái xiānsheng chúle shàng yīnyuè kè yǐwài, hái shàng diànnǎo kè.

1. 学英文◇学中文 — xué Yīngwén ◇ xué Zhōngwén
2. 会说中文◇会用中文写信 — huì shuō Zhōngwén ◇ huì yòng Zhōngwén xiě xìn
3. 喜欢唱歌◇喜欢跳舞 — xǐhuan chàng gē ◇ xǐhuan tiào wǔ
4. 能喝茶◇能喝咖啡 — néng hē chá ◇ néng hē kāfēi

I. 用 + tool/method/means + V(O)

Describe the use of the means in the action.

EXAMPLE: 写日记◇中文 — xiě rìjì ◇ Zhōngwén

→ 我们用中文写日记。 — Wǒmen yòng Zhōngwén xiě rìjì.

1. 写信◇英文 — xiě xìn ◇ Yīngwén
2. 做功课◇笔 — zuò gōngkè ◇ bǐ

3. 练习发音◇电脑	**3.** liànxí fāyīn ◇ diànnǎo
4. 喝茶◇咖啡杯	**4.** hē chá ◇ kāfēi bēi

J. Pair Activity

Work with a partner, and take turns asking each other:

你写信吗？	Nǐ xiě xìn ma?
你常常给谁写信？	Nǐ chángcháng gěi shéi xiě xìn?
你会用电脑写信吗？	Nǐ huì yòng diànnǎo xiě xìn ma?
你写日记吗？	Nǐ xiě rìjì ma?
你用中文写日记还是用英文写日记？	Nǐ yòng Zhōngwén xiě rìjì háishi yòng Yīngwén xiě rìjì?

HOW ABOUT YOU?

What is your major?

1.	历史	lìshǐ	n	history
2.	经济	jīngjì	n	economics
3.	化学	huàxué	n	chemistry
4.	数学	shùxué	n	mathematics
5.	物理	wùlǐ	n	physics
6.	语言学	yǔyánxué	n	linguistics
7.	工商管理	gōngshāng guǎnlǐ	n	business management
8.	亚洲研究	Yàzhōu yánjiū	n	Asian studies

If your major is not listed above, please ask your teacher and make a note here:

我的专业是 ____________

Wǒ de zhuānyè shì ____________

Culture Highlights

❶ The most common form of closing at the end of a letter in Chinese is 祝好 (zhù hǎo, I wish you well), with the character 祝 (zhù, to wish) following the final sentence of the letter and the character 好 (hǎo) at the very beginning of the next line.

However, it is not an uncommon practice, especially among younger people, to keep the two characters 祝好 unseparated.

祝您
佳节愉快，
新年好!!
学生
李润镜
苟文上
十二月十二日

Here a student closes her note with her good wishes.

❷ Colleges and universities in both mainland China and Taiwan are on the semester system. Typically, the fall semester starts in late August or early September, and ends in mid-January. The winter break lasts about a month. Since the Chinese New Year usually falls in late January or early February, college students can take advantage of the break to go home and celebrate the most important holiday of the year with their families. The spring semester starts around mid-February and lasts until early July. A semester at a Chinese college is about three weeks longer than that a typical American college semester.

English Text

An Entry from Li You's Diary

November 3, Tuesday

I was very busy and tired today. I got up at seven-thirty this morning. After taking a shower, I had breakfast. While I was eating, I listened to the sound recording. I went to the classroom at nine o'clock.

The first period was Chinese. The teacher taught us pronunciation, new vocabulary, and grammar. The teacher also taught us how to write Chinese characters, and gave us a new text. The text was very interesting. The second period was Computer Science. It was very difficult.

At noon I went to the cafeteria with my classmates for lunch. While we were eating, we practiced speaking Chinese. In the afternoon I went to the library to go online. At four o'clock, Wang Peng came looking for me to play ball. I had dinner at a quarter to six. At seven-thirty, I went to Bai Ying'ai's dorm for a chat. When I got there, she was doing her homework. I got home at eight-thirty. Before I went to bed, Gao Wenzhong called. He told me there'd be an exam tomorrow. I said I already knew that.

A Letter

(*The teacher asked the students to write a letter in Chinese as an assignment. Here's what Li You wrote to Gao Xiaoyin.*)

November 18

Dear Xiaoyin,

How are you? Long time no see. How are things recently?

This semester I've been busy. Besides the classes required for my major, I also need to study Chinese. Our Chinese class is really interesting. Because our Chinese teacher can only speak Chinese and does not know how to speak English, in the class we speak only Chinese, no English. At the beginning I felt it was very difficult. Later, Wang Peng often helped me practice Chinese, and I don't feel it is hard anymore.

Do you like to listen to music? Next Saturday there will be a concert at our school. I hope you can come. I do not write well in Chinese. Please don't make fun of me.

Best wishes,
Your friend,
Li You

PROGRESS CHECKLIST

Before proceeding to Lesson 9, be sure you can complete the following tasks in Chinese:

I am able to—

- ☑ Describe my daily routine at school;
- ☑ Write a simple diary entry in the proper format;
- ☑ Write a simple letter in the proper format;
- ☑ Express my modesty about my language abilities.

Please review the lesson if any of these tasks seem difficult.

LESSON 9 第九课 Dì jiǔ kè

Shopping 买东西 Mǎi dōngxi

LEARNING OBJECTIVES

In this lesson, you will learn to use Chinese to

- Speak about the color, size, and price of a purchase;
- Recognize Chinese currency;
- Pay bills in cash or with a credit card;
- Determine the proper change you should receive;
- Ask for a different size and/or color of merchandise;
- Exchange merchandise.

RELATE AND GET READY

In your own culture/community—

1. Do people haggle over prices in stores?
2. Can merchandise be returned or exchanged?
3. How do people pay for their purchases: in cash, with a check, or with a credit card?

Dialogue I: Shopping for Clothes

（李友在一个商店买东西，售货员问她…）

小姐，您要①买什么衣服？

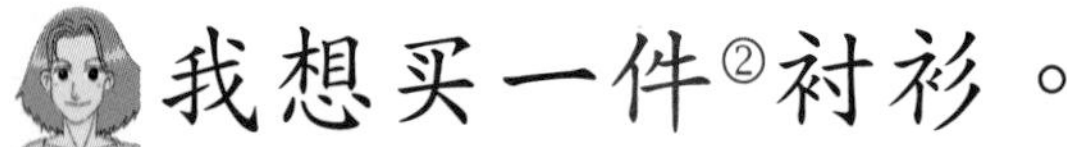
我想买一件②衬衫。

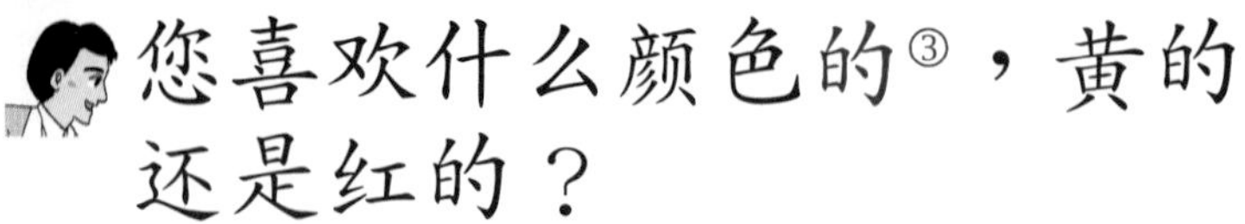
您喜欢什么颜色的③，黄的还是红的？

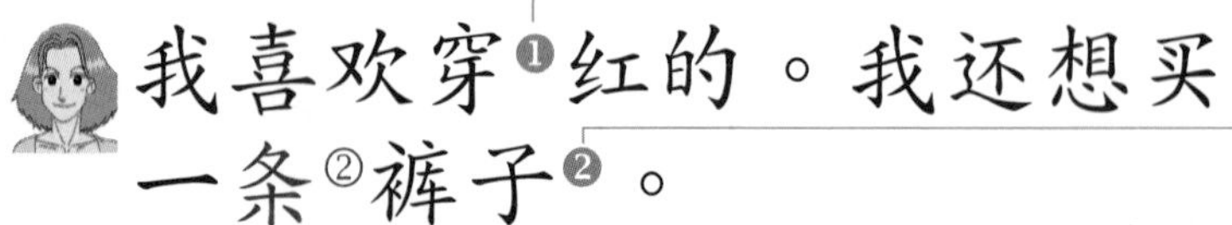
我喜欢穿❶红的。我还想买一条②裤子❷。

多④大的？大号的、中号的、还是小号的？

中号的。不要太贵的，也

LANGUAGE NOTES

❶ Note that the verb 穿 (chuān) can mean both "to wear" and "to put on." However, for most accessories, especially those for the upper part of the body, 戴 (dài) is used instead of 穿 (chuān).

❷ In Chinese, a pair of pants is just one single piece of clothing. Hence 一条裤子 (yì tiáo kùzi, literally, a trouser) instead of *一双裤子 (*yì shuāng kùzi, literally, a pair of trousers).

不要太便宜❸的。

这条裤子怎么样？

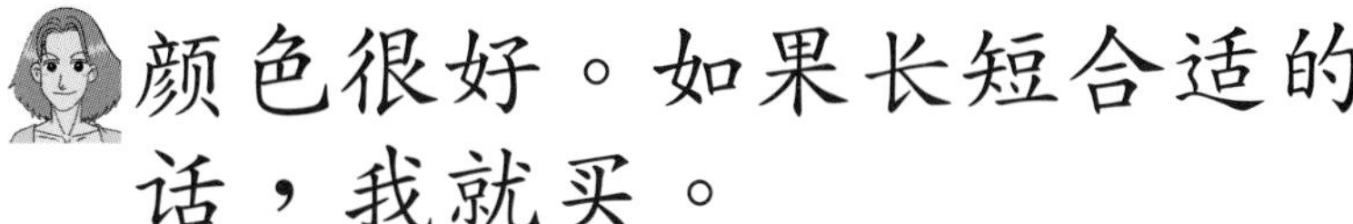
颜色很好。如果长短合适的话，我就买。

您试一下。

[*Li You checks the size on the label and measures the pants against her legs.*]

不用试。可以。

这件衬衫呢？

也不错。一共多少钱？

衬衫二十一块五，裤子三十二块九毛九，一共是五十四块四毛九分⑤。

好，这是一百块钱。

找您四十五块五毛一。谢谢。

❸ The character 便 in 便宜 (piányi, inexpensive) is pronounced "pián." But in 方便 (fangbiàn, convenient) the same character is pronounced "biàn." It is not uncommon in Chinese for the same character to be pronounced differently and carry different meanings. Other examples include: 乐 (yuè/lè) in 音乐 (yīnyuè, music), 可乐 (kělè, cola); and 觉 (jué/jiào) in 觉得 (juéde, to feel) and 睡觉 (shuì jiào, to sleep).

(Lǐ Yǒu zài yí ge shāngdiàn mǎi dōngxi, shòuhuòyuán wèn tā. . .)

Xiǎojiě, nín yào①mǎi shénme yīfu?

Wǒ xiǎng mǎi yí jiàn②chènshān.

Nín xǐhuan shénme yánsè de③, huáng de háishi hóng de?

Wǒ xǐhuan chuān❶ hóng de. Wǒ hái xiǎng mǎi yì tiáo②kùzi❷.

Duō④dà de? Dà hào de, zhōng hào de, háishi xiǎo hào de?

Zhōng hào de. Bú yào tài guì de, yě bú yào tài piányi❸ de.

 Zhè tiáo kùzi zěnmeyàng?

 Yánsè hěn hǎo, rúguǒ chángduǎn héshì de huà, wǒ jiù mǎi.

 Nín shì yi xia.

[*Li You checks the size on the label and measures the pants against her legs.*]

 Búyòng shì, kěyǐ.

 Zhè jiàn chènshān ne?

 Yě búcuò. Yígòng duōshao qián?

 Chènshān èrshíyī kuài wǔ, kùzi sānshí'èr kuài jiǔ máo jiǔ, yígòng shì wǔshísì kuài sì máo jiǔ fēn⑤ .

 Hǎo, zhè shì yìbǎi kuài qián.

 Zhǎo nín sìshíwǔ kuài wǔ máo yī. Xièxie.

VOCABULARY

1.	商店	shāngdiàn	n	store; shop
2.	买	mǎi	v	to buy
3.	东西	dōngxi	n	things; objects
4.	售货员	shòuhuòyuán	n	shop assistant; salesclerk
5.	衣服	yīfu	n	clothes
6.	件	jiàn	m	(measure word for shirts, dresses, jackets, coats, etc.)
7.	衬衫	chènshān	n	shirt
8.	颜色	yánsè	n	color
9.	黄	huáng	adj	yellow
10.	红	hóng	adj	red
11.	穿	chuān	v	to wear; to put on
12.	条	tiáo	m	(measure word for pants and long, thin objects)
13.	裤子	kùzi	n	pants
14.	号	hào	n	size
15.	中	zhōng	adj	medium; middle
16.	便宜	piányi	adj	cheap; inexpensive
17.	如果…的话	rúguǒ... de huà	conj	if

大家去商店买东西。
Dàjiā qù shāngdiàn mǎi dōngxi.

VOCABULARY

18.	长短	chángduǎn	n	length
	长	cháng	adj	long
	短	duǎn	adj	short
19.	合适	héshì	adj	suitable
20.	试	shì	v	to try
21.	不用	búyòng		need not
22.	一共	yígòng	adv	altogether
23.	多少	duōshao	qpr	how much/many
24.	钱	qián	n	money
25.	块	kuài	m	(measure word for the basic Chinese monetary unit)
26.	毛	máo	m	(measure word for 1/10 of a kuai, dime [in US money])
27.	分	fēn	m	(measure word for 1/100 of a kuai, cent)
28.	百	bǎi	nu	hundred
29.	找（钱）	zhǎo (qián)	v(o)	to give change

Grammar

1. The Modal Verb 要 (yào) (II)

[See also Lesson 6 Grammar 2.]

One of the meanings of 要 (yào) is "to desire to do something."

❶ 明天是周末，你要做什么？

Míngtiān shì zhōumò, nǐ yào zuò shénme?

(Tomorrow is the weekend. What do you want to do?)

❷ 我要去图书馆看书，你去不去？

Wǒ yào qù túshūguǎn kàn shū, nǐ qù bu qù?

(I want to go to the library to read. Are you going?)

❸ 我要喝可乐，他要喝茶。

Wǒ yào hē kělè, tā yào hē chá.

(I want to drink cola. He wants to drink tea.)

To negate it, use 不想 (bù xiǎng).

❹ 我不想去图书馆。

Wǒ bù xiǎng qù túshūguǎn.

(I don't feel like going to the library.)

❺ 今天我不想做功課。

Jīntiān wǒ bù xiǎng zuò gōngkè.
(I don't feel like doing my homework today.)

For (4), however, some Chinese speakers, particularly in the South, would say:

我不要去图书馆。

Wǒ bú yào qù túshūguǎn.

Both modal verbs 想 (xiǎng) and 要 (yào) can express a desire or an intention, but 要 (yào) carries a stronger tone.

2. Measure Words (II)

[See also Lesson 2 Grammar 2.]

The following are the "measure word + noun" combinations that we have covered so far. You have come across these measure words along with the nouns associated with them.

一个人	yí ge rén	a person
一位先生	yí wèi xiānsheng	a gentleman
一杯茶	yì bēi chá	a cup of tea
一瓶可乐	yì píng kělè	a bottle of cola
一枝笔	yì zhī bǐ	a pen
一张纸	yì zhāng zhǐ	a piece of paper
一节课	yì jié kè	a class period
一篇日记	yì piān rìjì	a diary entry
一封信	yì fēng xìn	a letter
一件衬衫	yí jiàn chènshān	a shirt
一条裤子	yì tiáo kùzi	a pair of pants
一双鞋	yì shuāng xié	a pair of shoes [See Dialogue 2 in Lesson 9.]
一块钱	yí kuài qián	one yuan
一毛钱	yì máo qián	1/10 of a yuan
一分钱	yì fēn qián	1/100 of a yuan, one cent

一分钱
yì fēn qián

Supplementary:

一本书	yì běn shū	a book
一只鞋	yì zhī xié	a shoe (one of a pair) [See also "a pair of shoes" above.]

3. The 的 (de) Structure (II)

We have a 的 (de) structure when a noun, a pronoun, or an adjective is followed by the structural particle 的 (de). Grammatically, a 的 (de) structure is equivalent to a noun, e.g., 老师的 (lǎoshī de, the teacher's), 我的 (wǒ de, mine), 大的 (dà de, the big one), etc. See also Grammar 8 in Lesson 7.

4. 多 (duō) Used Interrogatively

The adverb 多 (duō) is often used in a question asking about degree or extent, e.g.,

❶ 你今年多大？ [See Lesson 3.]

Nǐ jīnnián duō dà?

(How old are you this year?)

❷ 你穿多大的衣服？

Nǐ chuān duō dà de yīfu?

(What size clothes do you wear?)

❸ 你弟弟多高？

Nǐ dìdi duō gāo?

(How tall is your younger brother?)

The adjectives that follow 多 (duō) are typically those suggesting large extents such as 大 (dà, big), 高 (gāo, tall; high) and 远 (yuǎn, far), rather than those denoting small degrees such as 小 (xiǎo, small; little), 矮 (ǎi, short), and 近 (jìn, near).

5. Amounts of Money

Chinese monetary units are 元 (yuán), 角 (jiǎo, 1/10 of a yuan), and 分 (fēn, one cent or 1/100 of a yuan). In colloquial speech, alternative terms 块 (kuài) and 毛 (máo) are usually used instead of 元 (yuán) and 角 (jiǎo), but price markings in stores are likely to be in 元 (yuán) and 角 (jiǎo), and many store clerks also use 元 (yuán) in their speech. Using the colloquial terms, ¥ 5.99

is 五块九毛九分钱 (wǔ kuài jiǔ máo jiǔ fēn qián). However, in casual conversation abbreviated forms are often used.

The rules for abbreviation of monetary terms are as follows: begin by omitting the last element 钱 (qián) in the expression and then the second to last element: 五块九毛九分 (wǔ kuài jiǔ máo jiǔ fēn) omitting 钱 (qián), or 五块九毛九 (wǔ kuài jiǔ máo jiǔ) omitting both 钱 (qián) and 分 (fēn). Note that if 钱 is included, the preceding measure (e.g., 分) must also be included; one doesn't say *五块九毛九钱 (*wǔ kuài jiǔ máo jiǔ qián). One or more zeros occurring internally in a complex number are read as 零/〇 (líng, zero).

Rénmínbì: from top to bottom
五元、二角、一元
wǔ yuán, èr jiǎo, yì yuán

Xīntáibì
五十元
wǔshí yuán

❶ $8.55 八块五毛五(分)(钱)
bā kuài wǔ máo wǔ (fēn)(qián)

❷ $15.30 十五块三(毛)(钱)
shíwǔ kuài sān (máo) (qián)

❸ $103 一百零三块(钱)
yì bǎi líng sān kuài (qián)

❹ $100.30 一百块零三毛(钱)
yì bǎi kuài líng sān máo (qián)

❺ $100.03 一百块零三分(钱)
yìbǎi kuài líng sān fēn (qián)

To avoid ambiguity, 毛 (máo) and 分 (fēn) cannot be omitted in (4) or (5).

Language Practice

A. 要 (yào, to want to; to have a desire to)

Practice with a partner how to ask and answer what Little Wang wishes to do next week based on the following chart.

Monday	Tuesday	Wednesday	Thursday	Friday	Saturday

EXAMPLE: 星期一 xīngqīyī

→ **A:** 小王下个星期一要做什么？ **A:** Xiǎo Wáng xià ge xīngqīyī yào zuò shénme?

B: 小王下个星期一要去上课。 **B:** Xiǎo Wáng xià ge xīngqīyī yào qù shàng kè.

1. 星期二 xīngqīèr
2. 星期三 xīngqīsān
3. 星期四 xīngqīsì
4. 星期五 xīngqīwǔ
5. 星期六 xīngqīliù

B. 想 (xiǎng, to feel like; would like to)

Little Li likes window shopping, and always dreams about what she would like to buy. Say what's on her wish list based on the pictures.

EXAMPLE: 

→ 小李想买一件新衣服。 Xiǎo Lǐ xiǎng mǎi yí jiàn xīn yīfu.

1. 
2. 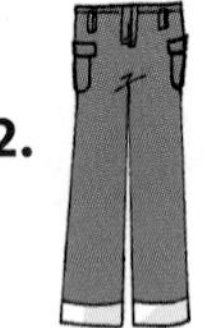
3. 
4. 

C. 的 (de) Structure

Practice how to ask and answer the following using the words given.

C1: Lost and Found: Identify to whom the objects belong.

EXAMPLE:

A: 

→ 这瓶可乐是谁的？ A: Zhè píng kělè shì shéi de?

B:  这瓶可乐是高文中的。 B: Zhè píng kělè shì Gāo Wénzhōng de.

1. 

2.  
3.  

C2: Identify the colors of Little Wang's belongings.

EXAMPLE:

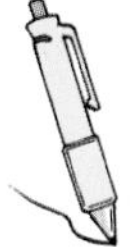

→ **A:** 小王的笔是什么颜色的？ → **A:** Xiǎo Wáng de bǐ shì shénme yánsè de?

B: 小王的笔是黄色的。 **B:** Xiǎo Wáng de bǐ shì huángsè de.

1.  **2.**  **3.** 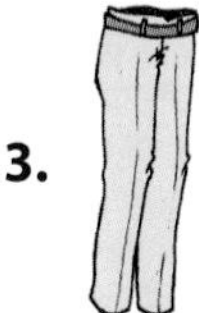

D. 多 (duō)

Practice how to ask about age, height, and how expensive things are.

How do you find out the following:

1. your friend's sibling's age
2. the price of your friend's pants
3. your teacher's height

E. Pair Activity

Is your partner a shopaholic? Find out your partner's shopping habits.

你喜欢买东西吗？ Nǐ xǐhuan mǎi dōngxi ma?

你常常去买东西吗？ Nǐ chángcháng qù mǎi dōngxi ma?

你喜欢买什么东西？ Nǐ xǐhuan mǎi shénme dōngxi?

你喜欢买衣服吗？ Nǐ xǐhuan mǎi yīfu ma?

你常常去哪儿买东西？ Nǐ chángcháng qù nǎr mǎi dōngxi?

你常常跟谁一起去买东西？ Nǐ chángcháng gēn shéi yìqǐ qù mǎi dōngxi?

你有几件衬衫？ Nǐ yǒu jǐ jiàn chènshān?

你有几条裤子？ Nǐ yǒu jǐ tiáo kùzi?

F. Pair Activity

Be a fashion commentator. Bring in a photo, or a clipping from a magazine, of your favorite celebrity. Work with a partner to ask and answer the following questions. Then report back to the class the information gathered regarding your partner's celebrity.

Celebrity's name 喜欢什么颜色？ Celebrity's name xǐhuan shénme yánsè?

她喜欢穿什么颜色的衣服？ Tā xǐhuan chuān shénme yánsè de yīfu?

她今天的衣服是什么颜色的？ Tā jīntiān de yīfu shì shénme yánsè de?

你觉得她今天的衣服长短合适不合适？ Nǐ juéde tā jīntiān de yīfu chángduǎn héshì bù héshì?

她的衣服多吗？ Tā de yīfu duō ma?

Dialogue II: Exchanging Shoes

 对不起，这双鞋太小了。能不能换一双？

 没问题。您看，这双怎么样？

 也不行，这双跟那双一样[6]大。

 那这双黑的呢？

 这双鞋虽然大小合适，可是[7]颜色不好。有没有咖啡色的？

 对不起，这种鞋只有黑的。

 这双鞋样子挺好的[1]，就是它吧[2]。你们这儿可以刷卡吗?

 对不起，我们不收信用卡。不过，这双的钱跟那双一样，您不用再付钱了。

LANGUAGE NOTES

❶ 挺+adj+的 (tǐng+adj+de) means "it's rather adj." The 的 (de) is optional.

❷ 就是它吧 (jiù shì tā ba) is an expression one often uses when making a decision at the end of a process of selection. It roughly means "This is it" or "I'll take it." [See That's How the Chinese Say It! after Lesson 10.]

Duìbuqǐ, zhè shuāng xié tài xiǎo le. Néng bu néng huàn yì shuāng?

 Méi wèntí. Nín kàn, zhè shuāng zěnmeyàng?

 Yě bù xíng, zhè shuāng gēn nà shuāng yíyàng⑥ dà.

 Nà zhè shuāng hēi de ne?

 Zhè shuāng xié suīrán dàxiǎo héshì, kěshì⑦ yánsè bù hǎo. Yǒu méiyǒu kāfēisè de?

 Duìbuqǐ, zhè zhǒng xié zhǐ yǒu hēi de.

 Zhè shuāng xié yàngzi tǐng hao de❶...jiù shì tā ba❷. Nǐmen zhèr kěyǐ shuā kǎ ma?

 Duìbuqǐ, wǒmen bù shōu xìnyòngkǎ. Búguò, zhè shuāng de qián gēn nà shuāng yíyàng, nín búyòng zài fù qián le.

鞋店
xié diàn

VOCABULARY

1.	双	shuāng	m	(measure word for a pair)
2.	鞋	xié	n	shoes
3.	换	huàn	v	to exchange; to change
4.	一样	yíyàng	adj	same; alike [See Grammar 6.]
5.	虽然	suīrán	conj	although [See Grammar 7.]
6.	大小	dàxiǎo	n	size
7.	咖啡色	kāfēisè	n	brown; coffee color
8.	种	zhǒng	m	(measure word for kinds, sorts, types)
9.	黑	hēi	adj	black
10.	样子	yàngzi	n	style
11.	挺	tǐng	adv	very; rather
12.	它	tā	pr	it
13.	这儿	zhèr	pr	here
14.	刷卡	shuā kǎ	vo	to pay with a credit card
	刷	shuā	v	to brush; to swipe
	卡	kǎ	n	card
15.	收	shōu	v	to receive; to accept
16.	信用卡	xìnyòngkǎ	n	credit card
17.	不过	búguò	conj	however; but
18.	再	zài	adv	again
19.	付钱	fù qián	vo	to pay money
	付	fù	v	to pay

收银台
shōuyín tái
在这儿付钱
zài zhèr fù qián

Grammar

6. 跟/和…(不)一样 (gēn/hé...{bù} yíyàng, {not} the same as...)

To express similarity or dissimilarity between objects, persons, or actions, we use the structure 跟/和…(不)一样 (gēn/hé... {bù} yíyàng).

❶ 你的衬衫跟我的一样。

Nǐ de chènshān gēn wǒ de yíyàng.

(Your shirt is the same as mine.)

❷ 贵的衣服和便宜的衣服不一样。

Guì de yīfu hé piányi de yīfu bù yíyàng.

(Expensive clothes are different from cheap ones.)

Following 一样 (yíyàng), an adjective can be used:

❸ 弟弟跟哥哥一样高。

Dìdi gēn gēge yíyàng gāo.

(The younger brother is as tall as the older one.)

❹ 这个电脑跟那个电脑一样新。

Zhè ge diànnǎo gēn nà ge diànnǎo yíyàng xīn.

(This computer is as new as that one.)

❺ 常老师写汉字写得跟王老师（写汉字写得）一样漂亮。

Cháng Lǎoshī xiě Hànzì xiě de gēn Wáng Lǎoshī (xiě Hànzì xiě de) yíyàng piàoliang.

Teacher Chang writes Chinese characters as nicely as Teacher Wang does.

7. 虽然…，可是/但是…(suīrán..., kěshì/dànshì..., although...yet...)

This pair of conjunctions links the two clauses in a complex sentence. Note, however, that 虽然 (suīrán) is often optional.

❶ 虽然这双鞋很便宜，可是大小不合适。

Suīrán zhè shuāng xié hěn piányi, kěshì dàxiǎo bù héshì.

(Although this pair of shoes is inexpensive, it's not the right size.)

中国布鞋
Zhōngguó bùxié
(Chinese cloth shoes)

❷ 这本书很有意思，可是太贵了。

Zhè běn shū hěn yǒu yìsi, kěshì tài guì le.

(This book is very interesting, but it's too expensive.)

❸ 中文不容易，但是很有意思。

Zhōngwén bù róngyì, dànshì hěn yǒu yìsi.

(Chinese is not easy, but it's very interesting.)

Whether or not 虽然 (suīrán) is used in the first clause, 可是/但是 (kěshì/dànshì) cannot be omitted in the second. The following sentence is, therefore, incorrect:

(2a) *虽然这本书很有意思，太贵了。

*Suīrán zhè běn shū hěn yǒu yìsi, tài guì le.

Language Practice

G. 跟…一样 (gēn...yíyàng, **the same as...**)

EXAMPLE: 这件衣服跟那件衣服一样漂亮。 Zhè jiàn yīfu gēn nà jiàn yīfu yíyàng piàoliang.

1. 这枝笔 ◇ 那枝笔 ◇ 便宜 — zhè zhī bǐ ◇ nà zhī bǐ ◇ piányi
2. 这条裤子 ◇ 那条裤子 ◇ 贵 — zhè tiáo kùzi ◇ nà tiáo kùzi ◇ guì
3. 这双鞋 ◇ 那双鞋 ◇ 合适 — zhè shuāng xié ◇ nà shuāng xié ◇ héshì
4. 这件衬衫 ◇ 那件衬衫 ◇ 大 — zhè jiàn chènshān ◇ nà jiàn chènshān ◇ dà
5. 第九课的语法 ◇ 第八课的语法 ◇ 难 — dì jiǔ kè de yǔfǎ ◇ dì bā kè de yǔfǎ ◇ nán

H. 虽然…可是/但是 (suīrán…kěshì/dànshì, although…yet)

EXAMPLE: 虽然中文很难，可是很有意思。 Suīrán Zhōngwén hěn nán, kěshì hěn yǒu yìsi.

1. 她的新衣服很多◇她都不穿 — tā de xīn yīfu hěn duō ◇ tā dōu bù chuān
2. 这条裤子很便宜◇长短不合适 — zhè tiáo kùzi hěn piányi ◇ chángduǎn bù héshì
3. 这件衬衫的颜色很好看◇有一点儿小 — zhè jiàn chènshān de yánsè hěn hǎokàn ◇ yǒu yìdiǎnr xiǎo
4. 这双鞋样子挺不错的◇太贵了 — zhè shuāng xié yàngzi tǐng búcuò de ◇ tài guì le
5. 这个商店不小◇不能刷卡 — zhè ge shāngdiàn bù xiǎo ◇ bù néng shuā kǎ

I. Identical Twins

Here's some information about two sisters who are identical twins. Describe the similarities between the two.

EXAMPLE: age: 14 14

→ 姐姐跟妹妹一样大。

1. height: 5′5″ 5′5″
2. shirts: size 6 size 6
3. pants: 30″ inseam 30″ inseam

J. Clothing Store

You own a small clothing store, and you want to plan your inventory. Survey your clients/everyone in the class about their color preferences and sizes and then decide how many pairs of shirts, pants, shoes, etc. you need to stock, and in what colors and sizes.

你喜欢穿什么颜色的	Nǐ xǐhuan chuān shénme yánsè de
鞋/衬衫/裤子？	xié/chènshān/kùzi?
你穿多大的	Nǐ chuān duō dà de
鞋/衬衫/裤子？	xié/chènshān/kùzi?

Write down your findings:

- shoes

____

- shirts

____

- pants

____

HOW ABOUT YOU?

What is your favorite color?

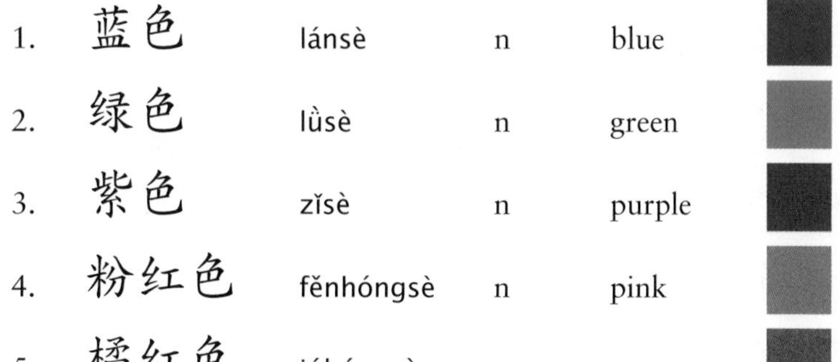

1.	蓝色	lánsè	n	blue
2.	绿色	lǜsè	n	green
3.	紫色	zǐsè	n	purple
4.	粉红色	fěnhóngsè	n	pink
5.	橘红色	júhóngsè	n	orange
6.	灰色	huīsè	n	gray

If your most favorite and least favorite colors are not listed above, ask your teacher and make a note here:

我最喜欢____________色。 Wǒ zuì xǐhuan __________sè.

我最不喜欢____________色。 Wǒ zuì bù xǐhuan __________sè.

What's in your wardrobe?

1.	上衣	shàngyī	n	upper garment
2.	大衣	dàyī	n	overcoat
3.	毛衣	máoyī	n	woolen sweater
4.	裙子	qúnzi	n	skirt
5.	夹克	jiákè	n	jacket
6.	外套	wàitào	n	outer garment; coat; jacket
7.	西装	xīzhuāng	n	(western-style) suit
8.	T恤衫	T-xùshān	n	T-shirt
9.	帽子	màozi	n	hat; cap
10.	袜子	wàzi	n	socks

If there are items in your wardrobe that are not mentioned above, ask your teacher and make a note here: ____________

Culture Highlights

1. In mainland China a salesperson in a department store is usually addressed as 售货员 (shòuhuòyuán), and a server in a restaurant is usually addressed as 服务员 (fúwùyuán, "Service Person"). In speaking to bus drivers or taxi drivers, as well as ticket sellers, the most common form of address (for women as well as men) is 师傅 (shīfu, an old term of respect for a master craftsman or skilled worker). However, these forms of address vary according to age and preference of the speaker as well as the status or function of the person spoken to, and usage is very much in flux in the early twenty-first century. As in so many matters of language usage, students should carefully observe actual usage and follow suit. In Taiwan, the terms 小姐 (xiǎojiě, Miss) and 先生 (xiānsheng, Mr.) have very broad usage, including the contexts mentioned above.

2. In mainland China prices are usually non-negotiable in supermarkets and large department stores, but bargaining is routine in street-side stalls and small shops. There is no sales tax in mainland China. It is also not customary to tip in a restaurant, although upscale restaurants often charge a service fee.

3. The traditional formal attire for Chinese men was a long robe called 长袍 (chángpáo, long gown) and a short jacket called 马褂 (mǎguà, Mandarin jacket), while women (in the cities) wore a modified Manchu-style dress called 旗袍 (qípáo, close-fitting woman's dress with a high neck and a slit skirt) until 1949 in mainland China and into the 1960s and 70s in Taiwan. Through the early decades of the People's Republic, men wore the 中山装 (Zhōngshānzhuāng, "Sun Yat-sen suit"), the top part of which came to be called in the West the "Mao jacket." Nowadays Chinese men and women dress in about the same way as Westerners, wearing suits and ties or dresses on formal occasions, and jeans and T-shirts for more casual purposes.

一件长袍
yí jiàn chángpáo

两件旗袍
liǎng jiàn qípáo

English Text

Dialogue I

(Shopping for clothes at a store)

Salesperson: Miss, what are you looking for?

Li You: I'd like to buy a shirt.

Salesperson: What color [shirt] do you like? Yellow or red?

Li You: I like red. I'd also like to get a pair of pants.

Salesperson: What size? Large, medium or small?

Li You: Medium. Something not too expensive, but not too cheap, either.

Salesperson: How about these pants?

Li You: The color is nice. If the size is right, I'll take them.

Salesperson: Please try them on.

[*Li You checks the size on the label, and measures the pants against her legs.*]

Li You: No need to try them. They'll do.

Salesperson: And how about this shirt?

Li You: It's not bad either. How much altogether?

Salesperson: Twenty one dollars and fifty cents for the shirt, and thirty-two ninety-nine for the pants. Fifty-four dollars and forty-nine cents altogether.

Li You: OK. Here's one hundred.

Salesperson: Forty-five fifty-one is your change. Thank you.

Dialogue II

Wang Peng: Excuse me, this pair of shoes is too small. Can I exchange them for another pair?

Salesperson: No problem. How about this pair?

Wang Peng: No, they won't do either. This pair is the same size as the other one.

Salesperson: What about this pair in black?

Wang Peng: This pair is the right size, but it's not a good color. Do you have any in brown?

Salesperson: I'm sorry. We only have black ones for this kind of shoes.

Wang Peng: The style of the pair is pretty nice. This is it. Can I use my credit card here?

Salesperson: I'm sorry, we don't take credit cards. But this pair is the same price as the other one. You don't need to pay again.

PROGRESS CHECKLIST

Before proceeding to Lesson 10, be sure you can complete the following tasks in Chinese:

I am able to—

- [x] Name my favorite color and other common colors;
- [x] Talk about clothing and shoe sizes;
- [x] Count money and determine the proper change;
- [x] Return or exchange items at a store.

Please review the lesson if any of these tasks seem difficult.

Transportation

LESSON 10

第十课 交通

Dì shí kè Jiāotōng

10

LEARNING OBJECTIVES

In this lesson, you will learn to use Chinese to

- Comment about several means of transportation;
- Explain how to travel from one station to another;
- Describe a traffic route;
- Express your gratitude after receiving a personal favor;
- Offer New Year's wishes.

RELATE AND GET READY

In your own culture/community,

1. What is the most popular means of public transportation?
2. Can people hail a taxi on the street easily or do they have to call one by phone?
3. How do people express their gratitude?
4. What do people say to each other on the New Year?

Dialogue: Going Home for the Winter Vacation

李友，寒假你回家吗？

对，我要回家。

飞机票你买了吗①？

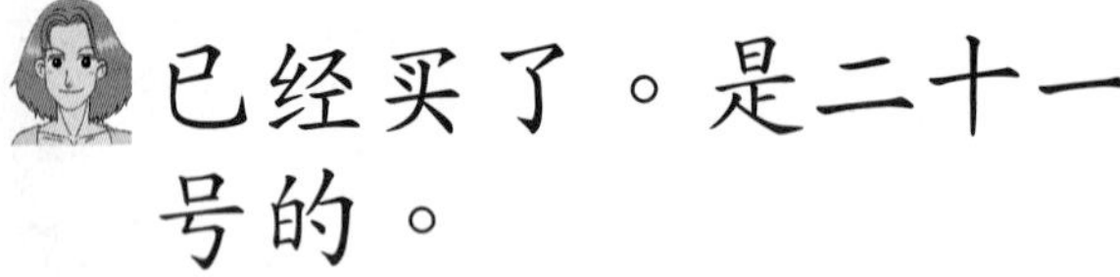
已经买了。是二十一号的。

飞机是几点的？

晚上八点的。

你怎么去❶机场？

我想坐公共汽车或者②坐地铁。你知道怎么走❶吗？

LANGUAGE NOTES

❶ 怎么去 (zěnme qù) asks the means of transportation and 怎么走 (zěnme zǒu) asks the detailed route or directions.

你先坐一路汽车，坐三站下车，然后换地铁。先坐红线，再③换绿线，最后换蓝线。

不行，不行，太麻烦了。我还是④打车❷吧。

❷ Taxicabs are called 计程车 (jìchéng chē, metered cars) in Taiwan but 出租(汽)车 (chūzū {qì}chē) in mainland China. To take a taxi is 打车 (dǎ chē).

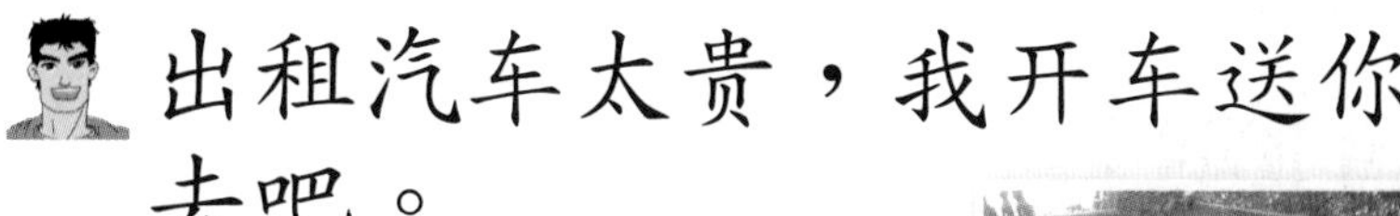

出租汽车太贵，我开车送你去吧。

谢谢你。

不用客气。

地铁站
dìtiě zhàn

Lǐ Yǒu, hánjià nǐ huí jiā ma?

Duì, wǒ yào huí jiā.

Fēijī piào nǐ mǎi le ma①?

Yǐjīng mǎi le. Shì èrshíyī hào de.

Fēijī shì jǐ diǎn de?

Wǎnshang bā diǎn de.

Nǐ zěnme qù❶ jīchǎng?

Wǒ xiǎng zuò gōnggòng qìchē huòzhě② zuò dìtiě. Nǐ zhīdao zěnme zǒu❶ ma?

Nǐ xiān zuò yī lù qìchē, zuò sān zhàn xià chē, ránhòu huàn dìtiě. Xiān zuò hóng xiàn, zài③ huàn lǜ xiàn, zuìhòu huàn lán xiàn.

Bù xíng, bù xíng, tài máfan le. Wǒ háishi④ dǎ chē❷ ba.

Chūzū qìchē tài guì, wǒ kāi chē sòng nǐ qù ba.

Xièxie nǐ.

Búyòng kèqi.

在这儿打车
zài zhèr dǎ chē

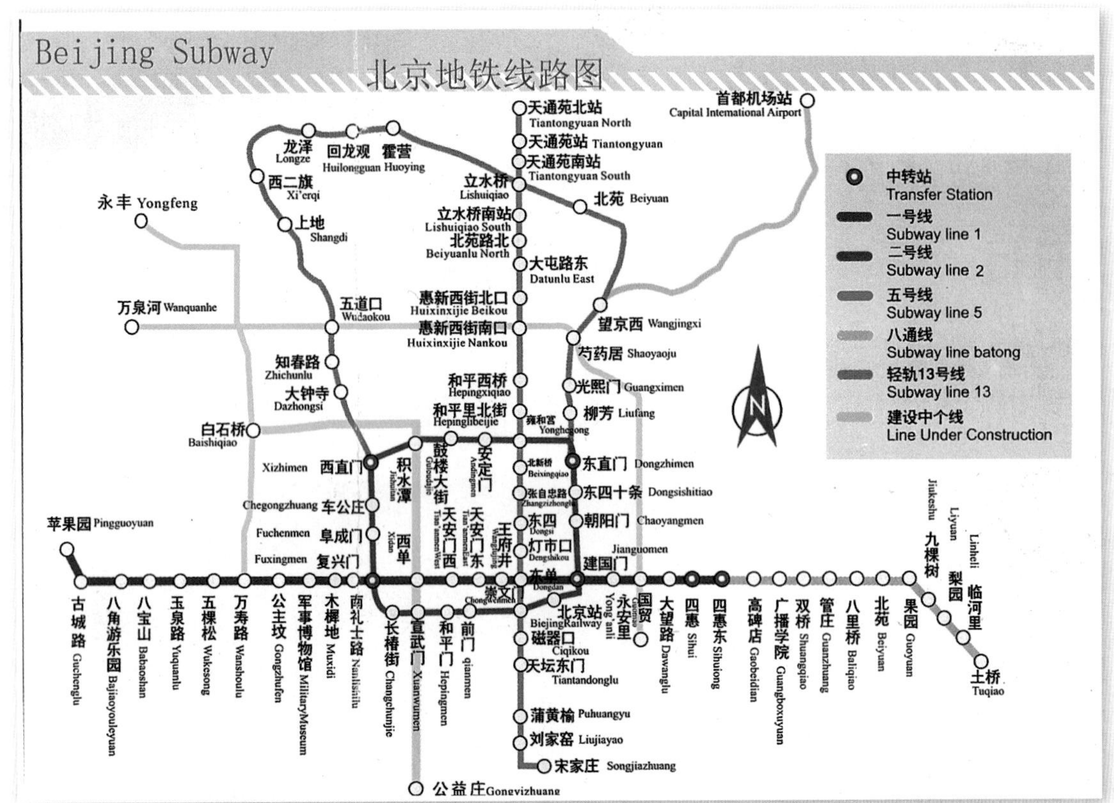

VOCABULARY

1.	寒假	hánjià	n	winter vacation
2.	飞机	fēijī	n	airplane
	飞	fēi	v	to fly
	机	jī	n	machine
3.	票	piào	n	ticket
4.	(飞)机场	(fēi)jīchǎng	n	airport
5.	坐	zuò	v	to travel by
6.	公共汽车	gōnggòng qìchē	n	bus
	公共	gōnggòng	adj	public
	汽车	qìchē	n	automobile
	车	chē	n	vehicle; car

VOCABULARY

7.	或者	huòzhě	conj	or [See Grammar 2.]
8.	地铁	dìtiě	n	subway
9.	走	zǒu	v	to go by way of; to walk
10.	先	xiān	adv	first [See Grammar 3.]
11.	站	zhàn	m	(measure word for stops of bus, train, etc.)
12.	下车	xià chē	vo	to get off (a bus, train, etc.)
13.	然后	ránhòu	adv	then
14.	绿	lǜ	adj	green
15.	线	xiàn	n	line
16.	最后	zuìhòu		final; last
17.	蓝	lán	adj	blue
18.	麻烦	máfan	adj	troublesome
19.	打车	dǎ chē	vo	to take a taxi
20.	出租汽车	chūzū qìchē	n	taxi
	出租	chūzū	v	to rent out; to let
	租	zū	v	to rent
21.	开车	kāi chē	vo	to drive a car
	开	kāi	v	to drive; to operate
22.	送	sòng	v	to see off or out; to take (someone somewhere)

北京机场
Běijīng jīchǎng

这张公共汽车票多少钱？
Zhè zhāng gōnggòng qìchē piào duōshao qián?

Grammar

1. Topic-Comment Sentences

When a noun or noun phrase has become established as a known element in a conversation, it can occur at the beginning of the sentence as the "topic," with the rest of the sentence functioning as a "comment" on it. This forms what is known as a "topic-comment sentence." In such a sentence the object of the verb can be brought forward to serve as the topic of the sentence.

❶ **A:** 我昨天买了一枝笔。

Wǒ zuótiān mǎi le yì zhī bǐ.

(I bought a pen yesterday.)

B: 那枝笔你用了吗？

Nà zhī bǐ nǐ yòng le ma?

(Have you used that pen?)

❷ A: 你知道我的衬衫在哪儿吗？

Nǐ zhīdao wǒ de chènshān zài nǎr ma?

(Do you know where my shirt is?)

B: 你的衬衫我给你妈妈了。

Nǐ de chènshān wǒ gěi nǐ māma le.

(I gave your shirt to your mother.)

❸ A: 你有朋友吗？

Nǐ yǒu péngyou ma?

(Do you have friends?)

B: 朋友我有很多，可是都不在这儿。

Péngyou wǒ yǒu hěn duō, kěshì dōu bú zài zhèr.

(I have many friends, but none of them are here.)

❹ 她不想去纽约，可是飞机票她妈妈已经帮她买了。

Tā bù xiǎng qù Niǔyuē, kěshì fēijī piào tā māma yǐjīng bāng tā mǎi le.

(She does not want to go to New York, but her mother has already bought the airplane ticket for her.)

2. 或者 (huòzhě, or) and 还是 (háishi, or)

While both 或者 (huòzhě, or) and 还是 (háishi, or) link up two words or phrases that indicate different alternatives, the former usually appears in statements, the latter in questions.

❶ A: 你今天晚上做什么？

Nǐ jīntiān wǎnshang zuò shénme?

(What are you going to do tonight?)

B: 听音乐或者看电影。

Tīng yīnyuè huòzhě kàn diànyǐng.

(Listen to music or watch a movie.)

❷ A: 你周末想看电影还是跳舞？

Nǐ zhōumò xiǎng kàn diànyǐng háishi tiào wǔ?

(Would you like to see a movie or go dancing this weekend?)

B: 看电影或者跳舞都行。

Kàn diànyǐng huòzhě tiào wǔ dōu xíng.

(Either seeing a movie or going dancing would be fine with me.)

❸ A: 你喜欢什么颜色的鞋？黑色的还是咖啡色的？

Nǐ xǐhuan shénme yánsè de xié? Hēisè de háishi kāfēisè de?

(What color shoes do you like? Black or brown ones?)

B: 黑色的或者咖啡色的我都不喜欢，我喜欢白的。

Hēisè de huòzhě kāfēisè de wǒ dōu bù xǐhuan, wǒ xǐhuan bái de.

(I don't like either black or brown; I like white ones.)

❹ 明天你去开会或者他去开会都可以。

Míngtiān nǐ qù kāi huì huòzhě tā qù kāi huì dōu kěyǐ.

(Either you or he may attend tomorrow's meeting.)

3. 先…再… (xiān...zài..., first..., then...)

Sometimes 再 (zài) indicates a sequence of actions rather than a repetition. 先看电影再吃饭 (xiān kàn diànyǐng zài chī fàn, first go to the movie, then eat) means 看电影以后吃饭 (kàn diànyǐng yǐhòu chī fàn, eat after seeing the movie).

MORE EXAMPLES:

❶ A: 你什么时候给妈妈打电话？

Nǐ shénme shíhou gěi māma dǎ diànhuà?

(When are you going to call Mom?)

B: 下课以后再打。

Xià kè yǐhòu zài dǎ.

(I'll call after class.)

❷ 我想先打球再去图书馆。

Wǒ xiǎng xiān dǎ qiú zài qù túshūguǎn.

(I'd like to play ball and then go to the library.)

❸ **A:** 弟弟常常先做功课再上网聊天儿。

Dìdi chángcháng xiān zuò gōngkè zài shàng wǎng liáo tiānr.

(My little brother often does his homework first and then chats online.)

As adverbs, 先 (xiān) and 再 (zài) must come immediately before a verb. They cannot be placed in front of the subject.

❹ 小王先买东西再吃晚饭。

Xiǎo Wáng xiān mǎi dōngxi zài chī wǎnfàn.

(Little Wang will shop first before having dinner.)

(4a) *先小王买东西再吃晚饭。

*Xiān Xiǎo Wáng mǎi dōngxi zài chī wǎnfàn.

4. 还是…(吧) (háishi...{ba}, had better)

The structure 还是…(吧) (háishi...{ba}, had better) can be used to signify making a selection after considering two or more options. Sometimes in making such a decision one is forced to give up one's preference.

❶ **A:** 你说，明天看电影还是看球？

Nǐ shuō, míngtiān kàn diànyǐng háishi kàn qiú?

(What do you think we should watch tomorrow, a movie or a ball game?)

B: 还是看电影吧。

Háishi kàn diànyǐng ba.

(Let's see a movie.)

❷ **A:** 我的车有问题。怎么办？

Wǒ de chē yǒu wèntí. Zěnme bàn?

(There is a problem with my car. What shall we do?)

B: 那别去听音乐会了。我们还是在家看电视吧。

Nà bié qù tīng yīnyuèhuì le. Wǒmen háishi zài jiā kàn diànshì ba.

(Let's not go to the concert then. We'd better stay home and watch TV.)

Language Practice

A. Topic-Comment Sentence

A brings up a piece of new information. That piece of information then becomes known/old information, or the topic of B's response. Let's practice.

EXAMPLE: **A:** 你喜欢我的这件衣服吗？ — **A:** Nǐ xǐhuan wǒ de zhè jiàn yīfu ma?

B: 这件衣服我不喜欢。 — **B:** Zhè jiàn yīfu wǒ bù xǐhuan.

1. **A:** 你会不会上网？ — **A:** Nǐ huì bu huì shàng wǎng?
2. **A:** 你复习课文了吗？ — **A:** Nǐ fùxí kèwén le ma?
3. **A:** 你现在想不想喝咖啡？ — **A:** Nǐ xiànzài xiǎng bu xiǎng hē kāfēi?
4. **A:** 你认识白英爱吗？ — **A:** Nǐ rènshi Bái Yīng'ài ma?

B. 或者 vs. 还是 (huòzhě **vs.** háishi)

Practice with a partner how to offer choices and how to be diplomatic or accommodating when answering.

EXAMPLE: 今天晚上做什么 — jīntiān wǎnshang zuò shénme

听音乐/看电视 — tīng yīnyuè/kàn diànshì

→ **A:** 我们今天晚上做什么？听音乐还是看电视？ → **A:** Wǒmen jīntiān wǎnshang zuò shénme? Tīng yīnyuè háishi kàn diànshì?

B: 听音乐或者看电视都行。 **B:** Tīng yīnyuè huòzhě kàn diànshì dōu xíng.

1. 明天下午做什么
   去打球/去跳舞
   míngtiān xiàwǔ zuò shénme
   qù dǎ qiú/qù tiào wǔ
2. 明天晚上做什么
   去商店买东西/去朋友家聊天儿
   míngtiān wǎnshang zuò shénme
   qù shāngdiàn mǎi dōngxi/qù péngyou jiā liáo tiānr
3. 这个周末怎么去机场
   坐地铁/打车
   zhège zhōumò zěnme qù jīchǎng
   zuò dìtiě/dǎ chē
4. 喝什么茶
   中国茶/英国茶
   hē shénme chá
   Zhōngguó chá/Yīngguó chá
5. 买什么颜色的车
   蓝的/黑的
   mǎi shénme yánsè de chē
   lán de/hēi de

C. 先…再…(xiān...zài...)

Let's practice how to place two actions in order.

→ 我先吃早饭，再去图书馆学习。 Wǒ xiān chī zǎofàn, zài qù túshūguǎn xuéxí.

D. 还是…吧 (háishi...ba)

With a partner, practice persuading each other to accept an alternative.

EXAMPLE: 听音乐◇复习生词语法 — tīng yīnyuè ◇ fùxí shēngcí yǔfǎ

→ **A:** 我们听音乐，好吗？ → **A:** Wǒmen tīng yīnyuè, hǎo ma?

B: 我们还是复习生词语法吧。 **B:** Wǒmen háishi fùxí shēngcí yǔfǎ ba.

1. 坐地铁去机场◇开车 — zuò dìtiě qù jīchǎng ◇ kāi chē
2. 坐公共汽车去买东西◇打车 — zuò gōnggòng qìchē qù mǎi dōngxi ◇ dǎ chē
3. 刷卡◇别用信用卡 — shuā kǎ ◇ bié yòng xìnyòngkǎ
4. 买黑色的衬衫◇买红色的 — mǎi hēisè de chènshān ◇ mǎi hóngsè de
5. 学中文专业◇学电脑专业 — xué Zhōngwén zhuānyè ◇ xué diànnǎo zhuānyè

E. Take turns directing your friend to...

1. Mr. Wang's office: Take the subway – the Red Line. Get off after 5 stops.

2. Mary's house: Take Bus #5. Get off after 4 stops. Then change to the subway. Take the Green Line first and then switch to the Red Line. Get off after 6 stops.

3. Mark's school: Take Bus # 29. Get off after 6 stops. Then switch to the subway. Take the Red Line first and then switch to the Blue Line. Get off after 3 stops.

This is a sign found at a bus stop. Can you locate the words meaning "getting on" and "getting off"?

An Email: Thanking Someone for a Ride

电子邮件❶

Date: 2008年12月20日

From: 李友

To: 王朋

Subject: 谢谢！

王朋：

谢谢你那天开车送我到机场。不过，让你花那么多时间，真不好意思。我这几天每天都⑤开车出去看老朋友。这个城市的人开车开得特别快。我在高速公路上开车，真有点儿紧张。可是这儿没

LANGUAGE NOTE

❶ The Chinese word for email, 电子邮件 (diànzǐ yóujiàn), literally means electronic mail. It is sometimes abbreviated as 电邮 (diàn yóu). More informal Chinese terms for email include 伊妹儿 (yīmèiér) and 伊媚儿 (yīmèiér); both are facetious transliterations of "email."

有公共汽车，也没有地铁，只能自己开车，很不方便。

有空儿的话打我的手机或者给我发短信，我想跟你聊天儿。

新年快要到了⑥，祝你新年快乐！

李友

Diànzǐ yóujiàn❶

Date: 2008 nián 12 yuè 20 rì

From: Lǐ Yǒu

To: Wáng Péng

Subject: Xièxie!

Wáng Péng:

Xièxie nǐ nà tiān kāi chē sòng wǒ dào jīchǎng. Búguò, ràng nǐ huā nàme duō shíjiān, zhēn bù hǎoyìsi. Wǒ zhè jǐ tiān měi tiān dōu⑤ kāi chē chūqu kàn lǎo péngyou. Zhè ge chéngshì de rén kāi chē kāi de tèbié kuài. Wǒ zài gāosù gōnglù shang kāi chē, zhēn yǒudiǎn(r) jǐnzhāng. Kěshì zhèr méiyǒu gōnggòng qìchē, yě méiyǒu dìtiě, zhǐ néng zìjǐ kāi chē, hěn bù fāngbiàn.

Yǒu kòngr de huà dǎ wǒ de shǒujī huòzhě gěi wǒ fā duǎnxìn, wǒ xiǎng gēn nǐ liáo tiānr.

Xīnnián kuài yào dào le⑥, zhù nǐ xīnnián kuàilè!

Lǐ Yǒu

VOCABULARY

1.	电子邮件	diànzǐ yóujiàn	n	email
	电子	diànzǐ	n	electron
2.	让	ràng	v	to allow or cause (somebody to do something)
3.	花	huā	v	to spend
4.	不好意思	bù hǎoyìsi		to feel embarrassed
5.	每	měi	pr	every; each [See Grammar 5.]
6.	城市	chéngshì	n	city
7.	特别	tèbié	adv	especially
8.	高速公路	gāosù gōnglù	n	highway
	高速	gāosù	adj	high speed
	公路	gōnglù	n	highway; public road
	路	lù	n	road; path
9.	紧张	jǐnzhāng	adj	nervous, anxious
10.	自己	zìjǐ	pr	oneself
11.	手机	shǒujī	n	cell phone
12.	发短信	fā duǎnxìn	vo	to send a text message; (lit.) to send a short message
13.	新年	xīnnián	n	new year
14.	快乐	kuàilè	adj	happy

中国的一个城市
Zhōngguó de yí ge chéngshì

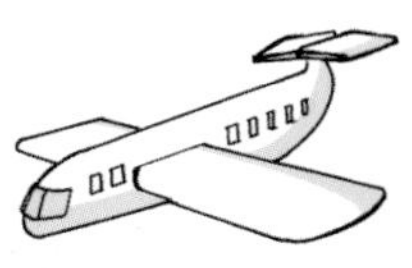

Describe the modes of transportation above.

Grammar

5. 每…都… (měi...dōu..., every)

In a sentence that contains the term 每 (měi, every), usually 都 (dōu, all) has to be inserted further along in the sentence, immediately in front of the verb.

❶ 他每天晚上都预习课文。

Tā měi tiān wǎnshang dōu yùxí kèwén.

(He studies the lessons in advance every night.)

❷ 我每节课都来。

Wǒ měi jié kè dōu lái.

(I come to every class.)

❸ 这儿每个人我都认识。

Zhèr měi ge rén wǒ dōu rènshi.

(I know everyone here.)

❹ 常老师的字每个都好看。

Cháng lǎoshī de zì měi ge dōu hǎokàn.

(Every one of Teacher Chang's characters looks nice.)

6. 要…了 (yào...le, soon)

The 要…了 (yào...le) structure indicates the imminence of an anticipated action or situation. It also appears in the form of 快要……了 (kuài yào...le).

❶ 新年快要到了，我们给爸爸妈妈写一封信吧。

Xīnnián kuài yào dào le, wǒmen gěi bàba māma xiě yì fēng xìn ba.

(New Year is around the corner. Let's write to Mom and Dad.)

❷ 寒假要到了，你要做什么？

Hánjià yào dào le, nǐ yào zuò shénme?

(It'll be winter break soon. What do you want to do?)

❸ 电影快要开始了，你买票了吗？

Diànyǐng kuài yào kāishǐ le, nǐ mǎi piào le ma?

(The movie is going to start soon. Did you get the tickets?)

❹ 快要考试了，我们大家得准备一下。

Kuài yào kǎo shì le, wǒmen dàjiā děi zhǔnbèi yí xià.

(The exam is coming. We have to study for it.)

Language Practice

F. 每…都 (měi…dōu…, **every**)

Look at the words given, and tell each other how predictable Little Bai is.

EXAMPLE: 晚上 ◇ 复习生词语法 EXAMPLE: wǎnshang ◇ fùxí shēngcí yǔfǎ

→ 小白每天晚上都复习生词语法。 → Xiǎo Bái měi tiān wǎnshang dōu fùxí shēngcí yǔfǎ.

1. 早上 ◇ 洗澡
2. 衬衫 ◇ 是白色的
3. 裤子 ◇ 是三十二号的
4. 周末 ◇ 去商店买东西
5. 寒假 ◇ 坐飞机回家

1. zǎoshang ◇ xǐ zǎo
2. chènshān ◇ shì báisè de
3. kùzi ◇ shì sānshíèr hào de
4. zhōumò ◇ qù shāngdiàn mǎi dōngxi
5. hánjià ◇ zuò fēijī huí jiā

G. Pair Activity

Is your partner a good driver? Find out!

你会开车吗？	Nǐ huì kāi chē ma?
你每天都开车吗？	Nǐ měitiān dōu kāi chē ma?
你开车开得快不快？	Nǐ kāi chē kāi de kuài bu kuài?
在高速公路上开车让你紧张吗？	Zài gāosù gōnglù shang kāi chē ràng nǐ jǐnzhāng ma?

HOW ABOUT YOU?

How do you get around?

1.	走路	zǒu lù	vo	to walk
2.	坐火车	zuò huǒchē	vo	to travel by train
3.	坐计程车	zuò jìchéngchē	vo	to take a taxi (in Taiwan)
4.	坐电车	zuò diànchē	vo	to take a cable car, trolley bus, or tram
5.	坐船	zuò chuán	vo	to travel by ship; to take a boat
6.	骑自行车	qí zìxíngchē	vo	to ride a bicycle
7.	骑摩托车	qí mótuōchē	vo	to ride a motorcycle

If the means of transportation of your choice is not listed above, ask your teacher and make a note here: ________________

Culture Highlights

1. Many taxi drivers in China, especially those in Beijing, are known to be very outgoing and talkative. If you go to China and your taxi driver happens to be a chatty one, it may be a good opportunity for you to learn about ordinary Chinese people's lives and their opinions on current affairs.

What kind of tickets do they sell here?

2. In China the railroad system has long constituted the principal means of travel and of transport in general. However, in recent years both the highway system and airline travel have expanded very rapidly. China now ranks second only to the United States in total miles of roadway in the highway system.

3. Chinese New Year, also known as 春节 (Chūnjié, Spring Festival), is the most important annual holiday in Chinese communities. It is determined by the lunar calendar and usually falls in late January or early February on the international solar calendar. However, nowadays the January 1 international New Year is also recognized. The most common New Year greetings are 新年好 (xīnnián hǎo) and 新年快乐 (xīnnián kuàilè), which can be used for both New Years, but for the Chinese New Year many people prefer the traditional greeting: 恭喜发财 (gōngxǐ fā cái). The phrase, which literally means "Congratulations and may you make a fortune," can be translated as "May you be happy and prosperous!"

大驾光临 请喝迎驾酒
迎驾集团
迎驾

English Text

Dialogue

Wang Peng: Are you going home during the winter break?
Li You: Yes, I am.
Wang Peng: Have you booked a plane ticket?
Li You: Yes, for the twenty-first.
Wang Peng: When is the plane leaving?
Li You: 8 p.m.
Wang Peng: How are you going to the airport?
Li You: I'm thinking of taking the bus or the subway. Do you know how to get there?
Wang Peng: You first take Bus No. 1. Get off after three stops. Then take the subway. First take the red line, then change to the green line, and finally change to the blue line.
Li You: Oh no. That's too much trouble. I'd better take a cab.
Wang Peng: It's too expensive to take a cab. I'll take you to the airport.
Li You: Thanks so much.
Wang Peng: Don't mention it.

An Email

Date: December 20, 2008
From: Li You
To: Wang Peng
Subject: Thank you

Wang Peng:
Thank you for driving me to the airport the other day. But I feel very bad for taking up so much of your time. The past few days I've been going out by car to see old friends. People in this city drive very fast. I am really nervous driving on the highway. But there are no buses or subway here. I have to drive. It's very inconvenient.
When you have time, please call my cell phone or send me a text message. I'd like to chat with you.
New Year is almost here. Happy New Year!

Li You

PROGRESS CHECKLIST

Before proceeding to Lesson 11, be sure you can complete the following tasks in Chinese:

I am able to—

- ☑ Speak about all common means of transportation;
- ☑ Discuss the most/least convenient way to get to a destination;
- ☑ Say if someone's driving makes me nervous;
- ☑ Thank someone for a favor;
- ☑ Extend New Year's greetings, both orally and in writing.

Please review the lesson if any of these tasks seem difficult.

That's How the Chinese Say It!

A Review of Functional Expressions from Lessons 6–10

After gauging your progress and before moving on to the next phase, let's take a break and see how some of the functional expressions that you have encountered really work!

I. 喂 (**wéi,** hello) [on the telephone] (Lesson 6)

This is how one starts a conversation on the telephone.

❶ A: 喂，哪位？

Wéi. Nǎ wèi?

(Hello! May I ask who's calling?)

B: 我是王朋。请问，李友在吗？

Wǒ shì Wáng Péng. Qǐng wèn, Lǐ Yǒu zài ma?

(This is Wang Peng. Is Li You there, please?)

A: 在，你等等，我去叫她。

Zài, nǐ děng deng, wǒ qù jiào tā.

(Yes. Wait a moment. I'll go get her.)

❷ A: 喂，你找谁？

Wéi, nǐ zhǎo shéi?

(Hello! Whom would you like to speak to?)

B: 我找小李。

Wǒ zhǎo Xiǎo Lǐ.

(I'd like to speak to Little Li.)

A: 我就是。你是哪位？

Wǒ jiù shì. Nǐ shì nǎ wèi?

(This is she. Who is this?)

B: 我是常老师。

Wǒ shì Cháng lǎoshī.

(This is Teacher Chang.)

❸ A: 喂，请问小王在吗？

Wéi, qǐng wèn Xiǎo Wáng zài ma?

(Is Little Wang there, please?)

B: 在，你是哪位？

Zài, nǐ shì nǎ wèi?

(Yes, he is. Who is this, please?)

A: 我是小李。

Wǒ shì Xiǎo Lǐ.

(This is Little Li.)

B: 好，请等一下。

Hǎo, qǐng děng yí xià.

(OK. Wait a second, please.)

II. 没问题 (**méi wèntí,** no problem) (Lesson 6)

You say this to put someone at ease that you will agree to do something that you've been asked to do, or you can say this to assure someone that there is no need to worry.

❶ 李友：王朋，你今天晚上帮我练习中文，好吗？

Lǐ Yǒu: Wáng Péng, nǐ jīntiān wǎnshang bāng wǒ liànxí Zhōngwén, hǎo ma?

(Li You: Wang Peng, would you help me practice Chinese this evening?)

王朋：没问题。晚上见。

Wáng Péng: Méi wèntí. Wǎnshang jiàn.

(Wang Peng: No problem. See you this evening.)

❷ A: 你给我介绍女朋友，好吗？

Nǐ gěi wǒ jièshào nǚpéngyou, hǎo ma?

(Can you find me a girlfriend?)

B: 没问题。

Méi wèntí.

(No problem.)

❸ A: 你下午有空儿帮我准备考试吗？要是你没时间，就算了。

Nǐ xiàwǔ yǒu kòngr bāng wǒ zhǔnbèi kǎoshì ma? Yàoshi nǐ méi shíjiān, jiù suàn le.

(Do you have time this afternoon to help me prepare for my test? Never mind if you are busy.)

B: 没问题，我有空儿。

Méi wèntí, wǒ yǒu kòngr.

(Don't worry, I have time.)

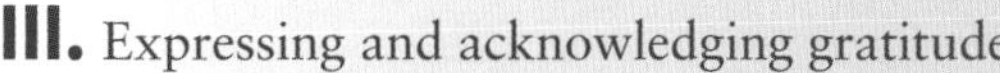

III. Expressing and acknowledging gratitude

❶ A: 小李，你的电话。

Xiǎo Lǐ, nǐ de diànhuà.

(Little Li, the call is for you.)

B: 谢谢！

Xièxie!

(Thanks!)

A: 不客气。

Bú kèqi.

(You're welcome.)

❷ A: 小高，请喝茶。

Xiǎo Gāo, qǐng hē chá.

(Please have some tea, Little Gao.)

B: 多谢！

Duō xiè.

(Thanks a lot.)

A: 不谢。

Bú xiè.

(No need to thank [me].)

❸ A: 王小姐，这是你的可乐。

Wáng xiǎojiě, zhè shì nǐ de kělè.

(Miss Wang, this is your cola.)

B: 谢谢！

Xièxie!

(Thanks!)

A: 没事儿。

Méi shìr.

(It's no big deal.)

❹ A: 白医生，你的书。

Bái Yīshēng, nǐ de shū.

(Dr. Bai, your book.)

B: 谢了。

Xiè le.

(Thanks.)

A: 不用谢。

Búyòng xiè.

(No need to thank [me].)

IV. 哪里，哪里 (**nǎli, nǎli,** you flatter me) or 是吗？(**shì ma,** Is that so?)

(Lesson 7)

When receiving a compliment, the Chinese often respond modestly that they are unworthy of the praise by using 哪里 (nǎli) or 是吗 (shì ma). But now some people will say 谢谢 (xièxie) instead.

❶ A: 你今天很漂亮。

Nǐ jīntiān hěn piàoliang.

(You are very pretty today.)

B: 哪里，哪里。

Nǎli, nǎli.

(You flatter me.)

❷ A: 你写汉字写得很漂亮。

Nǐ xiě Hànzì xiě de hěn piàoliang.

(You write Chinese characters beautifully.)

B: 哪里，写得不好。

Nǎli, xiě de bù hǎo.

(I wish that were true. My writing is not good.)

❸ A: 你说中文说得真好！

Nǐ shuō Zhōngwén shuō de zhēn hǎo!

(You speak Chinese really well!)

B: 是吗？我觉得我说得不好。

Shì ma? Wǒ juéde wǒ shuō de bù hǎo.

(Is that right? I don't think I speak very well.)

V. 就是它吧/就是他/她了 (Jiù shì tā ba/Jiù shì tā le, Let's go with that) (Lesson 9)

When you're finally making your choice, you can say 就是它吧 (Jiù shì tā ba) or 就是他/她了 (Jiù shì tā le) meaning "let's go with that" or "we'll go with him/her".

❶ A: 先生，你知道要哪一双了吗？

Xiānsheng, nǐ zhīdao yào nǎ yì shuāng le ma?

(Sir, do you know which pair you'd like?)

B: 就是它吧。

Jiù shì tā ba.

(I think I'll take that.)

❷ A: 王老師，小李打球打得不太好，你找别人跟你一起练习吧。

Wáng lǎoshī, Xiǎo Lǐ dǎ qiú dǎ de bú tài hǎo, nǐ zhǎo biérén gēn nǐ yìqǐ liànxí ba.

(Teacher Wang, Little Li is not a very good ball player. Why don't you find someone else to practice with?)

B: 就是他了。别人都没空儿。

Jiù shì tā le. Biérén dōu méi kòngr.

(We'll have to go with him. The others are all busy.)

VI. You can use 祝 **(zhù)** to offer good wishes. (Lesson 10)

❶ 祝你新年快乐！

Zhù nǐ xīnnián kuàilè!

(I wish you a happy New Year!)

❷ 祝你生日快乐！

Zhù nǐ shēngrì kuàilè!

(Happy Birthday to you!)

❸ 祝你考试考得好！

Zhù nǐ kǎoshì kǎo de hǎo!

(I wish you success on the exam!)

❹ 祝寒假快乐！

Zhù hánjià kuàilè!

(Have a happy winter break!)

❺ 祝感恩节快乐！

Zhù Gǎn'ēnjié kuàilè!

(Happy Thanksgiving!)

❻ 祝春节快乐！

Zhù Chūnjié kuàilè!

(Happy Chinese New Year!)

❼ 祝一路平安！

Zhù yí lù píng'ān!

(Have a safe trip!)

❽ 祝旅途愉快！

Zhù lǚtú yúkuài!

(Bon voyage!)

Any other useful expressions you would like to learn?

Please ask your teacher and make a note here:

Vocabulary Index (Chinese-English)

The Chinese-English index is alphabetized according to *pinyin*. Words containing the same Chinese characters are first grouped together. Homonyms appear in the order of their tonal pronunciation (i.e., first tones first, second tones second, third tones third, fourth tones fourth, and neutral tones last). Proper nouns from the dialogues and readings are shown in green. Supplementary vocabulary from the "How About You?" section is shown in blue.

Characters	Pinyin	Part of Speech	English	Lesson
A				
啊	a	p	(a sentence-final particle)	6
B				
爸爸	bàba	n	father, dad	2
吧	ba	p	(a sentence-final particle)	5
白英爱	Bái Yīng'ài	pn	(a personal name)	2
百	bǎi	nu	hundred	9
百事可乐	Bǎishìkělè	pn	Pepsi-Cola	5
半	bàn	nu	half; half an hour	3
办公室	bàngōngshì	n	office	6
帮	bāng	v	to help	6
杯	bēi	m	(measure word for cup and glass)	5
北京	Běijīng	pn	Beijing	1
本子	běnzi	n	notebook	7
笔	bǐ	n	pen	7
别	bié	adv	don't	6
别人	biérén	n	other people; another person	4
不	bù	adv	not; no	1
不错	búcuò	adj	pretty good	4
不过	búguò	conj	however; but	9
不好意思	bù hǎoyìsi		to feel embarrassed	10
不用	búyòng		need not	9
C				
才	cái	adv	not until, only then	5
菜	cài	n	dishes, cuisine	3

Characters	Pinyin	Part of Speech	English	Lesson
餐厅	cāntīng	n	dining room, cafeteria	8
茶	chá	n	tea	5
常常	chángcháng	adv	often	4
常老师	Cháng lǎoshī	pn	Teacher Chang	6
长短	chángduǎn	n	length	9
唱歌（儿）	chàng gē(r)	vo	to sing (a song)	4
衬衫	chènshān	n	shirt	9
城市	chéngshì	n	city	10
吃	chī	v	to eat	3
除了... 以外	chúle...yǐwài	conj	in addition to; besides	8
出租汽车	chūzū qìchē	n	taxi	10
穿	chuān	v	to wear; to put on	9
D				
打车	dǎ chē	vo	to take a taxi	10
打电话	dǎ diànhuà	vo	to make a phone call	6
打球	dǎ qiú	vo	to play ball	4
大	dà	adj	big; old	3
大哥	dàgē	n	eldest brother	2
大家	dàjiā	pr	everybody	7
大姐	dàjiě	n	eldest sister	2
大小	dàxiǎo	n	size	9
大学生	dàxuéshēng	n	college student	2
大衣	dàyī	n	overcoat	9
但是	dànshì	conj	but	6
到	dào	v	to go to; to arrive	6
德国	Déguó	pn	Germany	1
德文	Déwén	pn	the German language	6
的	de	p	(a possessive or descriptive particle)	2
得	de	p	(a structural particle)	7
得	děi	mv	must; to have to	6
等	děng	v	to wait; to wait for	6
第	dì	prefix	(prefix for ordinal numbers)	7
弟弟	dìdi	n	younger brother	2

Characters	Pinyin	Part of Speech	English	Lesson
地铁	dìtiě	n	subway	10
点	diǎn	m	o'clock (lit. dot, point, thus "points on the clock")	3
点(儿)	diǎn(r)	m	a little, a bit; some	5
电脑	diànnǎo	n	computer	8
电视	diànshì	n	television	4
电影	diànyǐng	n	movie	4
电子邮件	diànzǐ yóujiàn	n	email	10
东西	dōngxi	n	things; objects	9
懂	dǒng	v	to understand	7
都	dōu	adv	both; all	2
对	duì	adj	right; correct	4
对不起	duìbuqǐ	v	sorry	5
多	duō	adv	how many/much; to what extent	3
多	duō	adj	many; much	7
多少	duōshao	qpr	how much/many	9
E				
俄文	Éwén	pn	the Russian language	6
儿子	érzi	n	son	2
二姐	èrjiě	n	second oldest sister	2
F				
发短信	fā duǎnxìn	vo	to send a text message; (lit.) to send a short message	10
发音	fāyīn	n	pronunciation	8
法国	Fǎguó	pn	France	1
法文	Fǎwén	pn	the French language	6
饭	fàn	n	meal; (cooked) rice	3
方便	fāngbiàn	adj	convenient	6
飞机	fēijī	n	airplane	10
(飞)机场	(fēi)jīchǎng	n	airport	10
分	fēn	m	(measure word for 1/100 of a kuai, cent)	9
粉红色	fěnhóngsè	n	pink	9

Characters	Pinyin	Part of Speech	English	Lesson
封	fēng	m	(measure word for letters)	8
付钱	fù qián	vo	to pay money	9
父亲节	Fùqīnjié	pn	Father's Day	3
复习	fùxí	v	to review	7
G				
感恩节	Găn'ēnjié	pn	Thanksgiving	3
钢笔	gāngbĭ	n	fountain pen	7
高速公路	gāosù gōnglù	n	highway	10
高文中	Gāo Wénzhōng	pn	(a personal name)	2
高小音	Gāo Xiăoyīn	pn	(a personal name)	5
高兴	gāoxìng	adj	happy, pleased	5
告诉	gàosu	v	to tell	8
哥哥	gēge	n	older brother	2
个	gè/ge	m	(a measure word for many common everyday objects)	2
给	gěi	v	to give	5
给	gěi	prep	to; for	6
跟	gēn	prep	with	6
公共汽车	gōnggòng qìchē	n	bus	10
工程师	gōngchéngshī	n	engineer	2
工人	gōngrén	n	worker	2
工商管理	gōngshāng guănlĭ	n	business management	8
工作	gōngzuò	n/v	job; to work	2
功课	gōngkè	n	homework; schoolwork	7
逛街	guàng jiē	vo	to windowshop	4
贵	guì	adj	honorable; expensive	1
果汁	guŏzhī	n	fruit juice	5
H				
还	hái	adv	also; too; as well	3
还是	háishi	conj	or	3
孩子	háizi	n	child	2
韩国	Hánguó	pn	South Korea	1

Characters	Pinyin	Part of Speech	English	Lesson
韩文	Hánwén	pn	the Korean language	6
寒假	hánjià	n	winter vacation	10
汉字	Hànzì	n	Chinese characters	7
好	hǎo	adj	fine; good; nice; O.K.; it's settled	1
好久	hǎo jiǔ		a long time	4
号	hào	m	(measure word for number in a series; day of the month)	3
号	hào	n	size	9
喝	hē	v	to drink	5
和	hé	conj	and	2
合适	héshì	adj	suitable	9
黑	hēi	adj	black	9
很	hěn	adv	very	3
红	hóng	adj	red	9
后来	hòulái	t	later	8
护士	hùshi	n	nurse	2
花	huā	v	to spend	10
画画儿	huà huàr	vo	to draw; to paint	4
化学	huàxué	n	chemistry	8
换	huàn	v	to exchange; to change	9
黄	huáng	adj	yellow	9
灰色	huīsè	n	gray	9
回家	huí jiā	vo	to go home	5
回来	huí lai	vc	to come back	6
会	huì	mv	can; know how to	8
或者	huòzhě	conj	or	10
J				
几	jǐ	nu	how many; some; a few	2
家	jiā	n	family; home	2
加拿大	Jiā'nádà	pn	Canada	1
加州	Jiāzhōu	pn	California	1
夹克	jiákè	n	jacket	9
件	jiàn	m	(measure word for shirts, dresses, jackets, coats, etc.)	9

Characters	Pinyin	Part of Speech	English	Lesson
见	jiàn	v	to see	3
见面	jiàn miàn	vo	to meet up; to meet with	6
教	jiāo	v	to teach	7
教室	jiàoshì	n	classroom	8
教授	jiàoshòu	n	professor	2
叫	jiào	v	to be called; to call	1
节	jié	m	(measure word for class periods)	6
姐姐	jiějie	n	older sister	2
介绍	jièshào	v	to introduce	5
今年	jīnnián	t	this year	3
今天	jīntiān	t	today	3
紧张	jǐnzhāng	adj	nervous, anxious	10
进	jìn	v	to enter	5
进来	jìn lai	vc	to come in	5
经济	jīngjì	n	economics	8
经理	jīnglǐ	n	manager	2
九月	jiǔyuè	n	September	3
就	jiù	adv	precisely; exactly	6
橘红色	júhóngsè	n	orange (color)	9
觉得	juéde	v	to feel; to think	4
军人	jūnrén	n	soldier; military officer	2
K				
咖啡	kāfēi	n	coffee	5
咖啡色	kāfēisè	n	brown; coffee color	9
开车	kāi chē	vo	to drive a car	10
开会	kāi huì	vo	to have a meeting	6
开始	kāishǐ	v/n	to begin, to start; beginning	7
看	kàn	v	to watch; to look; to read	4
考试	kǎo shì	vo/n	to give or take a test; test	6
可口可乐	Kěkǒukělè	pn	Coca-Cola	5
可乐	kělè	n	[Coke or Pepsi] cola	5
可是	kěshì	conj	but	3
可以	kěyǐ	mv	can; may	5

Characters	Pinyin	Part of Speech	English	Lesson
刻	kè	m	quarter (of an hour)	3
课	kè	n	class; course; lesson	6
课本	kèběn	n	textbook	7
课文	kèwén	n	text of a lesson	7
客气	kèqi	adj	polite	6
空(儿)	kòng(r)	n	free time	6
口	kǒu	m	(measure word for number of family members)	2
酷	kù	adj	cool	7
裤子	kùzi	n	pants	9
快	kuài	adv/adj	quickly; fast, quick	5
快乐	kuàilè	adj	happy	10
块	kuài	m	(measure word for the basic Chinese monetary unit)	9
矿泉水	kuàngquánshuǐ	n	mineral water	5
L				
拉丁文	Lādīngwén	pn	the Latin language	6
来	lái	v	to come	5
蓝	lán	adj	blue	10
老师	lǎoshī	n	teacher	1
了	le	p	(a dynamic particle)	5
累	lèi	adj	tired	8
李友	Lǐ Yǒu	pn	(a personal name)	1
历史	lìshǐ	n	history	8
练习	liànxí	v	to practice	6
练习本	liànxíběn	n	exercise book	7
两	liǎng	nu	two; a couple of	2
聊天(儿)	liáo tiān(r)	vo	to chat	5
录音	lùyīn	n/vo	sound recording; to record	7
绿	lǜ	adj	green	10
律师	lǜshī	n	lawyer	2
M				
妈妈	māma	n	mother, mom	2
吗	ma	qp	(question particle)	1

Characters	Pinyin	Part of Speech	English	Lesson
麻烦	máfan	adj	troublesome	10
买	mǎi	v	to buy	9
慢	màn	adj	slow	7
忙	máng	adj	busy	3
毛	máo	m	(measure word for 1/10 of a kuai, dime (for US money))	9
毛笔	máobǐ	n	writing brush	7
毛衣	máoyī	n	woolen sweater	9
帽子	màozi	n	hat; cap	9
没	méi	adv	not	2
每	měi	pr	every; each	10
美国	Měiguó	pn	America	1
妹妹	mèimei	n	younger sister	2
明天	míngtiān	t	tomorrow	3
名字	míngzi	n	name	1
墨西哥	Mòxīgē	pn	Mexico	1
母亲节	Mǔqīnjié	pn	Mother's Day	3
N				
哪	nǎ/něi	qpr	which	6
哪里	nǎli	pr	where	7
哪儿	nǎr	qpr	where	5
那	nà	pr	that	2
那	nà	conj	in that case; then	4
那儿	nàr	pr	there	8
男	nán	adj	male	2
难	nán	adj	difficult	7
呢	ne	qp	(question particle)	1
能	néng	mv	can; to be able to	8
你	nǐ	pr	you	1
年级	niánjí	n	grade in school	6
念	niàn	v	to read aloud	7
您	nín	pr	you (honorific for)	6
纽约	Niǔyuē	pn	New York	1

Characters	Pinyin	Part of Speech	English	Lesson
农民	nóngmín	n	farmer; peasant	2
女	nǚ	adj	female	2
女儿	nǚ'ér	n	daughter	2
P				
朋友	péngyou	n	friend	3
篇	piān	m	(measure word for essays, articles, etc.)	8
便宜	piányi	adj	cheap; inexpensive	9
票	piào	n	ticket	10
漂亮	piàoliang	adj	pretty	5
瓶	píng	m/n	(measure word for bottles); bottle	5
平常	píngcháng	adv	usually	7
葡萄牙文	Pútáoyáwén	pn	the Portuguese language	6
Q				
骑摩托车	qí mótuōchē	vo	to ride a motorcycle	10
骑自行车	qí zìxíngchē	vo	to ride a bicycle	10
起床	qǐ chuáng	vo	to get up	8
汽水(儿)	qìshuǐ(r)	n	soft drink; soda pop	5
铅笔	qiānbǐ	n	pencil	7
钱	qián	n	money	9
情人节	Qíngrénjié	pn	Valentine's Day	3
请	qǐng	v	please (polite form of request); to treat or to invite (somebody)	1
请客	qǐng kè	vo	to invite someone (to dinner, coffee, etc.); to play the host	4
去	qù	v	to go	4
裙子	qúnzi	n	skirt	9
R				
然后	ránhòu	adv	then	10
让	ràng	v	to allow or cause (somebody to do something)	10

Characters	Pinyin	Part of Speech	English	Lesson
人	rén	n	people; person	1
认识	rènshi	v	to be acquainted with; recognize	3
日本	Rìběn	pn	Japan	1
日记	rìjì	n	diary	8
日文	Rìwén	pn	the Japanese language	6
容易	róngyì	adj	easy	7
如果…的话	rúguǒ... de huà	conj	if	9
S				
商店	shāngdiàn	n	store; shop	9
商人	shāngrén	n	merchant; businessperson	2
上个	shàng ge		the previous one	7
上海	Shànghǎi	pn	Shanghai	1
上课	shàng kè	vo	to go to a class; to start a class; to be in class	7
上网	shàng wǎng	vo	to go online; to surf the internet	8
上午	shàngwǔ	t	morning	6
上衣	shàngyī	n	upper garment	9
谁	shéi	qpr	who	2
什么	shénme	qpr	what	1
生词	shēngcí	n	new words; vocabulary	7
生日	shēngrì	n	birthday	3
十八	shíbā	nu	eighteen	3
十二	shí'èr	nu	twelve	3
时候	shíhou	n	(a point in) time; moment; (a duration of) time	4
时间	shíjiān	n	time	6
试	shì	v	to try	9
是	shì	v	to be	1
事（儿）	shì(r)	n	matter; affair; event	3
收	shōu	v	to receive; to accept	9
手机	shǒujī	n	cell phone	10
售货员	shòuhuòyuán	n	shop assistant; salesclerk	9
书	shū	n	book	4

Characters	Pinyin	Part of Speech	English	Lesson
数学	shùxué	n	mathematics	8
刷卡	shuā kǎ	vo	to pay with a credit card	9
帅	shuài	adj	handsome	7
双	shuāng	m	(measure word for a pair)	9
水	shuǐ	n	water	5
睡觉	shuì jiào	vo	to sleep	4
说	shuō	v	to say; to speak	6
说话	shuō huà	vo	to talk	7
送	sòng	v	to see off or out; to take (someone somewhere)	10
宿舍	sùshè	n	dormitory	8
算了	suàn le		forget it; never mind	4
虽然	suīrán	conj	although	9
岁	suì	n	year (of age)	3
所以	suǒyǐ	conj	so	4
T				
T恤衫	T-xùshān	n	T-shirt	9
他	tā	pr	he; him	2
她	tā	pr	she; her	2
它	tā	pr	it	9
太...了	tài...le		too; extremely	3
特别	tèbié	adv	especially	10
天	tiān	n	day	3
条	tiáo	m	(measure word for pants and long, thin objects)	9
跳舞	tiào wǔ	vo	to dance	4
听	tīng	v	to listen	4
挺	tǐng	adv	very; rather	9
同学	tóngxué	n	classmate	3
图书馆	túshūguǎn	n	library	5
W				
袜子	wàzi	n	socks	9
外国	wàiguó	n	foreign country	4

Characters	Pinyin	Part of Speech	English	Lesson
外套	wàitào	n	outer garment; coat; jacket	9
玩(儿)	wán(r)	v	to have fun; to play	5
玩游戏机	wán yóuxìjī	vo	to play videogames	4
晚	wǎn	adj	late	7
晚饭	wǎnfàn	n	dinner; supper	3
晚上	wǎnshang	t/n	evening; night	3
王朋	Wáng Péng	pn	(a personal name)	1
喂	wéi/wèi	interj	(on telephone) Hello!; Hey!	6
位	wèi	m	(polite measure word for people)	6
为什么	wèishénme	qpr	why	3
问	wèn	v	to ask (a question)	1
问题	wèntí	n	question; problem	6
我	wǒ	pr	I; me	1
我们	wǒmen	pr	we	3
午饭	wǔfàn	n	lunch, midday meal	8
物理	wùlǐ	n	physics	8
X				
西班牙文	Xībānyáwén	pn	the Spanish language	6
西装	xīzhuāng	n	(western-style) suit	9
希腊文	Xīlàwén	pn	the Greek language	6
希望	xīwàng	v/n	to hope; hope	8
喜欢	xǐhuan	v	to like	3
洗澡	xǐ zǎo	vo	to take a bath/shower	8
下车	xià chē	vo	to get off (a bus, train, etc.)	10
下个	xià ge		next one	6
下棋	xià qí	vo	to play chess	4
下午	xiàwǔ	t	afternoon	6
夏威夷	Xiàwēiyí	pn	Hawaii	1
先	xiān	adv	first	10
先生	xiānsheng	n	Mr.; husband; teacher	1
线	xiàn	n	line	10
现在	xiànzài	t	now	3
想	xiǎng	mv	to want to; would like to; to think	4

Characters	Pinyin	Part of Speech	English	Lesson
小	xiǎo	adj	small; little	4
小姐	xiǎojiě	n	Miss; young lady	1
笑	xiào	v	to laugh at; to laugh; to smile	8
鞋	xié	n	shoes	9
写	xiě	v	to write	7
谢谢	xièxie	v	to thank	3
新	xīn	adj	new	8
新年	xīnnián	n	new year	10
信	xìn	n	letter (correspondence)	8
信用卡	xìnyòngkǎ	n	credit card	9
星期	xīngqī	n	week	3
星期四	xīngqīsì	n	Thursday	3
行	xíng	v	all right; O.K.	6
姓	xìng	v/n	(one's) surname is...; to be surnamed; surname	1
学	xué	v	to study; to learn	7
学期	xuéqī	n	school term; semester/quarter	8
学生	xuésheng	n	student	1
学习	xuéxí	v	to study; to learn	7
学校	xuéxiào	n	school	5
雪碧	Xuěbì	pn	Sprite	5
Y				
呀	ya	p	(interjectory particle used to soften a question)	5
亚洲研究	Yàzhōu yánjiū	n	Asian studies	8
颜色	yánsè	n	color	9
样子	yàngzi	n	style	9
要	yào	v	to want	5
要	yào	mv	will, to be going to; to want to, to have a desire to	6
要是	yàoshi	conj	if	6
也	yě	adv	too; also	1
一边	yìbiān	adv	simultaneously; at the same time	8
一共	yígòng	adv	altogether	9

Characters	Pinyin	Part of Speech	English	Lesson
一起	yìqǐ	adv	together	5
一下	yí xià	n+m	once; a bit	5
一样	yíyàng	adj	same; alike	9
衣服	yīfu	n	clothes	9
医生	yīshēng	n	doctor; physician	2
以后	yǐhòu	t	after	6
以前	yǐqián	t	before	8
已经	yǐjīng	adv	already	8
意大利文	Yìdàlìwén	pn	the Italian language	6
因为	yīnwèi	conj	because	3
音乐	yīnyuè	n	music	4
音乐会	yīnyuèhuì	n	concert	8
印度	Yìndù	pn	India	1
英国	Yīngguó	pn	Britain; England	3
英文	Yīngwén	pn	English (language)	2
用	yòng	v	to use	8
有	yǒu	v	to have; to exist	2
有的	yǒude	pr	some	4
有意思	yǒu yìsi	adj	interesting	4
语法	yǔfǎ	n	grammar	7
语言学	yǔyánxué	n	linguistics	8
预习	yùxí	v	to preview	7
圆珠笔	yuánzhūbǐ	n	ballpoint pen	7
月	yuè	n	month	3
越南	Yuènán	pn	Vietnam	1

Z

Characters	Pinyin	Part of Speech	English	Lesson
在	zài	prep	at; in; on	5
在	zài	v	to be present; to be at (a place)	6
再	zài	adv	again	9
再见	zàijiàn	v	goodbye; see you again	3
早	zǎo	adj	early	7
早饭	zǎofàn	n	breakfast	8
早上	zǎoshang	t	morning	7

Characters	Pinyin	Part of Speech	English	Lesson
怎么	zěnme	qpr	how; how come	7
怎么样	zěnmeyàng	qpr	Is it O.K.? How is that? How does that sound?	3
站	zhàn	m	(measure word for stops of bus, train, etc.)	
张	zhāng	m	(measure word for flat objects, paper, pictures, etc.)	7
找	zhǎo	v	to look for	4
找（钱）	zhǎo (qián)	v(o)	to give change	9
照片	zhàopiàn	n	picture; photo	2
这	zhè	pr	this	2
这么	zhème	pr	so; such	7
这儿	zhèr	pr	here	9
真	zhēn	adv	really	7
正在	zhèngzài	adv	in the middle of (doing something)	8
枝	zhī	m	(measure word for long, thin, inflexible objects, pens, rifles, etc.)	7
知道	zhīdao	v	to know	8
只	zhǐ	adv	only	4
纸	zhǐ	n	paper	7
中	zhōng	adj	medium; middle	9
中国	Zhōngguó	pn	China	1
中文	Zhōngwén	pn	Chinese (language)	6
中午	zhōngwǔ	n	noon	8
种	zhǒng	m	(measure word for kinds, sorts, types)	9
周末	zhōumò	n	weekend	4
祝	zhù	v	to wish (well)	8
专业	zhuānyè	n	major (in college); specialty	8
准备	zhǔnbèi	v	to prepare	6
紫色	zǐsè	n	purple	9
字	zì	n	character	7
字典	zìdiǎn	n	dictionary	7

Characters	Pinyin	Part of Speech	English	Lesson
自己	zìjǐ	pr	oneself	10
走	zǒu	v	to go by way of; to walk	10
走路	zǒu lù	vo	to walk	10
最后	zuìhòu		final; last	10
最近	zuìjìn	t	recently	8
昨天	zuótiān	t	yesterday	4
做	zuò	v	to do	2
坐	zuò	v	to sit	5
坐	zuò	v	to travel by	10
坐船	zuò chuán	vo	to travel by ship; to take a boat	10
坐电车	zuò diànchē	vo	to take a cable car, trolley bus, or tram	10
坐火车	zuò huǒchē	vo	to travel by train	10
坐计程车	zuò jìchéngchē	vo	to take a taxi (in Taiwan)	10

Vocabulary Index (English-Chinese)

Proper nouns from the dialogues and readings are shown in green. Supplementary vocabulary from the "How About You?" section is shown in blue.

English	Characters	Pinyin	Part of Speech	Lesson
A				
a little, a bit; some	点(儿)	diǎn(r)	m	5
a long time	好久	hǎo jiǔ		4
after	以后	yǐhòu	t	6
afternoon	下午	xiàwǔ	t	6
again	再	zài	adv	9
airplane	飞机	fēijī	n	10
airport	(飞)机场	(fēi)jīchǎng	n	10
all right; O.K.	行	xíng	v	6
allow or cause (somebody to do something)	让	ràng	v	10
already	已经	yǐjīng	adv	8
also; too; as well	还	hái	adv	3
although	虽然	suīrán	conj	9
altogether	一共	yígòng	adv	9
America	美国	Měiguó	pn	1
and	和	hé	conj	2
Asian studies	亚洲研究	Yàzhōu yánjiū	n	8
ask (a question)	问	wèn	v	1
at; in; on	在	zài	prep	5
B				
Bai Ying'ai	白英爱	Bái Yīng'ài (a personal name)	pn	2
ballpoint pen	圆珠笔	yuánzhūbǐ	n	7
be	是	shì	v	1
be acquainted with; recognize	认识	rènshi	v	3
be called; call	叫	jiào	v	1
be present; be at (a place)	在	zài	v	6
because	因为	yīnwèi	conj	3

English	Characters	Pinyin	Part of Speech	Lesson
before	以前	yǐqián	t	8
begin, start; beginning	开始	kāishǐ	v/n	7
Beijing	北京	Běijīng	pn	1
big; old	大	dà	adj	3
birthday	生日	shēngrì	n	3
black	黑	hēi	adj	9
blue	蓝	lán	adj	10
book	书	shū	n	4
both; all	都	dōu	adv	2
breakfast	早饭	zǎofàn	n	8
Britain; England	英国	Yīngguó	pn	3
brown; coffee colored	咖啡色	kāfēisè	n	9
bus	公共汽车	gōnggòng qìchē	n	10
business management	工商管理	gōngshāng guǎnlǐ	n	8
busy	忙	máng	adj	3
but	但是	dànshì	conj	6
but	可是	kěshì	conj	3
buy	买	mǎi	v	9

C

English	Characters	Pinyin	Part of Speech	Lesson
California	加州	Jiāzhōu	pn	1
can; able to	能	néng	mv	8
can; know how to	会	huì	mv	8
can; may	可以	kěyǐ	mv	5
Canada	加拿大	Jiā'nádà	pn	1
cell phone	手机	shǒujī	n	10
character	字	zì	n	7
chat	聊天(儿)	liáo tiān(r)	vo	5
cheap; inexpensive	便宜	piányi	adj	9
chemistry	化学	huàxué	n	8
child	孩子	háizi	n	2
China	中国	Zhōngguó	pn	1
Chinese characters	汉字	Hànzì	n	7

English	Characters	Pinyin	Part of Speech	Lesson
Chinese (language)	中文	Zhōngwén	pn	6
city	城市	chéngshì	n	10
class; course; lesson	课	kè	n	6
classmate	同学	tóngxué	n	3
classroom	教室	jiàoshì	n	8
clothes	衣服	yīfu	n	9
Coca-Cola	可口可乐	Kěkǒukělè	pn	5
coffee	咖啡	kāfēi	n	5
[Coke or Pepsi] cola	可乐	kělè	n	5
college student	大学生	dàxuéshēng	n	2
color	颜色	yánsè	n	9
come	来	lái	v	5
come back	回来	huí lai	vc	6
come in	进来	jìn lai	vc	5
computer	电脑	diànnǎo	n	8
concert	音乐会	yīnyuèhuì	n	8
convenient	方便	fāngbiàn	adj	6
cool	酷	kù	adj	7
credit card	信用卡	xìnyòngkǎ	n	9

D

English	Characters	Pinyin	Part of Speech	Lesson
dance	跳舞	tiào wǔ	vo	4
daughter	女儿	nǚ'ér	n	2
day	天	tiān	n	3
diary	日记	rìjì	n	8
dictionary	字典	zìdiǎn	n	7
difficult	难	nán	adj	7
dining room, cafeteria	餐厅	cāntīng	n	8
dinner; supper	晚饭	wǎnfàn	n	3
dishes, cuisine	菜	cài	n	3
do	做	zuò	v	2
doctor; physician	医生	yīshēng	n	2
don't	别	bié	adv	6
dormitory	宿舍	sùshè	n	8

English	Characters	Pinyin	Part of Speech	Lesson
draw; paint	画画儿	huà huàr	vo	4
drink	喝	hē	v	5
drive a car	开车	kāi chē	vo	10
(dynamic particle)	了	le	p	5
E				
early	早	zǎo	adj	7
easy	容易	róngyì	adj	7
eat	吃	chī	v	3
economics	经济	jīngjì	n	8
eighteen	十八	shíbā	nu	3
eldest brother	大哥	dàgē	n	2
eldest sister	大姐	dàjiě	n	2
email	电子邮件	diànzǐ yóujiàn	n	10
engineer	工程师	gōngchéngshī	n	2
England; Britain	英国	Yīngguó	pn	3
English (language)	英文	Yīngwén	pn	2
enter	进	jìn	v	5
especially	特别	tèbié	adv	10
evening; night	晚上	wǎnshang	t/n	3
every; each	每	měi	pr	10
everybody	大家	dàjiā	pr	7
exchange; change	换	huàn	v	9
exercise book	练习本	liànxíběn	n	7
F				
family; home	家	jiā	n	2
farmer; peasant	农民	nóngmín	n	2
father, dad	爸爸	bàba	n	2
Father's Day	父亲节	Fùqīnjié	pn	3
feel; think	觉得	juéde	v	4
feel embarrassed	不好意思	bù hǎoyìsi		10
female	女	nǔ	adj	2
final; last	最后	zuìhòu		10

English	Characters	Pinyin	Part of Speech	Lesson
fine; good; nice; O.K.; it's settled	好	hǎo	adj	1
first	先	xiān	adv	10
foreign country	外国	wàiguó	n	4
forget it; never mind	算了	suàn le		4
fountain pen	钢笔	gāngbǐ	n	7
France	法国	Fǎguó	pn	1
free time	空(儿)	kòng(r)	n	6
French language	法文	Fǎwén	n	6
friend	朋友	péngyou	n	3
fruit juice	果汁	guǒzhī	n	5
G				
Gao Wenzhong	高文中	Gāo Wénzhōng	pn	2
Gao Xiaoyin	高小音	Gāo Xiǎoyīn	pn	5
Germany	德国	Déguó	pn	1
German language	德文	Déwén	pn	6
get off (a bus, train, etc.)	下车	xià chē	vo	10
get up	起床	qǐ chuáng	vo	8
give	给	gěi	v	5
give change	找（钱）	zhǎo (qián)	v(o)	9
give or take a test; test	考试	kǎo shì	vo/n	6
go	去	qù	v	4
go by way of; walk	走	zǒu	v	10
go home	回家	huí jiā	vo	5
go online; surf the internet	上网	shàng wǎng	vo	8
go to; arrive	到	dào	v	6
go to a class; start a class; be in class	上课	shàng kè	vo	7
goodbye; see you again	再见	zàijiàn	v	3
grade in school	年级	niánjí	n	6
grammar	语法	yǔfǎ	n	7
gray	灰色	huīsè	n	9
Greek language	希腊文	Xīlàwén	pn	6
green	绿	lǜ	adj	10

English	Characters	Pinyin	Part of Speech	Lesson
H				
half; half an hour	半	bàn	nu	3
handsome	帅	shuài	adj	7
happy	快乐	kuàilè	adj	10
happy, pleased	高兴	gāoxìng	adj	5
hat; cap	帽子	màozi	n	9
have; exist	有	yǒu	v	2
have a meeting	开会	kāi huì	vo	6
have fun; play	玩(儿)	wán(r)	v	5
Hawaii	夏威夷	Xiàwēiyí	pn	1
he; him	他	tā	pr	2
Hello!; Hey! (on telephone)	喂	wéi/wèi	interj	6
help	帮	bāng	v	6
here	这儿	zhèr	pr	9
highway	高速公路	gāosù gōnglù	n	10
history	历史	lìshǐ	n	8
homework; schoolwork	功课	gōngkè	n	7
honorable; expensive	贵	guì	adj	1
hope; hope	希望	xīwàng	v/n	8
how; how come	怎么	zěnme	qpr	7
How is that? How does that sound? Is it O.K.?	怎么样	zěnmeyàng	qpr	3
how many; some; a few	几	jǐ	nu	2
how many/much; to what extent	多	duō	adv	3
how much/many	多少	duōshao	qpr	9
however; but	不过	búguò	conj	9
hundred	百	bǎi	nu	9
I				
I; me	我	wǒ	pr	1
if	要是	yàoshi	conj	6
if	如果…的话	rúguǒ… de huà	conj	9
in addition to; besides	除了…以外	chúle...yǐwài	conj	8

English	Characters	Pinyin	Part of Speech	Lesson
in that case; then	那	nà	conj	4
in the middle of (doing something)	正在	zhèngzài	adv	8
India	印度	Yìndù	pn	1
interesting	有意思	yǒu yìsi	adj	4
(interjectory particle used to soften a question)	呀	ya	p	5
introduce	介绍	jièshào	v	5
invite someone (to dinner, coffee, etc.); play the host	请客	qǐng kè	vo	4
Is it O.K.? How is that? How does that sound?	怎么样	zěnmeyàng	qpr	3
it	它	tā	pr	9
Italian language	意大利文	Yìdàlìwén	pn	6

J

English	Characters	Pinyin	Part of Speech	Lesson
jacket	夹克	jiákè	n	9
Japan	日本	Rìběn	pn	1
Japanese language	日文	Rìwén	pn	6
job; work	工作	gōngzuò	n/v	2

K

English	Characters	Pinyin	Part of Speech	Lesson
know	知道	zhīdao	v	8
Korea (South)	韩国	Hánguó	pn	1
Korean language	韩文	Hánwén	pn	6

L

English	Characters	Pinyin	Part of Speech	Lesson
late	晚	wǎn	adj	7
later	后来	hòulái	t	8
Latin language	拉丁文	Lādīngwén	pn	6
laugh at; laugh; smile	笑	xiào	v	8
lawyer	律师	lǜshī	n	2
length	长短	chángduǎn	n	9
letter (correspondence)	信	xìn	n	8
Li You	李友	Lǐ Yǒu	pn	1
library	图书馆	túshūguǎn	n	5

English	Characters	Pinyin	Part of Speech	Lesson
like	喜欢	xǐhuan	v	3
line	线	xiàn	n	10
linguistics	语言学	yǔyánxué	n	8
listen	听	tīng	v	4
look for	找	zhǎo	v	4
lunch, midday meal	午饭	wǔfàn	n	8

M

English	Characters	Pinyin	Part of Speech	Lesson
major (in college); specialty	专业	zhuānyè	n	8
make a phone call	打电话	dǎ diànhuà	vo	6
male	男	nán	adj	2
manager	经理	jīnglǐ	n	2
many; much	多	duō	adj	7
mathematics	数学	shùxué	n	8
matter; affair; event	事（儿）	shì(r)	n	3
meal; (cooked) rice	饭	fàn	n	3
(measure word for a pair)	双	shuāng	m	9
(measure word for bottles); bottle	瓶	píng	m/n	5
(measure word for class periods)	节	jié	m	6
(measure word for cup and glass)	杯	bēi	m	5
(measure word for essays, articles, etc.)	篇	piān	m	8
(measure word for flat objects, paper, pictures, etc.)	张	zhāng	m	7
(measure word for kinds, sorts, types)	种	zhǒng	m	9
(measure word for letters)	封	fēng	m	8
(measure word for long, thin, inflexible objects, pens, rifles, etc.)	枝	zhī	m	7
(measure word for many common everyday objects)	个	gè/ge	m	2
(measure word for number in a series; day of the month)	号	hào	m	3
(measure word for number of family members)	口	kǒu	m	2
(measure word for 1/100 of a kuai, cent)	分	fēn	m	9

English	Characters	Pinyin	Part of Speech	Lesson
(measure word for 1/10 of a kuai, dime (for US money))	毛	máo	m	9
(measure word for pants and long, thin objects)	条	tiáo	m	9
(measure word for people (polite))	位	wèi	m	6
(measure word for quarter (of an hour))	刻	kè	m	3
(measure word for shirts, dresses, jackets, coats, etc.)	件	jiàn	m	9
(measure word for stops of a bus, train, etc.)	站	zhàn	m	10
(measure word for the basic Chinese monetary unit)	块	kuài	m	9
medium; middle	中	zhōng	adj	9
meet up; meet with	见面	jiàn miàn	vo	6
merchant; businessperson	商人	shāngrén	n	2
Mexico	墨西哥	Mòxīgē	pn	1
mineral water	矿泉水	kuàngquánshuǐ	n	5
Miss; young lady	小姐	xiǎojiě	n	1
money	钱	qián	n	9
month	月	yuè	n	3
morning	上午	shàngwǔ	t	6
morning	早上	zǎoshang	t	7
mother, mom	妈妈	māma	n	2
Mother's Day	母亲节	Mǔqīnjié	pn	3
movie	电影	diànyǐng	n	4
Mr.; husband; teacher	先生	xiānsheng	n	1
music	音乐	yīnyuè	n	4
must; have to	得	děi	mv	6

N

English	Characters	Pinyin	Part of Speech	Lesson
name	名字	míngzi	n	1
need not	不用	búyòng		9
nervous, anxious	紧张	jǐnzhāng	adj	10
new	新	xīn	adj	8

English	Characters	Pinyin	Part of Speech	Lesson
new words; vocabulary	生词	shēngcí	n	7
new year	新年	xīnnián	n	10
New York	纽约	Niǔyuē	pn	1
next one	下个	xià ge		6
noon	中午	zhōngwǔ	n	8
not	没	méi	adv	2
not; no	不	bù	adv	1
not until, only then	才	cái	adv	5
notebook	本子	běnzi	n	7
now	现在	xiànzài	t	3
nurse	护士	hùshi	n	2

O

English	Characters	Pinyin	Part of Speech	Lesson
o'clock (lit. dot, point, thus "points on the clock")	点	diǎn	m	3
office	办公室	bàngōngshì	n	6
often	常常	chángcháng	adv	4
older brother	哥哥	gēge	n	2
older sister	姐姐	jiějie	n	2
once; a bit	一下	yí xià	n+m	5
oneself	自己	zìjǐ	pr	10
only	只	zhǐ	adv	4
or	还是	háishi	conj	3
or	或者	huòzhě	conj	10
orange (color)	橘红色	júhóngsè	n	9
other people; another person	别人	biérén	n	4
outer garment; coat; jacket	外套	wàitào	n	9
overcoat	大衣	dàyī	n	9

P

English	Characters	Pinyin	Part of Speech	Lesson
pants	裤子	kùzi	n	9
paper	纸	zhǐ	n	7
pay money	付钱	fù qián	vo	9
pay with a credit card	刷卡	shuā kǎ	vo	9

English	Characters	Pinyin	Part of Speech	Lesson
pen	笔	bǐ	n	7
pencil	铅笔	qiānbǐ	n	7
people; person	人	rén	n	1
Pepsi-Cola	百事可乐	Bǎishìkělè	pn	5
physics	物理	wùlǐ	n	8
picture; photo	照片	zhàopiàn	n	2
pink	粉红色	fěnhóngsè	n	9
play ball	打球	dǎ qiú	vo	4
play chess	下棋	xià qí	vo	4
play videogames	玩游戏机	wán yóuxìjī	vo	4
please (polite form of request); to treat or to invite (somebody)	请	qǐng	v	1
polite	客气	kèqi	adj	6
Portuguese language	葡萄牙文	Pútáoyáwén	pn	6
(possessive or descriptive particle)	的	de	p	2
practice	练习	liànxí	v	6
precisely; exactly	就	jiù	adv	6
(prefix for ordinal numbers)	第	dì	prefix	7
prepare	准备	zhǔnbèi	v	6
pretty	漂亮	piàoliang	adj	5
pretty good	不错	búcuò	adj	4
preview	预习	yùxí	v	7
previous one	上个	shàng ge		7
professor	教授	jiàoshòu	n	2
pronunciation	发音	fāyīn	n	8
purple	紫色	zǐsè	n	9

Q

English	Characters	Pinyin	Part of Speech	Lesson
quarter (of an hour)	刻	kè	m	4
question; problem	问题	wèntí	n	6
(question particle)	吗	ma	qp	1
(question particle)	呢	ne	qp	1
quickly, fast, quick	快	kuài	adv/adj	5

English	Characters	Pinyin	Part of Speech	Lesson
R				
read aloud	念	niàn	v	7
really	真	zhēn	adv	7
receive; accept	收	shōu	v	9
recently	最近	zuìjìn	t	8
red	红	hóng	adj	9
review	复习	fùxí	v	7
ride a bicycle	骑自行车	qí zìxíngchē	vo	10
ride a motorcycle	骑摩托车	qí mótuōchē	vo	10
right; correct	对	duì	adj	4
Russian language	俄文	Éwén	pn	6
S				
same; alike	一样	yíyàng	adj	9
say; speak	说	shuō	v	6
school	学校	xuéxiào	n	5
school term; semester/quarter	学期	xuéqī	n	8
second oldest sister	二姐	èrjiě	n	2
see	见	jiàn	v	3
see off or out; take (someone somewhere)	送	sòng	v	10
send a text message; (lit.) send a short message	发短信	fā duǎnxìn	vo	10
(sentence-final particle)	啊	a	p	6
(sentence-final particle)	吧	ba	p	5
September	九月	jiǔyuè	n	3
Shanghai	上海	Shànghǎi	pn	1
she; her	她	tā	pr	2
shirt	衬衫	chènshān	n	9
shoes	鞋	xié	n	9
shop assistant; salesclerk	售货员	shòuhuòyuán	n	9
skirt	裙子	qúnzi	n	9
simultaneously; at the same time	一边	yìbiān	adv	8
sing (a song)	唱歌（儿）	chàng gē(r)	vo	4

English	Characters	Pinyin	Part of Speech	Lesson
sit	坐	zuò	v	5
size	大小	dàxiǎo	n	9
size	号	hào	n	9
sleep	睡觉	shuì jiào	vo	4
slow	慢	màn	adj	7
small; little	小	xiǎo	adj	4
so	所以	suǒyǐ	conj	4
so; such	这么	zhème	pr	7
socks	袜子	wàzi	n	9
soda pop; soft drink	汽水（儿）	qìshuǐ(r)	n	5
soldier; military officer	军人	jūnrén	n	2
some	有的	yǒude	pr	4
son	儿子	érzi	n	2
sorry	对不起	duìbuqǐ	v	5
sound recording; record	录音	lùyīn	n/vo	7
Spanish language	西班牙文	Xībānyáwén	pn	6
spend	花	huā	v	10
Sprite	雪碧	Xuěbì	pn	5
store; shop	商店	shāngdiàn	n	9
(structural particle)	得	de	p	7
student	学生	xuésheng	n	1
study; learn	学	xué	v	7
study; learn	学习	xuéxí	v	7
style	样子	yàngzi	n	9
subway	地铁	dìtiě	n	10
suit (western-style)	西装	xīzhuāng	n	9
suitable	合适	héshì	adj	9
(one's) surname is...; be surnamed; surname	姓	xìng	v/n	1
sweater (woolen)	毛衣	máoyī	n	9
T				
T-shirt	T恤衫	T-xùshān	n	9
take a bath/shower	洗澡	xǐ zǎo	vo	8

English	Characters	Pinyin	Part of Speech	Lesson
take a cable car, trolley bus, or tram	坐电车	zuò diànchē	vo	10
take a taxi	打车	dǎ chē	vo	10
take a taxi (in Taiwan)	坐计程车	zuò jìchéngchē	vo	10
talk	说话	shuō huà	vo	7
taxi	出租汽车	chūzū qìchē	n	10
tea	茶	chá	n	5
teach	教	jiāo	v	7
teacher	老师	lǎoshī	n	1
Teacher Chang	常老师	Cháng lǎoshī	pn	6
television	电视	diànshì	n	4
tell	告诉	gàosu	v	8
textbook	课本	kèběn	n	7
text of a lesson	课文	kèwén	n	7
thank	谢谢	xièxie	v	3
Thanksgiving	感恩节	Gǎn'ēnjié	pn	3
that	那	nà	pr	2
then	然后	ránhòu	adv	10
there	那儿	nàr	pr	8
things; objects	东西	dōngxi	n	9
this	这	zhè	pr	2
this year	今年	jīnnián	t	3
Thursday	星期四	xīngqīsì	n	3
ticket	票	piào	n	10
time	时间	shíjiān	n	6
time (a point in); moment; time (a duration of)	时候	shíhou	n	4
tired	累	lèi	adj	8
to; for	给	gěi	prep	6
today	今天	jīntiān	t	3
together	一起	yìqǐ	adv	5
tomorrow	明天	míngtiān	t	3
too; also	也	yě	adv	1
too; extremely	太...了	tài...le		3

English	Characters	Pinyin	Part of Speech	Lesson
travel by	坐	zuò	v	10
travel by train	坐火车	zuò huǒchē	vo	10
travel by ship; take a boat	坐船	zuò chuán	vo	10
troublesome	麻烦	máfan	adj	10
try	试	shì	v	9
twelve	十二	shí'èr	nu	3
two; a couple of	两	liǎng	nu	2
U				
understand	懂	dǒng	v	7
upper garment	上衣	shàngyī	n	9
use	用	yòng	v	8
usually	平常	píngcháng	adv	7
V				
Valentine's Day	情人节	Qíngrénjié	pn	3
very	很	hěn	adv	3
very; rather	挺	tǐng	adv	9
Vietnam	越南	Yuènán	pn	1
W				
wait; wait for	等	děng	v	6
walk	走路	zǒu lù	vo	10
Wang Peng	王朋	Wáng Péng	pn	1
want	要	yào	v	5
want to; would like to; think	想	xiǎng	mv	4
watch; look; read	看	kàn	v	4
water	水	shuǐ	n	5
we	我们	wǒmen	pr	3
wear; put on	穿	chuān	v	9
week	星期	xīngqī	n	3
weekend	周末	zhōumò	n	4
what	什么	shénme	qpr	1
where	哪里	nǎli	pr	7

English	Characters	Pinyin	Part of Speech	Lesson
where	哪儿	nǎr	qpr	5
which	哪	nǎ/něi	qpr	6
who	谁	shéi	qpr	2
why	为什么	wèishénme	qpr	3
will; be going to; want to, have a desire to	要	yào	mv	6
windowshop	逛街	guàng jiē	vo	4
winter vacation	寒假	hánjià	n	10
wish (well)	祝	zhù	v	8
with	跟	gēn	prep	6
worker	工人	gōngrén	n	2
write	写	xiě	v	7
writing brush	毛笔	máobǐ	n	7

Y

English	Characters	Pinyin	Part of Speech	Lesson
year (of age)	岁	suì	n	3
yellow	黄	huáng	adj	9
yesterday	昨天	zuótiān	t	4
you	你	nǐ	pr	1
you (honorific for 你)	您	nín	pr	6
younger brother	弟弟	dìdi	n	2
younger sister	妹妹	mèimei	n	2

Vocabulary by Grammar Category and by Lesson

Lesson & Section	noun	measure word	pronoun	numeral	verb	modal verb
L1-1	小姐 名字 先生		你 我 什么		请 问 姓 叫	
L1-2	老师 学生 人				是	
L2-1	照片 爸爸 妈妈 孩子 姐姐 弟弟 大哥 儿子 女儿	个	那 这 谁 她 他		有	
L2-2	家 哥哥 妹妹 大姐 二姐 工作 律师 英文 大学生 医生	口		几 两	做	
L3-1	九月 月 星期 星期四 天 生日 岁 饭 菜	号 点	怎么样 我们	十二 十八 半	吃 谢谢 喜欢 见 再见	
L3-2	事(儿) 晚饭 同学 朋友	刻	为什么		认识	

	adjective	adverb	preposition	conjunction	time word	particle	others	proper noun
	好 贵					呢		李友 王朋
		不 也				吗		中国 北京 美国 纽约
	女 男	没				的		高文中
		都		和				白英爱
	大	多		还是 可是	今年 晚上		太…了	英国
	忙	很 还		因为	现在 今天 明天			

Lesson & Section	noun	measure word	pronoun	numeral	verb	modal verb
L4-1	周末 电视 音乐 书 时候 电影 外国		有的		打球 看 唱歌 跳舞 听 去 请客	
L4-2	别人				觉得 睡觉 找	想
L5-1	学校 茶 咖啡 可乐 水	点(儿) 瓶 杯	哪儿		进 进来 来 介绍 坐 喝 要 对不起 给	可以
L5-2	图书馆				玩(儿) 聊天(儿) 回家	
L6-1	时间 问题 课 年级 空儿 办公室	位 节	您 哪		打电话 在 开会 考试 到 行 等	要
L6-2	中文				帮 准备 练习 说 见面 回来	得
L7-1	字 笔 纸 语法 生词 汉字	枝 张	怎么 哪里		说话 复习 写 教 懂 预习 学	
L7-2	功课 课文 录音		这么 大家		上课 开始 念 学习	

	adjective	adverb	preposition	conjunction	time word	particle	others	proper noun
	对	常常		那 所以	昨天			
	小 不错 有意思	只					好久 算了	
	高兴 漂亮	快	在			呀 吧	一下	高小音
		一起 才				了		
	方便 客气	就 别	给	要是	下午 上午 以后		喂	常老师
			跟	但是		啊	下个	
	慢 容易 多 难	真				得	上个 第	
	早 晚 帅 酷	平常			早上			

Lesson & Section	noun	measure word	pronoun	numeral	verb	modal verb
L8-1	日记 早饭 教室 发音 电脑 餐厅 午饭 宿舍	篇	那儿		起床 洗澡 上网 告诉 知道	
L8-2	信 学期 专业 音乐会	封			希望 用 笑 祝	会 能
L9-1	商店 东西 售货员 衣服 衬衫 颜色 裤子 号 长短 钱	件 条 块 毛 分	多少	百	买 穿 试 找（钱）	
L9-2	鞋 大小 咖啡色 样子 信用卡	双 种	它 这儿		换 刷卡 收 付钱	
L10-1	寒假 飞机 票 (飞)机场 公共汽车 地铁 线 出租汽车	站			坐 走 下车 打车 开车 送	
L10-2	电子邮件 城市 高速公路 手机 新年		每 自己		让 花 发短信	

	adjective	adverb	preposition	conjunction	time word	particle	others	proper noun
	累 新	一边 正在 已经			中午 以前			
				除了… 以外	最近 后来			
	黄 红 中 便宜 合适	一共		如果… 的话			不用	
	一样 黑	挺 再		虽然 不过				
	绿 蓝 麻烦	先 然后		或者			最后	
	紧张 快乐	特别					不好意思	

Alternate Characters (Texts in Traditional Form)

Lesson 1

Dialogue I: Exchanging Greetings

你好❶！

你好！

請問❷，你❸貴姓？

我姓①李。你呢②？

我姓王。李小姐❹，你叫③什麼名字？

我叫李友。王先生，你叫什麼名字？

我叫王朋。

Dialogue II: Asking about Someone's Nationality

王先生，你是④老師嗎⑤？

我不⑥❶是老師，我是學生。李友，你呢？

我也⑦是學生。你是中國人嗎？

是，我是北京人。你是美國人嗎？

是，我是紐約人。

Lesson 2

Dialogue I: Looking at a Family Photo

(Wang Peng is in Gao Wenzhong's room and points to a picture on the wall.)

高文中，那是你的①照片嗎？

(They both walk toward the picture and then stand in front of it.)

是。這是我爸爸，這是我媽媽。

這❶個②女孩子是誰③？

她是我姐姐。

這個男孩子是你弟弟嗎？

不是，他是我大哥的兒子❷。

你大哥有④女兒嗎？

他沒有女兒。

Dialogue II: Asking about Someone's Family

白英愛，你家❶有⑤幾口❷人？

我家有六口人。我爸爸、我媽媽、一❸個哥哥、兩⑥個妹妹和❹我❺。李友，你家有幾口人？

我家有五口人。爸爸、媽媽、大姐、二姐和我。你爸爸媽媽做什麼工作？

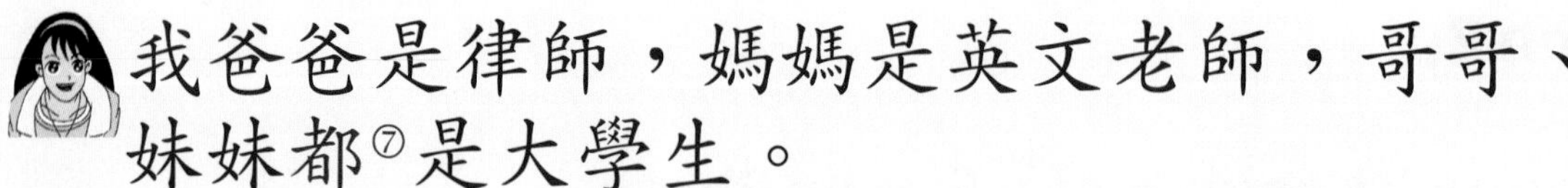

我爸爸是律師，媽媽是英文老師，哥哥、妹妹都⑦是大學生。

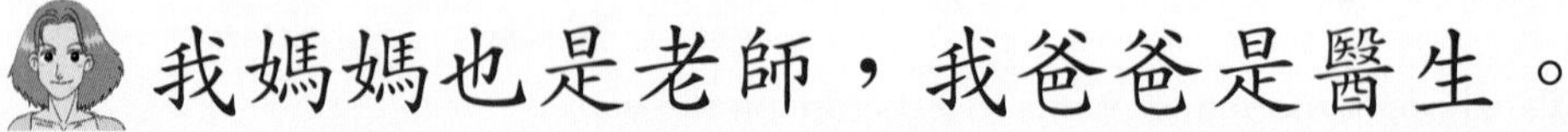

我媽媽也是老師，我爸爸是醫生。

Lesson 3

Dialogue I: Taking Someone Out to Eat on His/Her Birthday

(Gao Wenzhong is talking to Bai Ying'ai.)

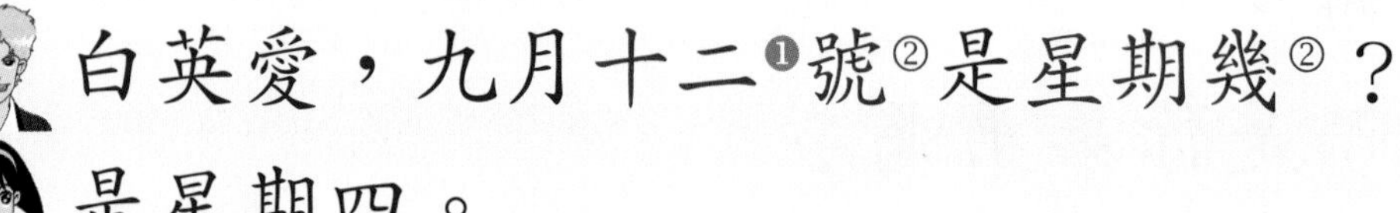

白英愛，九月十二❶號②是星期幾②？

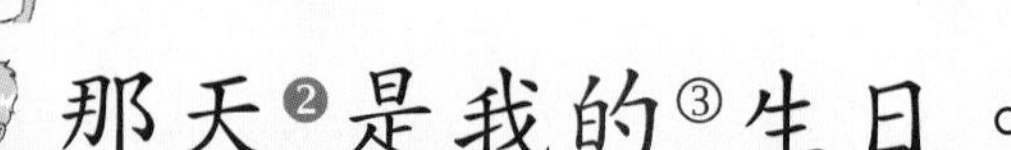

是星期四。

那天❷是我的③生日。

是嗎？你今年多大❸？

十八歲❹。

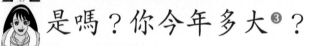

我星期四請你吃飯④，怎麼樣？

太好了。謝謝，謝謝❺。

你喜歡吃中國菜還是⑤美國菜？

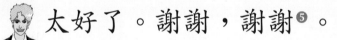

我是英國人，可是我喜歡吃中國菜。

好，我們吃中國菜。

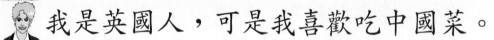

星期四幾點？

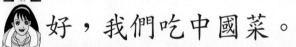

七點半怎麼樣？

好，星期四晚上見。

再見！

Dialogue II: Inviting Someone to Dinner

白英愛，現在幾點？

五點三刻。

我六點一刻有事兒。

你今天很忙❶，明天忙不忙⑥？

我今天很忙，可是明天不忙。有事兒嗎？

明天我請你吃晚飯，怎麼樣？

你為什麼請我吃飯？

因為明天是高文中的生日。

是嗎？好。還⑦請誰？

還請我的同學李友。

那太好了，我認識李友，她也是我的朋友。明天幾點？

明天晚上七點半。

好，明天七點半見。

Lesson 4

Dialogue I: Talking about Hobbies

白英愛，你週末喜歡做什麼①？

我喜歡打球、看電視❶。你呢？

我喜歡唱歌、跳舞，還喜歡聽音樂。你也喜歡看書，對不對？

對，有的時候也喜歡看書。

你喜歡不喜歡②看電影？

喜歡。我週末常常看電影。

那③我們今天晚上去看④一個外國電影，怎麼樣？我請客。

為什麼你請客？

因為昨天你請我吃飯，所以今天我請你看電影。

那你也請王朋、李友，好嗎⑤？

…好。

Dialogue II: Would You Like to Play Ball?

(Wang Peng is talking to Gao Wenzhong.)

小高❶，好久不見❷，你好嗎❸？

我很好。你怎麼樣？

我也不錯。這個週末你想⑥做什麼？想不想去打球？

打球？我不喜歡打球。

那我們去看球，怎麼樣？

看球？我覺得❹看球也沒有意思。

那你這個週末想做什麼？

我只想吃飯、睡覺❺⑦。

算了，我去找別人。

Lesson 5

Dialogue: Visiting a Friend's Home

(The doorbell rings.)

誰呀？

是我，王朋，還有李友。

請進，請進，快進來！來，我介紹一下①，這是我姐姐，高小音。

小音，你好。認識你很高興。

認識你們我也很高興。

你們家很大②，也很漂亮。

是嗎？❶請坐，請坐。

 小音，你在③哪兒❷工作？

 我在學校工作。你們想喝點兒①什麼？喝茶還是喝咖啡？

 我喝茶吧④。

 我要一瓶可樂，可以嗎？

 對不起，我們家没有可樂。

 那給我一杯水吧。

Narrative: At a Friend's House

昨天晚上，王朋和李友去高文中家玩兒。在高文中家，他們認識了⑤高文中的姐姐。她叫高小音，在學校的圖書館工作。她請王朋喝❶茶，王朋喝了兩杯。李友不喝茶，只喝了一杯水。他們一起聊天兒、看電視。王朋和李友晚上十二點才⑥回家。

Lesson 6

Dialogue I: Calling One's Teacher

（李友給①常老師打電話）

 喂？

 喂，請問，常老師在嗎？

 我就是。您❶是哪位？

老師，您好。我是李友。

李友，有事兒嗎？

老師，今天下午您有時間❷嗎？我想問❸您幾個問題。

對不起，今天下午我要②開會。

明天呢？

明天上午我有兩節❹課，下午三點要給二年級考試。

您什麼時候❺有空兒？

明天四點以後❻才有空兒。

要是❼您方便，四點半我到您的辦公室去，行嗎？

四點半，沒問題❽。我在辦公室等你。

謝謝您。

別③客氣。

Dialogue II: Calling a Friend for Help

喂，請問，王朋在嗎？

我就是。你是李友吧❶？

王朋，我下個星期④要考中文，你幫我準備一下，跟我練習說中文，好嗎？

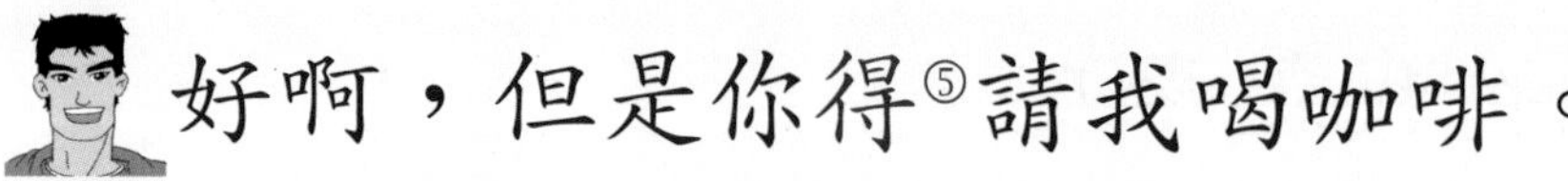

好啊，但是你得⑤請我喝咖啡。

喝咖啡，沒問題。那我什麼時候跟你見面？你今天晚上有空兒嗎？

今天晚上白英愛請我吃飯。

是嗎？白英愛請你吃飯？

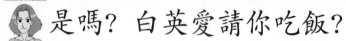

對。我回來⑥以後給你打電話。

好，我等你的電話。

Lesson 7

Dialogue I: How Did You Do on the Exam?

（王朋跟李友説話）

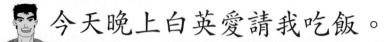

李友，你上個星期考試考得①怎麼樣？

因為你幫我復習，所以考得不錯。但是我寫中國字寫得太②慢了！

是嗎？以後我跟你一起練習寫字，好不好❶？

那太好了！我們現在就③ 寫，怎麼樣？

好，給我一枝筆④、一張紙。寫什麼字？

你教我怎麼寫“懂”字吧。

好吧。

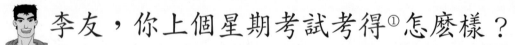

你寫字寫得真②好，真快。

哪裏，哪裏❷。你明天有中文課嗎？我幫你預習。

明天我們學第七⑤課。第七課的語法很容易，我都懂，可是生詞太多，漢字也有一點兒⑥難。

没問題，我幫你。

Dialogue II: Preparing for a Chinese Class

（李友跟白英愛説話）

白英愛，你平常來得很早，今天怎麽⑦這麽晚？

我昨天預習中文，早上❶四點才③睡覺，你也睡得很晚嗎？

我昨天十點就③睡了。因為王朋幫我練習中文，所以我功課做得很快。

有個中國朋友真好。

（上中文課）

大家早❷，現在我們開始上課。第七課你們都預習了嗎？

預習了。

李友，請你念課文。...念得很好。你昨天晚上聽錄音了吧？

 我没聽。

 但是她的朋友昨天晚上幫她學習了。

 你的朋友是中國人嗎？

 是。

 他是一個男的[8]，很帥[❸]，很酷，叫王朋。[9]

Lesson 8

A Diary: A Typical School Day

An Entry from Li You's Diary

李友的一篇日記

十一月三日　星期二

今天我很忙，很累。早上七點半起床[1]，洗了澡以後就[2]吃早飯。我一邊吃飯，一邊[3]聽錄音。九點到教室去上課[4]。

第一節課是中文，老師教我們發音、生詞和語法，也教我們寫字，還給了[5]我們一篇新課文[6]，這篇課文很有意思。第二節是電腦[❶]課，很難。

中午我和同學們一起到餐廳去吃午飯。我們一邊吃，一邊練習説中文。下午我到圖書館去上網。四點王朋來找我打球。五點三刻吃晚飯。七點半我去白英愛的宿舍跟她聊天(兒)。到那兒的時候，她正在⑦做功課。我八點半回家。睡覺以前，高文中給我打了一個電話，告訴我明天要考試，我說我已經知道了。

A Letter: Talking about Studying Chinese

A Letter

一封信

(The teacher asked the students to write their friends a letter in Chinese as a homework assignment. Here's what Li You wrote to Gao Xiaoyin.)

小音：

你好！好久不見，最近怎麽樣？

這個學期我很忙，除了專業課以外，還⑧得學中文。我們的中文課很有意思。因為我們的中文老師只會⑨說中文，不會說英文，所以上課的時候我們只說中文，不說英文。開始我覺得很難，後來❶，王朋常常幫我練習中文，就⑩覺得不難了❷。

你喜歡聽音樂嗎？下個星期六，我們學校有一個音樂會，希望你能⑨來。我用中文寫信寫得很不好，請別笑我。祝

好

你的朋友

李友

十一月十八日

Lesson 9

Dialogue I: Shopping for Clothes

（李友在一個商店買東西，售貨員問她...）

小姐，您要①買什麼衣服？

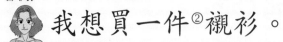

我想買一件②襯衫。

您喜歡什麼顏色的③，黄的還是紅的？

我喜歡穿❶紅的。我還想買一條②褲子❷。

多④大的？大號的、中號的、還是小號的？

中號的。不要太貴的，也不要太便宜❸的。

這條褲子怎麼樣？

顏色很好。如果長短合適的話，我就買。

您試一下。

[Li You checks the size on the label and measures the pants against her legs.]

不用試。可以。

這件襯衫呢？

也不錯。一共多少錢？

襯衫二十一塊五，褲子三十二塊九毛九，
一共是五十四塊四毛九分⑤。

好，這是一百塊錢。

找您四十五塊五毛一。謝謝。

Dialogue II: Exchanging Shoes

對不起，這雙鞋太小了。能不能換一雙？

沒問題。您看，這雙怎麼樣？

也不行，這雙跟那雙一樣⑥大。

那這雙黑的呢？

這雙鞋雖然大小合適，可是⑦ 顏色不好。有沒有咖啡色的？

對不起，這種鞋只有黑的。

這雙鞋樣子挺好的❶，就是它吧❷。你們這兒可以刷卡嗎?

對不起，我們不收信用卡。不過，這雙的錢跟那雙一樣，您不用再付錢了。

Lesson 10

Dialogue: Going Home for the Winter Vacation

李友，寒假你回家嗎？

對，我要回家。

飛機票你買了嗎①？

已經買了。是二十一號的。

飛機是幾點的？

晚上八點的。

你怎麼去❶機場？

我想坐公共汽車或者②坐地鐵。你知道怎麼走❶嗎？

你先坐一路汽車，坐三站下車，然後換地鐵。先坐紅綫，再③換綠綫，最後換藍綫。

不行，不行，太麻煩了。我還是④打車❷吧。

出租汽車太貴，我開車送你去吧。

謝謝你。

不用客氣。

An Email: Thanking Someone for a Ride

電子郵件❶

Date: 2008年12月20日

From: 李友

To: 王朋

Subject: 謝謝！

王朋：

謝謝你那天開車送我到機場。不過，讓你花那麼多時間，真不好意思。我這幾天每天都⑤開車出去看老朋友。這個城市的人開車開得特別快。我在高速公路上開車，真有點兒緊張。可是這兒没有公共汽車，也没有地鐵，只能自己開車，很不方便。

有空兒的話打我的手機或者給我發短信，我想跟你聊天兒。

新年快要到了⑥，祝你新年快樂！

李友